ELIZABETHAN PLAYWRIGHTS

ELIZABETHAN PLAYWRIGHTS

A Short History of the English Drama from
Mediæval Times *to the Closing of the*
Theaters in 1642

BY

FELIX E. SCHELLING

Benjamin Blom

First published by Harper & Bros., 1925
Copyright renewed by Mrs. Gertrude B. Schelling, 1952
Reissued by Benjamin Blom, Inc., 1965 by arrangement with Mrs. G. B. Schelling
Library of Congress Catalog Card No. 64-18788

Printed in U.S.A. by
NOBLE OFFSET PRINTERS, INC.
NEW YORK 3, N. Y.

TO MY FELLOW-TEACHERS OF ENGLISH
IN THE UNIVERSITY OF PENNSYLVANIA

CONTENTS

PREFACE

It has been the present author's fortune to have dealt
with the story of our older English drama, in whole or in
part, more than once before: most extensively in his *Elizabethan Drama*, 2 vols., 1908. Since that date, scholarship
has added to our stores of knowledge and cleared up much
that had hitherto been understood less clearly. *The Cambridge History of English Literature* in the volumes which
deal with the drama, the work as to the stage, especially
of Reynolds, Graves, Thorndike, and Adams in America;
the bibliographical and other work of Pollard, Greg, Chambers, and many more in England; that of Reyher and
Feuillerat in particular in France—all this has added to
our stores, not to mention many other valuable contributions. And now, subsequent to the first draft of the present
book, appears Dr. Chambers's eagerly awaited *Elizabethan Stage*, which cannot but be taken into serious
account, alike for its learning and the weight to be attached
at all times to this eminent scholar's critical decisions.

In any work of scholarly cast, we may decide, as some
have decided, to accept nothing whatever that other scholars have done, but to go down to the bedrock of original
material and demonstrate once more the justice of the
acceptance of the multiplication table. The other extreme
gives us a history of former critical opinion expressed
with that evasive particularity which leaves things exactly
where they were. There is perhaps a third course which,
on the basis of a first-hand knowledge of the materials in
question and with a diligent endeavor to become acquainted
with other superstructures that scholarship has reared
upon them, makes a selective rather than an exhaustive
use of these materials, and is less emulous of singularity

ix

than of a modest effort to get at and present, as nearly as possible, the truth. This last has been the ideal in this case. It is too much to hope that any ideal can reach more than a qualified fulfillment.

This book has been written mainly abroad, and the author has therefore been denied the intimacy of his own library and that of his own university. But this loss has been compensated and more by the courtesies of others in that republic of scholarship and letters that knows no aliens. My acknowledgments are due to the authorities of the British Museum and those of the London Library, particularly to Mr. C. T. Hagberg Wright, librarian of the latter, and to Mr. Gorham P. Stevens and Dr. E. D. Van Buren, the director and librarian, respectively, of the American Academy in Rome, in the congenial atmosphere of which, however distant from England and Elizabeth, many of the pages of this book were written. Nearer home, I record my appreciation of the encouragement of my friend and colleague, Professor Arthur H. Quinn who, as general editor of the series of which this book is one, procured the writing of it. The Index has been prepared by my wife, the ever best of all helpers.

FELIX E. SCHELLING.

INTRODUCTION

Ours is the pleasing task to trace once more the fascinating story of the rise, the flourish, and the decline of that splendid drama in the midst of which towers the genius of Shakespeare. The range of the plays which this age produced is the range of Elizabethan life itself; and that life was the fullest, the most varied and picturesque, the most significant in promise and fulfillment which England had ever known. Elizabethan drama is conspicuous in that it is representative of the totality of the age, and naïvely so representative. For that drama mirrors alike the glitter of the court and the gossip of the presence chamber, the bustling, merry life of London's prosperous citizens and that wholesome rural living which has always been typically English. It did more; for it chronicled, too, martial and other adventure abroad and, levying on the literature of the ages, made to live once again the heroes of other peoples and the stories of other times. In the plays of Shakespeare's age we shall find a range of ideas, an inventiveness, a contrast and variety in dramatic art unparalleled elsewhere. There is scarcely a kind of drama, a method of expressing it, a way of reading in that volume of complexities, the manner in which men live, in which Elizabethan playwrights have not stood forth conspicuous for their originality and resource. The wit of ingenuity of Jonson and Fletcher each in his different way, Webster's power of phrase, with Shakespeare combining these qualities and more: we shall look far before we find again a conjunction such as this.

Actual drama involving a professional stage and the professional writing of plays did not come to exist in Lyly, the poetry of Marlowe and Dekker, the dramatic

INTRODUCTION

England until Queen Elizabeth had been nearly a generation on her throne. Earlier Tudor days, with their changes and dissensions in church and state, were little conducive to the cultivation of popular arts, although the elements of gentler living and of culture were not unknown to the boisterous court of Henry VIII. It is in domestic security that the arts flourish; and that came after the Armada, the gift of Elizabeth to her people. Besides this, the spirit of inquiry which revived a knowledge of the ancients and quickened the arts of the modern world, had come late into England, like a delayed and inclement northern spring; while the sweet Pagan learning of Italy was rendered bitter from the first by moral questionings and yearnings, and by theological dissensions as well. None the less, the drama of Elizabeth had its roots deep in the past and could not have been what it became save for mediæval preparation. Correspondingly, the impetus which begot the tragedy of Kyd and Marlowe and the comedy of Greene continued in flood to the end of Elizabeth's reign and far into that of her successor, to ebb under Charles in the shadow of the political differences soon to involve the nation in civil war. With these considerations in view, it is not illogical to employ the word "Elizabethan" as generally accepted as to literature, so that it may include the immediate sources of the drama in England, beginnings which in orderly development reached their flower in the latter years of the great queen; and correspondingly to trace the continuance of these same characteristics until the social and intellectual break, occasioned by the victory of the Commonwealth. With the drama in the Middle Ages we shall be concerned only in so far as it was a preparation for what was to come. The drama after Shakespeare, up to the closing of the theaters, as well as Shakespeare himself, his predecessors and contemporaries, this is our story.

In the absence of newspapers and periodicals, with fiction

as yet not come into its own, the drama in Elizabeth's time exerted an influence far more powerful than that of today. Elizabethan drama has been called a great national utterance because in it spoke the spirit of England, despite all its imitations and borrowings from alien sources. Indeed, the frankness with which the material of the world was transformed into the terms of that immediate present is one of the salient characteristics of this drama from Shakespeare to the least of his fellows. It is not only that on the boards—Diogenes, Julius Cæsar, Macbeth, Rosalind, or Romeo—the doublet and hose clothed them all, but that the actions of these people of the stage are those of their creators, transferred from the life about them in its impetuousness and diversity, their thoughts, too, as well, in their depth, their brilliancy and daring. With all its artifice and convention there has never been a drama so near to the life that it mirrored. And there has never been an age which so immediately responded to an artistic appeal.

Elizabethan activity in the projecting, writing, and acting of plays was simply amazing. London was a small city as yet. It was not until the reign of James that its numbers reached 200,000; and Puritan prejudice was strong and growing against the theater, while that terrible visitant, the plague, shut down all places of assembly every six or seven years for months at a time, leaving the returns of the actors precarious and intermittent at best. While an accurate estimate of this dramatic "output" is impossible because of the incompleteness of our information, the lack of evidence as to many things and the enormous loss in the way of printed books and manuscripts of plays which time has worked, it is not too much to say that the total body of these dramatic writings must have constituted something like 2,500 titles between the accession of the queen and the conclusion of the old drama. Of this reconstructed mass rather less than half came to print, and not many more than half of these are still extant, to

be read by the industrious and the curious.[1] As to authorship, while that of many plays remains unknown or at
least indistinguishable, it is easy to list some fourscore
names, more or less active within this period in the writing,
adaptation, and translation of drama.

To expect a uniform degree of excellence in such a mass
is preposterous. The range of Elizabethan drama is not
only marked by a constituency that extended from the
queen on her throne to the veriest tapster and vagrant of
the street, but it was likewise the work of men representing
almost every walk of English life, from noblemen whose
gravity took them to the council board, lawyers who sat
on the woolsack, or scholars who graced the universities,
to actors, musicians, and even professional clowns. There
is much dull and uninspired writing in this old drama, and
it panders only too often to low and vulgar tastes. There
is an easy amateurishness also about many of these plays,
and they may be criticized for crudity, tastelessness, and
a want of art. But no one can read far into Elizabethan
drama and find that this is all; and, judged by their intent,
with some acquaintance of conditions which invoked them
and a spirit that looks rather for what is admirable than
for defects to carp at, this body of plays represents a
degree of discernment into human nature, a success in representing human life, a sense of design, an artistry and
poetry which is unexcelled in the drama of any other age
or tongue.

The only way in which to become acquainted with any
literature is faithfully to read it, not about it. This book
is offered merely for guidance, and by one who may plead
in justification that he has sojourned somewhat in the
pleasant Elizabethan land and wishes that more may come
veritably to know it not only in its capital, but likewise
beyond the regal precincts of Shakespeare.

[1] See E. K. Chambers, *The Elizabethan Stage*, iii, 177-183, for an enumeration of the plays between 1559 and 1616; his Index discloses some
1,330 titles, including fragments and translations, between these dates.

ELIZABETHAN PLAYWRIGHTS

CHAPTER I

The Church and the Stage

IT IS the best opinion that the literary drama of ancient Greece and Rome exerted no influence on the dramas which arose in mediæval Europe until the revival of learning affected the stage as it affected nearly every other intellectual activity of modern life. But there were other links with the past, and the suggestion of some of these, together with a recognition of the dramatic spirit and activities inherent in racial custom and cult, are our immediate topics.

Dr. E. K. Chambers, in his learned and fascinating book, *The Mediæval Stage*, shows how, in the fourth century, on the downfall of the stage, the *mimi* or actors of degenerate Roman farces and pantomimes, degenerated still further into wandering tumblers, jugglers and buffoons;[1] and, tracing a far greater decline from the dignified northern Teutonic scop and gleeman, companion of his king in arms and singer of heroic deeds at his table, finds in the union and confusion of mime with the gleeman, the later wandering minstrel, that universal entertainer of the Middle Ages. The designation *minstrel* included everything from an original poet or musician to a dancer, a mimic, a juggler or a clown, from a dignified servant of his king, on a fixed and liberal stipend, to a tattered wanderer from tavern to tavern, dependent on his wit for a dinner. And the variety of the minstrel's talents compassed the variety of his entertainment, serious or trivial, artistic or banal, as circumstances might dictate. While

Mime, scop and minstrel

[1] See E. Faral, *Les Jongleurs en France au Moyen Age*, 1910, for a modification of this view.

1

this variety of status and function is recognized at times and even the Church vacillates from a qualified acceptance of minstrelsy to fulmination against it, the minstrel in general was held in increasing disrepute and handed down to the Elizabethan player an inheritance of obloquy and contempt.

Drama in minstrelsy   That elements of drama enter into the repertory of the minstrel is attested by the frequency of dialogue in both lyric and narrative minstrelsy. Sometimes we have the *aube*, or lovers' parting, such as that of Romeo and Juliet on the break of day, sometimes a pastoral, more or less rude and comic, between shepherds. More in the nature of actual comedy are the *débates* and *estrifs* or strifes, carried on in dialogue and often serious and even religious in tone. But minstrelsy offers us impersonation, as well as dialogue achieved by means of mask and costume; and impersonation in costume suggests inevitably a distribution of parts. Actable farce, indeed, must have been far from unknown in the heyday of minstrelsy in England. It was doubtless both crude and unliterary and for the most part therefore unrecorded. A specimen of such we may well believe that we have in the fragment of the oriental tale of *Dame Siriz*, involving a dialogue between Clericus and Puella, and dating from the middle of the thirteenth century.[1]

Drama of the folk   Another root of drama, running even deeper into antiquity, is that which accompanied the immemorial traditions that maintained the early religion of the folk. These took innumerable forms, such as "the observance of the morn of May," with its garlanding of houses, its processions bearing flowers, dancing, the Maypole and chosen king or queen, or that of the harvest when the last wain was conducted home with rejoicings. Many processional customs, such as ridings, shows, watches, bonfires, Midsummer's Day and the like, preserved these and other

[1] G. H. McKnight, *Middle English Humorous Tales*, 1913, p. xxxvii, who agrees with W. Heuser, *Anglia* xxx, that "the fabliau is based upon an original interlude."

2

festivals of the folk throughout England as well as the rest of Europe; and ancient magic and sacrificial customs frequently entered into them, later to be translated into the terms of meaningless procedure, rural merrymaking and horse-play. While the Church was often severe in its condemnation of the vanities of the minstrel, it would appear that ancient heathen ritual, where it fell short of desecration or a trespass on public decency, was treated more leniently. It was easier to convert these pagan customs to Christian uses than to destroy them; and in many a procession of Catholic Europe the image of the saint succeeded to the place once occupied by the doll or other anthropomorphic image of the goddess of fertility.

But the village festival, whatever its origin in heathen ritual or subsequent conversion into conformity with Christian cult, was not all solemn procedure. *Play* is well defined as that species of human activity which serves no end beyond itself; and the element of play enters into human institutions from the first, whether it be represented in the skull of the sacrificial ox kicked about a field, the progenitor of football, or in the dignified athletic contests of Homeric times, signalizing the funeral of a hero. With play comes make-belief and mimicry, and both are of the life-blood of drama. The relation of games, sports and even the unguarded pastimes of children to the mimetic impulse is close and intricate, but it cannot detain us here. Suffice it to say that in the sword dance with the related morris dance and other mummers' plays, we have what may properly be "called folk drama, because they are derived with a minimum of literary intervention from the dramatic tendencies latent in folk-festivals of a very primitive type." [1] Only less directly of the folk are pastoral dialogues like the French *Robin and Marion*, the ballad deeds of Robin Hood in dialogue form, known to have been acted as far back as the time of the War of the Roses, and spectacles involving a mock fight "expressed

"Play" and folk drama

---

[1] E. K. Chambers, *The Mediæval Stage*, i, 218.

3

in actions and rhymes," such as the *Hox Tuesday Play*, revived for Queen Elizabeth on her visit to the Earl of Leicester at Kenilworth in 1575.

The Feast of Fools There remains among the teeming mediæval manifestations of the dramatic instinct, the many varieties of feasting, reveling, mockery and masking which grew out of the New Year's festival commemorating the beginning of winter. Among them, prominent on the Continent and especially in France, was the Feast of Fools in which the lower clergy mimicked and parodied the procedures of the Church and, inverting their own status and that of their betters, indulged in licence of behavior, often in the church itself, to the scandal of their order and honest men. In England the Feast of Fools never attained the popularity nor involved the abuses that came to stigmatize it in France; but the not dissimilar festivity of the Boy Bishop took its place. This was a custom among choirboys, who assumed the right, in seasons of revel, to choose a "bishop" from among their number, to burlesque divine service and in mock solemnity levy tribute to support "the bishop's" state. The diffusion of this practice in cathedrals, lesser churches, monasteries and schools was extraordinary, and only the youth of the participants in it prevented the scandalous excesses of the Feast of Fools.

Lay revelry Obviously this species of revelry was not to be confined to the clergy. It was paralleled before long and imitated by the laity; and guilds were instituted which widened this burlesque of the solemnities of the Church into a parody of society at large. Such acting and satirizing guilds are best exampled in the amateur *sociétés joyeuses* of France, the *Enfants sans Souci* and their like and even more serious literary societies fell into the vogue of satire, if not burlesque on the stage.[1] But inevitable was the contact of such societies with professional minstrelsy, and it was the repertory of the minstrel which often supplied the

[1] *Ibid., The Mediæval Stage,* i, 375, where abundant references are given.

merry monologue known as the *sermon joyeux*, the *farce*, *débat* or *sottie*, a comedy of fools, as well as song, dance and other organized mirth. There are few traces of the *société joyeuse* in England, where such jollity was less fully organized; but masking, mumming, as it was called, and disguising, with much of their attendant mock ceremony, burlesque and licence, became a feature of the season of Christmas at court, in the halls of noblemen and gentry, at schools and universities and among the citizens of towns as well. The annals are full of descriptions of these revelings, which rose at times to the dignity of serious pageantry and the organization of a mock court under a Lord of Misrule, and sunk at others to the lowest forms of itinerant and impromptu buffoonery. It would appear that spoken words were not in earlier times a feature of these lay revels, and it has been thought that it was the poet John Lydgate, in the earlier half of the fifteenth century, who first, in England, gave a literary direction to mumming.[1] By the time of the Tudors, speeches, songs and dialogue had become common to them, and at court the need for a regulation of all these activities brought about, in 1545, the creation of the Office of the Revels, which functions so importantly in the history of Elizabethan drama. A lesser outcome of these ancient revels was the recognition of the professional fool, a personage quite distinct from the clown of mediæval festival, and one destined to play an important rôle in the development of later drama.

Up to this point our concern has been with play and the mimetic impulse which that inherent human instinct transmitted down the ages in a bewildering variety of ways. This may be likened to the preparation of the soil for actual drama, and there is danger that with some, like Grimm long ago, we may attach too much importance to it. But we have likewise found in minstrelsy a professional

Major sources of drama

[1] E. K. Chambers, *The Mediæval Stage*, i, 396; E. P. Hammond, in *Anglia* xxii, 864; R. Brotanek, *Die englischen Maskenspiele*, 1902, p. 306.

and creative spirit which, however inarticulate or expressing itself merely in narrative or lyrically, at times begot premonitions and approaches to veritable drama. But the capital sources of modern drama are not thus tenuously to be traced back to these successors, however remote, of the farces of the mimes, even if this influence is not wholly to be rejected. The major sources of modern drama are really two and the line of their evolution is well defined. These are the ecclesiastical liturgy, out of which came mediæval sacred drama, and the classical revivals of the humanists. The former claims the rest of this chapter.

Liturgical drama

In strict ecclesiastical language the term, *liturgy*, signifies that part of Christian service which is devoted specifically to the celebration of the Eucharist. In common parlance, however, *liturgy* means no more than "a collection of formularies for the conduct of divine service." *Liturgical drama* is the somewhat unhappy title which has been applied to certain amplifications of parts of the services of the Church which involved mimetic action, symbolic costume and the suggestion of dialogue by way of antiphonal chant. In the beginning, these were very slender and it is only in the light of their subsequent expansion that we can recognize their dramatic possibilities. These amplifications by way of illustration or emphasis were called *tropes*, and they were first written to supply words to certain new melodies called *neumae*, which had been similarly interpolated by way of amplification in parts of the *Antiphonary* or book of anthems. Earlier *tropes* were usually taken direct from the words of the *Vulgate*. Some of them developed in time into notable mediæval hymns; others proved barren. By no means were all capable of dramatic development; and this development often only began when a given *trope* was transferred from the position in the service in which it had originated to some other place more favorable to such growth. In the origin

6

of modern drama there are two such points, Easter and Christmas; and the former is by far the more important.

The Easter *Quem quaeritis*, as it is called from the first two words of this *trope*, originated in the Benedictine abbey of St. Gall, as far back as the middle of the ninth century. It represented a simple chanted colloquy between voices of the choir, signifying the two Maries and the responding angel. Soon these personages were visualized by means of trailing vestments, wings for the angel, and the like; and a visit was made within the church to an actual structure representing the sepulcher, a device which became common in mediæval churches. Thus attached to the ceremony of the sepulcher, the *Quem quaeritis* soon added scene to scene, until it came to include, in some places, the announcement of the Resurrection, the visit to the sepulcher, the appearance of the risen Christ to Mary Magdalene, and even occasionally a comedy scene in which ointment is purchased of an *unguentarius*, or oil merchant, for the anointment of the dead. The place of the *Quem quaeritis* became that of the Easter sepulcher on Good Friday and its spread was far and wide. *The Easter trope*

The second important *trope* was that of the *Stella*, otherwise known as the *Tres Reges*, or the *Magi*. In its simplest form the Wise Men enter the church from different quarters, following the star to where it gleams over the altar, and, meeting there, comment in dialogue on the star as the sign foretold of the coming of the Saviour. But here, too, came growth and expansion, including the meeting of the Magi with Herod, his sending of his scribes, the angelic warning to the Magi not to return the same way, the raging of Herod and even the massacre of the innocents. An earlier *trope*, too, that of the *Pastores*, or shepherds, in which a visit to the *praesepe*, or cradle, closely follows the visit to the sepulcher of the *Quem quaeritis*, was often joined or adapted to the *Stella*, just as the *Perigrinus*, in which the figure of Christ appears armed with the Resurrection cross, united with the *Quem quaeritis*. *The Christmas trope*

7

Still another liturgical dramatic origin is found in the *Prophetæ*, originally a *lectio* or reading, not a chant, in which the prophets of the Jews are cited to speak in turn, testifying to the Christ. This was finally converted into dramatic form and the citation among the prophets of Balaam and his ass brought it in touch, in later times, with the Feast of the Ass and profane plays. The evolution of all these *tropes* into what cannot but be called drama was complete by the middle of the thirteenth century, and such was the solidarity of the mediæval Church that what is true of the Continent is equally true of England, as sufficient remains of English material attest. Like topics soon presented themselves to the inventiveness and ingenuity of the time. Hilarius, a pupil of Abelard about 1125, is the author of three Latin plays, on St. Nicholas, Lazarus, and Daniel, the last apparently an offshoot of the *Prophetæ*; and all show but a slender hold on any fixed position in the liturgy. The earlier unknown authors of the beginnings of drama were clerics attached to church or monastery. Hilarius, who was possibly of English birth, was more than probably a vagrant scholar.[1] The *Sponsus*, a French play on the wise and foolish virgins, still links on to the Christmas service; while in the elaborate spectacle of the German *Antichristus* of 1160, based on the second Epistle of St. Paul to the Thessalonians, we have so satirical and anticlerical a production that that alone is enough to take it out of the liturgical into independent drama.

As to performance, the choir was clearly the first stage. But, losing touch with the service, there was need of a greater space, and the action soon spread into the nave of the church. While there was no decoration, certain properties became, as Thorndike calls them, "centers of dramatic interest," the cross, the sepulcher, the manger.

Amplification of tropes

Performance of religious drama

[1] G. R. Coffman, *A New Theory Concerning the Origin of the Miracle Play*, Chicago Thesis, 1914, finds these origins in the musical services of particular saints' days and in an application of the dramatic method to the legend.

8

About them and between them, the action took place; and this led to the recognition of certain fixed positions, called *loca, sedes,* or *domus,* occupied by individual actors and localized by means of special designations. This left a neutral space between, called the *platea.* In such an arrangement there was neither entrance nor exit for any actor; he was before his audience, which was on all sides of him, for the duration of the play. Several places could be represented in their several positions simultaneously and without change, and the *platea,* being devoid of properties or of local designation, might serve for any place at all. To visualize an example, in the Abbey of St. Martial at Limoges in France the parable of the wise and foolish virgins was staged under title of the *Sponsus,* possibly somewhat in this way. Before the door leading from the body of the church to the choir stood two little groups of figures signifying young women, one sedate and ready with their lamps all trimmed, the other chattering and giggling, careless, their lamps unfilled, untrimmed. When from behind the gate there resounds the voice of the Angel Gabriel announcing, "Ere long the Bridegroom cometh." The wise virgins kneel in ready obedience; the foolish ones flutter distracted, seeking through the crowd the oil merchant who, sitting at his little table, dispenses his wares leisurely to each, and, we may well believe, not without wise and witty admonition. And they hurry back, only to find, alas! that the Bridegroom has come, the guests are entered, and the doors are shut against them. There the parable ends, but the mediæval mind demands completeness and comedy as well. So, as they are bewailing their unhappy neglect and complaining to one another, dark figures, hoofed and horned and tailed, dart out from behind the pillars and carry off the foolish and now lost maidens, to eternal punishment. Several old cuts and plans survive to disclose the nature of the setting and arrangement of these old plays. A passion play at Donaueschingen was elaborately staged on twenty-two platforms, among them the Garden of Gethsemane, the palaces of Herod and Pilate, the pillar of the scourging, and the pillar on the top of which stood the cock that crew to the tragic undoing of Peter. The play began in the nave and passed from station to station, through the choir to the sanctuary. The holy sepulcher, the cross, and heaven stood appropriately there; hell was placed afar off in the nave, where it remains in its realistic details, a permanent feature of some old continental churches. A still later performance of the passion play at Valenciennes, in 1547, represents the pageants for the whole play gathered together on one platform, elaborately displaying Nazareth, Jerusalem, the house of Caïphas, the Golden Gate, and Limbo or purgatory. The device of a real ship, floating in a real sea a dozen feet square, seems a triumph of scenic effect. A globular crystalline structure over one of the houses represents Paradise, the Trinity figured therein surrounded with angels. While at the opposite end stood hell with gaping mouth, its monsters, chambers of torture, Ixion on his wheel, and other great sinners, the whole illuminated with a realistic conflagration.

Development into the miracle play
But long before these later elaborations, a process of secularization had set in, which, most active between 1250 and 1350, transformed an office of worship, conducted by the clergy as a part of the service and in the church, into a popular spectacle, acted and controlled by lay guilds and staged in the market-place. This change was brought about by a further expansion and coalescence of liturgical dramatic material. As to the Christmas play, the *Stella* did not develop; but the *Prophetæ*, taking Adam and the creation of man as of the prophetic type, stretched back the theme to the Garden of Eden, and forward to the fall of the angels. The Easter play likewise expanded, adding such scenes as the incredulity of Thomas, Christ stepping forth from the sepulcher and his visit to the lower regions to save by his grace the souls of the righteous who, dying before his coming, could not have known him. This topic,

derived from the Apocryphal gospel of Nicodemus and known as *The Harrowing of Hell*, exists in an Anglo-Saxon poem of the eighth or ninth century, and by some has been thought to be an actual drama—if such, the earliest in England. But better opinion considers this version of *The Harrowing* a *débat* or *estrif*, to be declaimed, not acted. The Easter play further developed in adding to its theme that of the passion. The Passion play is earliest traceable to 1200 at Sienna, and its origin was not liturgical. In this earliest form it includes the descent from the cross, the healing of Longinus and the burial of Christ. An interesting addition is a scene of comedy in which figures Mary Magdalene before her conversion and a merchant, from whom she purchases cosmetics. The Passion play united with that of the Nativity, with the *Old Testament* material for prologue and the ascension to last judgment to succeed, realizes the mighty range and sweep of the cosmic miracle play which thus conceives the whole story of man, his creation, fall, and redemption in the sacrifice of Christ, the life of the Saviour in the promises of his coming, his converse with men and ministrations among them, his death and resurrection: a design unequaled in its comprehensiveness, inspired with a central dramatic motive unparalleled and unsurpassed. This process of growth and cohesion was complete by the opening of the fourteenth century. Thereafter only episodic amplification was possible.

The secularization of the sacred play involved several features of importance to the history of the drama. When guilds of laymen and literary societies, such as the *puy* in France, took over the acting of religious plays, the vernacular gradually worked its way into the texts, to the partial, at last to all but the complete, exclusion of Latin, the language of the Church. This took from the drama that cosmopolitan character which the solidarity of the Church throughout Christendom had given it; and after the fourteenth century there is a separate national devel-

Secularization of religious drama

11

opment of the sacred drama in France, Italy, England, and elsewhere. Still again, the step which took the drama out of the church quickened the growth of comedy. The liturgical pre-drama was not without comedy figures: the *unguentarius, mercator,* Herod, type of the braggart, perhaps even Mary Magdalene in her unregenerate state. The devil is personified in one of the earliest ceremonies, that of the *Tollite portas,* or opening of the doors, as hiding in the church and fleeing from it on the demand of the clergy in procession to enter; and he was early utilized as a fun-maker, even at times as a species of guard or policeman with a cudgel to keep back the crowd; however the figure of Satan or Lucifer remained tragic and dignified. But when all has been said, it was the transfer of the plays, not only from the services, but from their place in the calendar to Corpus Christi day, and their combination with the ecclesiastical and lay procession which signalized that celebration, that transformed them into the stupendous spectacles which they became. The feast of Corpus Christi was instituted by Pope Urban IV in 1264, confirmed by Clement V in 1311, and an office was compiled for it by Thomas Aquinas. It was fixed for Thursday after Trinity Sunday and hence was likely to fall in pleasant spring weather. As a celebration "in honor of the mystery of the transubstantiated sacrament" it represents the very essence of the tragedy of the life and sacrifice of Christ, and gave unity to a theme the importance and universality of which were most fittingly commemorated in drama.

Nature of its evolution In this brief sketch of the evolution of the miracle play it is carefully to be remembered that the steps detailed did not ensue with any historical order or regularity. Indeed, nearly all the stages of this development existed at some time or other simultaneously, the completed cycle, the various types of dramas derived from the liturgical *tropes,* even specimens of the liturgical beginnings themselves, at times in very late survivals. Besides this, episodes of longer plays broke off and other plays were devised out of material derived from the Apocrypha and from legends of saints, such as St. Nicholas, St. Catherine, St. George, and many others. This led to much in later times. To instance only one example, the transfer of the play of St. George from its ecclesiastical associations to a popular drama involving procession, pageantry, and the slaying of the dragon, became a natural process when that personage was identified with the patron saint of England. As a mummers' play, confused with the sword dance, if not related to it, the play of St. George has lasted down to modern times.[1]

We have now before us the idea of a theatrical representation of Bible story, appropriately costumed after the notions of the time, if not after ours, staged and involving dialogue and action. Various words were employed in the Middle Ages to denote this sort of thing. Of these *representatio* or *representatio miraculi* was the most usual; and this was commonly cut down to *miraculum* or *miracle*, which came, in England at least, to stand for any religious play. As the idea of amusement or diversion gradually entered into competition with that of devotion, *ludus*, or the vernacular *jeu*, *Spiel*, *play*, was more and more frequently used. Despite its analogy to the French *mystère*, the term *mystery* or *mystery play*, thus applied to an English mediæval drama, is wholly indefensible, as it was unknown in English until its appearance as an academic coinage in the preface to *Dodsley's Old English Plays*, in 1744. The term *saint play*, involved in such titles as *Ludus de Sancta Katerina*, for example, is useful to distinguish religious plays thus founded on extra-biblical material.

Use of terms

As to England, there seems no good reason to believe that actual sacred drama was known before the Norman Conquest. The earliest mention of such a play, which is

Early sacred drama in England

---

[1] A. W. Pollard, *English Miracle Plays, Moralities and Interludes*, seventh ed. 1923.

by Matthew Paris about 1240, takes us back to 1119 at least before which time a play concerning St. Catherine was acted at Dunstable. About 1182, Fitzstephen, in his *Life of Thomas à Becket*, draws a contrast between theatrical spectacles of ancient Rome and the holier plays of London "which represented miracles and the sufferings of confessors and martyrs of the Church." No Latin miracle plays, written in England, are extant; and we have not sufficient evidence to be sure that French miracle plays were ever written or acted there. From a statement made in one of the manuscripts of the *Chester Plays* their date has been referred back to 1328 and their authorship, or revision at least, to the famous Ralph Higden, author of *Polychronicon*. In 1377 is the earliest mention of the now lost Corpus Christi plays of Beverley which flourished into the reign of Queen Mary. The York craft guild plays are first named in the next year; those of Coventry, in 1392. *The Towneley Plays*, supposedly acted at Wakefield, Pollard believes to have been complete by 1420. Such mentions and the scores of others lead to the inference of a far earlier period for the beginnings of this vogue in England and point to a diffusion extraordinarily wide.

The cosmic miracle or cycle

At its height the English miracle play was a cycle of dramas, given yearly under the direction of the civic authorities in a series of separate scenes or pageants, as they were called, each intrusted to the guild of some particular craft or occupation and acted by its members. To the town belonged the publication of the "banns" or proclamation of the play and a register or copy of the text was preserved among its archives. It was the town which acted as arbiter in disputes between the guilds and it demanded that the plays be properly given, by sufficient actors, enforcing its demands at need by fine. Supervision of the stations for performance and the entertainment of guests lay also with the civic authorities; but they seem not to have incurred the expenses of the pageants themselves, their furnishing or costuming, save in exceptional cases, all these matters belonging to the guilds. As substantially every resident of a town was a member of some guild, the maintenance of the cycle fell upon all. This democracy in sustenance was extended beyond the guilds as disclosed in records which tell of the assignment of scenes to the "priests," to the "gentlemen" at Beverley, to the "cathedral clergy" at Lincoln, and even to "the worshipful wives of this town," at York. There were, of course, many variations from these general conditions; for plays were acted singly and in cycles elsewhere than in towns, and guilds were formed to sustain town plays where, as in London, the civic authorities did not provide for them.

The typical English cycle was acted, as at York, on movable pageants—in this case to the number of forty-eight—drawn from place to place, the play of each pageant repeated again and again. But stationary pageants in smaller towns and for lesser cycles were not unknown. Indeed, the *Ludus Coventriæ*, the cycle next longest to that of York, was probably so acted, where within the eastern midlands is not certain, although all are agreed that this cycle had nothing to do with Coventry, which had one of its own. At Chester a cycle made up of some twenty-five plays was acted by craft guilds at Whitsuntide. This cycle shows a closer relation to the *Mystère du Viel Testament* than do other remains in English; and it likewise admits more apocryphal and legendary material.[1] Finally in the *Towneley Plays*, thirty-two in number, we have a composite collection, believed to have been acted variously by crafts at Wakefield or at one of the great fairs of the neighborhood. From a literary point of view, none of these old efforts to realize on the stage the familiar stories of the Bible can be rated very high. Mediæval drama, as an art, stands on no such level as mediæval architecture, for example. But some of these scenes ex-

Extant English cycles

---

[1] A. C. Baugh, in *Schelling Anniversary Papers*, 1923.

hibit an attractive naturalness, a human feeling, a groping
after, if seldom the grasp, of dramatic situation which
neither their language, to us often uncouth, nor their
forced and elaborate versification, can wholly impair. Rising conspicuously above their kind are some half dozen
of the *Towneley Plays*, among them *Noah*, the *Magi*, and
two plays on the Shepherds, conspicuously the second;
for here it is that we find a dramatist of verve, dramatic
sensibility, and humor emerging out of this welter of
Bible story remade, no unworthy fellow exponent of an
era which gave Chaucer to the world. We do not know
his name; for the sacred drama had evolved (save for the
solitary name of Ralph Higden) very much in the manner
of the ballad, the work of authors unnamed and unknown,
but expressing the feeling and the ideas of their class,
whether clergy or guild, and developing only as these ideas
were successfully representative. The *Chester Plays*, then,
those of *York*, the *Towneley Plays* and the *Ludus Coventriæ* (sometimes called the *Hegge Plays* from the name
of a sometime owner, but certainly not of Coventry),[1] these
constitute the four cosmic cycles of miracle plays which
remain to us in various manuscripts, practically complete; and to these may be added a Cornish cycle which
takes us beyond our subject. From single plays and fragments of cycles once acted at Coventry, Newcastle, Norwich, Shrewsbury, and other places, and from traces by
way of mention and allusion, we have reason to believe
that the diffusion of the sacred drama in its cosmic form
was exceedingly wide in fourteenth and fifteenth century
England, and that for more than two hundred years there
was scarcely a town of importance, a cathedral, a church,
or a monastery without its celebration, on Corpus Christi
day, on Whitsuntide or on some other holiday of the
Church, of either a cycle or of some variety, at least, of
the lesser kindred of the miracle play.

[1]See *Mediæval Stage*, ii, 321, for a comparative table of the contents
of the four cycles.

As to presentation, at Chester, " 'the banns' were pro- claimed on St. George's day by the city crier with whom rode the stewards of each craft," and a proclamation was made "against all disturbers of the peace." Then followed the pageants, the first of them beginning at the Abbey Gate and repeating at other stations, until nine were playing simultaneously in as many different places. It took three days at Chester to complete the cycle. A late contemporary describes the pageant wagon itself as "a high place made like a house with two rooms, being open on the top. [In] the lower room they apparelled and dressed themselves, and in the higher room they played. And they [the wagons] stood upon six wheels." In this system of processional performances, the action was by no means confined to the pageants themselves, but took place at times between them, as in the *plateæ* of church performance. Of curtain there is little trace except as to that which was hung at times from the lower story of the pageant to conceal the tiring or dressing room. Though in the *Ludus Coventriæ* a curtain is employed occasionally to discover the actors and a certain sense of off stage and on was developed. Costume was the simplest, however elaborate at times, and the idea of any manner of clothing other than that of their own time and climate does not seem to have occurred to the projectors of these plays. It is easier for us to dilate on the crudeness and childishness of these rude performances than to appreciate the tremendous effect which their vogue must have had on the mediæval man and woman. From the point of view of the drama, never has a national soil been better prepared than was that of England by these plays. And while undoubtedly the spectacular was their chief attraction to the crowd, there are not wanting evidences of sinners brought to repentance by their powerful appeal.

The attitude of the clergy towards the miracle play throughout the Middle Ages was in the main that of encouragement and approval. Occasional reforming prelates

17

such as Robert Grosseteste, Bishop of Lincoln, might stretch the prohibition of Innocent III as to the clergy's participation in the Feast of Fools and like secular *ludi* to include miracle plays, or a zealous follower of Wyclif, later, fulminate against them; but the sacred drama had grown, like mediæval art, music, and architecture, out of the corporate soul of Christendom; like the other arts, it was the expression of that splendid Catholic solidarity in struggle to express in the concrete the spiritual yearnings of a world as yet undivided by schism and untouched with doubt. While we cannot grant to these stuttering efforts at literary expression the success which the Middle Ages attained in gothic architecture, for example, we can see in the dignity of the sacred figures of these old plays, in their humanity and occasional pathos, in the humor of their realization every now and then of the actualities about them, the inherent qualities of veritable drama. Whatever the trivialities of detail into which it lapsed at times, never has there been a finer central theme than this of the sacrifice of Christ that men might live, presented on the great canvas of Bible story. Under kinder auspices and in gentler times, above all, with one great tragic genius, the peer of the comic spirit of the unknown playwright of Wakefield, such a drama might have developed into an achievement to hold its place beside that of ancient Greece or of Elizabethan England.

CHAPTER II

HUMANISM AND THE DRAMA

IN the miracle play the Church was always present. Miracle and Moral Though lay guilds might handle the matter and the cosmic cycle become at times a spectacle, the spirit of religion was over it all. With the moral play, however religious its primary intent, this was changed. The priest had become the teacher. The exposition of Bible story with its figurative suggestiveness of divine mysteries, was superseded by exhortation to correct and godly living, often inventively figured forth by way of parable, by satire, which always stalks in the shadow of the moralist, at last by the rancor of controversy and schism.

Almost from the first the miracle play had reached out Extra biblical material for material beyond Bible story. Putting aside the tone of mockery, which is born elsewhere, it has been well observed that the governing spirit of the miracle play is not tragic, but that of comedy, kindly, pathetic, reconciling, and humane.[1] This effect is produced by familiar touches, bringing these scenes, supposed to depict alien times in an alien age, into contact with mediæval daily life. Thus Cain is developed, as this scene is again and again rewritten, from a niggardly boor into a shrewd scoundrel inclined to argue dialectically in self-justification with his Maker. The note of conjugal difference is thrust into the play of *Noah and the Ark;* and Gyb, the wife, heads the long list of diverting stage shrews. The relations of filial piety are touchingly set forth in *Abraham and Isaac* and the tenderness bordering on humor and the humor that borders tears are depicted in the relations of Joseph and

---

[1] C. M. Gayley, *Plays of Our Forefathers,* 1907, p. 144.

Mary. That much of this was more or less unconsciously done does not take from its merit or its effectiveness. But there was another line of growth for the miracle play besides this of the dramatic development of personage and incident, and this lay in novelty of material. England never possessed an analogue to the extensive literature of the legends of the saints and the miracles of the Virgin, which the cult of the Mother of God produced in France. However, an English example of this kind of drama is the *Croxton Play* of the conversion of Sir Jonathus the Jew by miracle of the Blessed Sacrament, an elaborate performance displaying elements both moral and comic. Other such plays are *Mary Magdalene* and *The Conversion of St. Paul*, both of the Digby Manuscript, and interesting from their independence of the cycle and from their concentration upon a new dramatic interest.[1] In the former there is much in method and matter derived from the contemporary moral play, and the story is extended to include Mary's unregenerate days as well as her conversion of the King of Marcylle, and her subsequent life as an anchorite in the desert. Both plays combine mediæval saint-story with scriptural tradition. But extra-biblical material was not derived alone from the Apocryphal gospels. Sources such as the *Cursor Mundi* and *The Golden Legend* entered more or less into all the cycles, and both enrich and dislocate biblical history with popular lore and legend. It is inaccurate to speak of the moral play as either an outgrowth of the miracle or its successor. For, to instance England only, a guild for the production of a *Paternoster* play or *Play of the Lord's Prayer* was in existence as early as 1378. The play is described as one in which "all manner of vices and sins were held up to scorn and the virtues were held up to praise." And a *Play of the Creed*, in which each apostle sets forth an article of the "Apostles' Creed," was acted, likewise at York, from 1446 to more than a century later. None the less, it was out of extra-

---

[1] As to the Digby MS., see *The Mediæval Stage*, ii, 428.

HUMANISM AND THE DRAMA

biblical material that the suggestion of the moral play came, for with this extension of matter, inventiveness was encouraged; and the inventiveness of the Middle Ages expressed itself in allegory.

The moral play may be defined as a drama of didactic intention, presenting life by way of allegory and by means of personages designed to figure forth certain abstract qualities of body or mind. The motives of allegorical drama have been discerned in Latin literature, and it is usual on this topic to mention the elaborate allegorical poem, *Psychomachia,* of Prudentius dating A. D. 400, to refer to the reconciliation of the heavenly virtues in the eighty-fifth Psalm, to St. Paul's allusion to the armor of the Christian in *Ephesians* and the like. But there were other contemporary influences. Allegory is the breath of popular mediæval romance such as the *Roman de la Rose.* The widely diffused play of *Antichristus* dates back to the twelfth century with its allegorical figures of Heresy, Pity, and the Church. And there is the vogue in art and literature and the striking realism of the *danse macabre,* representing Death as the constant and inevitable companion of man. Let us take the familiar example, *The Summoning of Everyman,* in print "at least four times early in the sixteenth century." [1] The title declares it "a treatise how the High Father of heaven sendeth Death to summon every creature to come and give an account of their lives in this world"; and the Messenger, who speaks the prologue, announces: "Here you shall see how Fellowship, Jollity, Strength, Pleasure and Beauty will fade away from thee as flowers in May." Somewhat mitigated as to length and sincerely staged, this old moral has an appeal in its simplicity, its fervor, and its truth today, all of this abundantly illustrated a few years ago in its revival on the modern stage. More, *Everyman* became in

The moral play

[1] Pollard, as above, p. 1. where the English version is acknowledged a "translation from the Dutch *Elkerlijk,* and the source referred, with Ten Brink, to a "Buddhist parable known to Europeans through the legend of Barlaam and Josaphat."

21

our time the inspiration of a considerable number of plays, many of them popular, thus declaring that the spirit of allegory is as yet far from dead.

Varieties of the moral play

We have, then, in the moral play, not only presentation by way of abstraction, but man conceived of as beset by vices and defended by virtues in an incessant struggle for his soul. Some of the older moral plays, such as *The World and the Child*, give us this struggle under guise of the appropriate temptations belonging to successive periods of life from childhood to old age, and imitate in this the wide range of the miracle play. Others, like *Everyman* itself, or Skelton's somewhat overrated *Magnificence*, are of more limited scope, fixing attention on some one episode in human life. Various classifications of the moral play have been attempted. They are mostly misleading, because the moral, like other drama, shades imperceptibly species into species and enters into the make-up of plays otherwise planned. Enumeration of the list of English moral plays must remain as foreign to our purpose as attempted classification. It is enough to note how such plays range from elaborate performances made up of a series of pageants emulating the miracle cycle to slight productions which only their didactic intention distinguishes from mere interludes. An important group of these last is that which dilates on the life and the temptations of the young, and in this presages the comedy of manners. Such is the subject of *Hickscorner* (c. 1513), which points out the path of that scoffer at religion, egged on by Freewill and Imagination; another is *Youth* (1513-29), misled by Riot, Pride, and Abominable Living. The spirit here is that of the later group of plays that exploit the parable of the prodigal son, favorite theme of the humanists and the school drama.

Staging of the moral play

As to the staging of these many kinds of moral plays, *The Pride of Life*, which dates not long after the death of Chaucer, was acted out of doors, and so was *The Castle of*

Perseverance, which belongs to much the same period.[1] In this latter this stronghold is realistically reared in the midst of a circular field, with a couch for Mankind beneath it and five outlying "skafolds," for "God, the World, the Flesh, Covetousness, and Belial." [2] Even more elaborate outdoor performances were those of Sir David Lindsay's *Satire of the Three Estates*, between 1540 and 1554, at least one of them on a jousting field before the king and the gathered nobility of Scotland, an affair equaling in importance and preparation a mediæval tournament. In such performances the places for individual scenes were often a considerable distance apart and much of the action took place in the indeterminable open field between them. More usually moral plays were acted within doors, and this in itself entailed a simpler staging. Some morals disclose two or more "houses" on the stage at the same time, as in *Wit and Wisdom*, in which we have the house of Wantonness, the den of Irksomeness, a prison, and Mother Bee's house, the action proceeding from one to the other. But many more might have been successfully acted, like the interludes which existed with them and followed them, on a bare stage or even on the floor of the hall before the screen, with its convenient doors, for a background, and such articles as were at hand for occasional properties.

From the very first the moral play was prone to a satirical bias. A forbidding group were begotten in the bitter controversies and the proselytizing zeal which marked the earlier days of the Reformation; and foremost among them are those of John Bale, sometime Protestant Bishop of Ossory in Ireland, a writer as vociferous as he was persistent and voluminous. Three of the extant dramatic works of Bale are in the nature of miracle plays. Unlike others of their kind, these are Protestant in bias; and their controversial spirit Bale maintained in his two

Bale and the controversial moral play

[1] W. K. Smart, *Manly Anniversary Studies*, 1923, p. 43, dates this play 1405 and places it near Lincoln.
[2] See the familiar diagram reproduced from the contemporary manuscript first by T. Sharp, *A Dissertation on the Pageants*, etc., 1825.

23

moral plays, *The Three Laws of Christ*, peculiarly bitter
in its denunciations of Rome, and *King Johan*, an interesting departure from the moral type in that its subject
is the history of an English king, here distorted into that
of a premature champion of the Protestant cause and surrounded with such figures as Dissimulation, Private
Wealth, and England personified. Bale was a zealot,
variously in orders in the Roman and the English Church,
or in flight on the Continent, but remarkable in his deliberate diversion of the stage to the propaganda of Protest-
antism.[1] On the day of the accession to the throne of
Queen Mary, he had some of his plays defiantly acted at
the market cross of Kilkenny; and he lived on, a prebend
of Canterbury, into Elizabeth's reign. There were other
moral plays of controversy; *Lusty Juventus* by R. Wever,
a disciple of Bale, is such, wherein the hero, led away from
the principles of the Reformation, is rescued by Knowledge and Good Counsel; and *New Custom*, which declares
against "Mass, Popery, Purgatory and Pardons." Most
of these plays were printed in the first two decades of
Elizabeth's reign; and it is quite likely that the majority
were didactic exercises rather than pieces from the actual
repertories of acting companies.[2] Many are anonymous,
like the two just named; but some attach the author's
name, such as *The Life and Repentance of Mary Magdalene*, by Louis Wager, in which biblical and allegorical
characters appear cheek by jowl, or Ulpian Fulwell's
Like Will to Like, in which figures a personage named
Ralph Roister, later to give his name to a more important production, and a Vice who, after the manner of his
kind, is ridden away on the back of the Devil. For
reasons obvious, but one controversial moral play has come
down to us on the Roman Catholic side, and this is *Respub-*

---

[1] Chambers, *Elizabethan Stage*, i, 242, finds Bale a "principal agent of
Cromwell's statecraft in what was probably a deliberate attempt to
capture so powerful an engine as the stage in the interests of Protestant-
ism." The plays acted at Kilkenny were *God's Promise* and *John the
Baptist*. Both are extant. Bale died in 1563.
[2] *Ibid.*, iii, 179.

lica, dating from the reign of Queen Mary, authorship and other provenance unknown.

Of the contents of moral plays, enough has been said. The characters in them, though abstract in name and as to the qualities figured, often gain, when individualized by the actor, so as to produce the effect of real personages. Thus Pauper in Lyndsay's *Satire of the Three Estates,* bewailing the exactions of landlord and clergy, becomes almost as genuine a person as Mak, the thievish knave and the shepherds whom he cheats, in the *Towneley* "Second Shepherds' Play." Nor was the moral play without power in its day. Lyndsay's *Satire* so moved his king as to certain wrongs in the state that he declared justice should be done though some sweat for it. A moral performed by students of Gray's Inn, before Cardinal Wolsey and called *Lord Governance,* was so pointed in its political allusiveness that his eminence took offense and ordered the author, John Roo, and some of the actors to the Fleet prison.[1] Among the general personages of the moral play, while the Devil still figures variously, his faculties for clever agile mischief are shared by the Vice, who in turn shades off into the stage Fool, if indeed the Vice be not a cousin-german of the original in life of that ubiquitous personage.[2]

Reality of moral figures

Among moral plays written in the reign of Henry VIII, the schoolmaster and the censor of morals comes more and more completely to supersede the preacher. In the interlude of *The Four Elements* (1517), for example, authority speaks informingly in praise of learning, declaring among "many proper points of philosophy . . . certain conclusions that the earth must needs be round," and how "within these twenty year westward he found new lands that we never heard tell of before." This well-written didactic moral is the work of John Rastell, described as "printer, lawyer, dramatist, and enthusiast." Rastell was

Rastell and the circle of More

[1] Halle's *Chronicle,* ed. H. Ellis, 1809, p. 719.
[2] A recent monograph is *Studies in the Development of the Fool in Elizabethan Drama,* 1923, by Miss O. M. Busby.

brother-in-law of Sir Thomas More, England's first lay
chancellor. A moral play of not dissimilar type is Henry
Medwall's *Nature*. Medwall was one of the chaplains of
the humanist prelate, Cardinal Morton, in whose household More was reared, where, it is related that "he would
suddenly sometimes step in among the players, and, never
studying for the matter, make a part of his own . . .
which made the lookers-on more sport than all the players
beside."[1] To this group interested in drama, Medwall
and Rastell writing plays and the latter publishing them
and exploiting them, we may add John Heywood, the
writer of interludes, who became Rastell's son-in-law and
perhaps owed his first advancement at court to More.
Rastell seems even to have anticipated the building of the
Theater by some fifty years, with a stage which he erected
for open-air plays in his garden, as early as 1524.[2]

John Hey-
wood and
the inter-
lude

We have carried forward the tale of the moral play to
a point at which it becomes confused with the interlude.
Interludium, or *interlude*, has been variously defined. The
older notion of it as a slight mimetic or dramatic representation, falling—like the comedy of Mak in the *Towneley
Plays*—between the acts of a longer and more serious
play, or between the courses of a feast, has recently been
strengthened by the rediscovery of Medwall's interlude of
Fulgens and Lucres, the prologue of which makes unmistakable allusion to such a use. This is contrary to Chambers's view of the interlude as simply a *ludus*, or play, *inter*,
or between, two or more persons and hence merely a dialogue. Whatever the original significance, the term
interlude came gradually to be used as to a play of more
or less secular contents, until, in the application of the

---

[1] J. Roper, *Life of More*, ed. S. W. Singer, 1822, p. 4, and see the interesting application of this anecdote in a scene of the play, *Sir Thomas
More*.
[2] A. W. Reed, *John Heywood and his Friends*, 1917, and *The Beginnings
of the English Secular and Romantic Drama*, 1922. For the "pleadings
in a theatrical lawsuit" in which a "stage for players in Rastell's Ground
Beside Finsbury" is named, E. Arber, *Fifteenth Century Prose and
Verse*, p. 319.

word to Heywood's farces of mediæval type, we have this usage fully confirmed. John Heywood, who wrote much besides drama, really began his career as a singer and player on the virginals in the court of Henry VIII. As such his descent is from the minstrel, precisely as the inspiration of his interludes and dialogues is the French *fabliaux.* Heywood is first heard of at court in 1519, where he was actively engaged, as the records show, up to 1528. He was a yeoman of the crown in 1520 and sewer of the chamber at the time of King Edward's funeral in 1553. Heywood's devotion to the older faith sent him into exile on the accession of Queen Elizabeth; and, born in 1497, he died, a very old man, about 1580, abroad. Of the six dramatic productions with safety to be attributed to Heywood's pen, two, *Love* and *Wit and Folly,* are argumentative dialogues "in the manner of an interlude." The other four are pure farce, notable among them, *The Four P's,* a debate between a pardoner, a palmer, and a 'poticary "as to which shall take the best place," determined by tall talk and imaginative lying, decided by a pedlar. But of no less humor, vigor, and liveliness is the practical joke on a stupid husband, *The Merry Play of John, Tyb and Sir John,* and the scandalous altercation between *The Pardoner and the Frere,* both of whom attempt to preach in a church at the same time for something more tangible than the saving of souls. *The Play of the Weather* is more elaborate and returns somewhat to the methods of the moral, with Merry Report, a species of good-humored Vice, mustering various complainants as to the weather before the throne of Jupiter for redress. To the modern reader these interludes, with all their vigor, are repellent for their humor of filth, a species of beastliness which Heywood shared with his redoubtable contemporary Skelton; and, besides, they partake in goodly part of the wearisome disputatiousness that was equally characteristic of these moral and school-ridden days. But with Heywood we leave two things behind us, allegory and all ul-

27

terior religious and moral purposes. In this unabashed return to the spirit of farce the artistic impulse is set free, and we have, for the first time in England, a dramatic production intended wholly and simply to amuse.

Pageantry, mumming, and disguising
Coincident with the development of the dialogue and the interlude, the Middle Ages offer, from very early times, examples of almost every conceivable form of pageantry, in which mere ceremonial advanced, with the aid of architectural design, disguise, color, speech, and song, into the domain of actual drama. Pageantry, indeed, was generally incidental to courtly or civic occasion, the entertainment of a prince or his welcome to a foreign embassy, civic functions or even private courtesies; and the devices of pageantry, its banners, escutcheons, drapery, and blaze of color had always embellished the assemblies of chivalry, the tourney, and the tilt. Prominent among mediæval entertainments was mumming or disguising, in simple form little more than the entry of a band of gentlemen, fantastically dressed, to dance, in some form, prearranged or extempore, with the ladies. The pageant itself often involved a movable device, a ship, a castle, or the like, wheeled into the hall and arranged in accordance with some allegorical significance appropriate to the complete effect. Dumb show in action and speech-making could obviously be incorporated in either the disguise or the pageant; and the step to a more or less coherent scene involving action was an easy one. Whether the derivation was through the older drama of a serious intention to the interlude, or merely the emergence of the dramatic element inherent in pageantry and disguising, with the transfer of plays from the market-place to the banqueting hall came a twofold transformation: the drama ceased even in pretence to be anything more than an entertainment and its performances aspired more and more to professional standards.[1]

[1] As to the particulars of early masking, see *The Elizabethan Stage,* chap. v.; and R. Withington, *English Pageantry.* 1918, 1920.

HUMANISM AND THE DRAMA

This is not the place in which to discuss, either historically or critically, that interesting outcome of the renaissance called humanism. It is sufficient to our purpose to recall that the ideals of the humanists, like those of the Church, were international, and its language, at least at first, Latin. Humanism was speculative in thought and social in inclination, not ascetic and cloistral. The humanist loved not learning alone for itself, but also for its power as a means of education, culture, and refinement. He was, therefore, the born teacher and in the communication of his ideas, the exchange of thought, the guidance of those who needed him—and of some who did not—lay his function and his pleasure.

One of the results of humanist interest in the revival of the classics was the restoration to the world of classical tragedy and comedy, a knowledge of which, except for the comedies of Terence, appears to have been lost to the Middle Ages. As to Terence, his works had been remarkably adapted to moral and religious purposes in the tenth century by Roswitha, the nun of Gandersheim, thus anticipating the "Christianized Terence" of the humanists by four or five hundred years.[1] In the early fourteenth century Mussato wrote his *Ecerinis*, the first of a long series of modern tragedies inspired by those of Seneca; and the discovery of a dozen comedies of Plautus, hitherto unknown, a century later, added another Roman model. These earlier Latin imitations of classical drama were probably not acted, but read; and despite much uncertainty of information, it is not to be questioned that the example of the miracle play, the moral and vernacular interludes, which we know were early acted by students, encouraged the performance of Latin plays. By the middle of the fifteenth century such performances had ceased to be unusual in Italy, and the practice soon spread over Europe, taken up eagerly by schoolmasters

---

[1] Roswitha, as he modernizes the name, has been excellently translated by C. St. John, 1923; and by H. J. H. Tillyard, same date.

for its pedagogical utility, combining, as it did, the inculcation of the virtues, industry and obedience, and improvement in the students' knowledge of the forms and idioms of Latin, the universal language of scholarship. Thus the Scotch humanist and Latin poet, George Buchanan, while a teacher at Bordeaux (c. 1540), translated and had performed by his students the *Medea* and the *Alcestis* of Euripides. Buchanan was led by Greek rather than Latin tradition, and extended his dramatic art to a treatment of Bible story in like classical manner, in his *Baptistes* and in the story of Jephthes, the latter a tragedy which came deservedly to enjoy a great repute.[1] Less lofty in his inspiration, the French professor at Paris, who Latinized his name into Ravisius Textor, wrote Latin morals and farces of which two found their way into English translation as *Thersites* and *The Disobedient Child*.[2] In Holland the humanist drama turned chiefly to the application of Terence to subjects of religious and moral edification, developing especially the theme of the prodigal son, exampled in the *Asotus* of Macropedius, which inspired an effective English comedy, entitled *Misogonus*, of uncertain authorship in the middle 'sixties. The *Acolastus* of Gnaphaeus is an even more famous example, as it was long used as a school book in England. Dutch Erasmus, Spanish Vives, and Italian Bruno all sojourned in England; and each touched at least the edge of drama: Erasmus in his famous *Colloquies*, Vives in his delightful pedagogical dialogues, and Bruno, in a comedy that inspired no less a play than Jonson's *Alchemist*.[3] In the wider reaches of humanism, quite the most elaborate English play of the type is Gascoigne's *Glass of Government*, 1575, in which the careers of two good boys and two bad are happily, if

School drama

---

[1] On the subject at large, see the Introduction to *The Poetical Works of Sir William Alexander*, by L. E. Kastner and H. B. Charlton, 1921.
[2] J. Bolte, *Vahlon-Festschrift*, 594; but also A. Brandl, *Quellen des weltlichen Dramas*, 1898, p. lxxiii.
[3] For a specimen of the touch of Vives with drama, see F. Watson's translation of some of the dialogues in *Tudor Schoolboy Life*, 1908. Bruno's *Candelaio* has not been translated, so far as I know.

lengthily, contrasted in a series of Terentian situations; and with this the school drama as such ends in England.

But long before this time, plays of Seneca and Plautus had been acted in English schools and universities; and the imitations of both, in Latin and in English, had ceased to be unusual. Between 1540 and 1550 we hear of comedies and tragedies by Ralph Radcliff, Nicholas Grimald, and Nicholas Udall. Radcliff and Udall were schoolmasters who wrote primarily for their scholars. Grimald, best known as the editor of *Tottel's Miscellany* of lyrical verse, was a lecturer at Oxford, where two of his Latin plays were acted; in the story of the Reformation later he was to play no creditable part.[1] Of the many recorded performances of classical drama, imitated or original, at the universities, it is not possible here to speak in any degree of fullness. A performance of the *Pax* of Aristophanes is among them in which the later famous Doctor Dee contrived the flight of a huge scarabeus across the stage and perhaps laid thereby the foundations of a reputation for magic.[2]

English imitations of classical drama

While the performance of classical plays must have been influenced from the first by current mediæval methods of staging, the discovery in humanists' times of the writings of the Roman architect, Vitruvius, containing a celebrated and obscure passage on the arrangement of the classical stage, was eagerly seized on by scholars and followed so far as it was understood. According to Vitruvius, it would appear that the classical Roman stage was provided, across the back and facing the audience, with a permanent architectural structure furnished with three doors and capable of being, in some wise, variously decorated by certain prospects painted in perspective. In addition to the three doors mentioned, there were two other exits from the stage

Vitruvius and the renaissance stage

---

[1] Grimald's two Latin plays are *Christus Redivivus*, 1543, and *Archipropheta*, 1548. See L. R. Merrill, *Publ. Mod. Lang. Asso.* xxxvii, 1922, where Grimald is called "the Judas of the reformation."

[2] Doctor Dee relates this exploit in stage mechanics in his "Compendious Rehearsal," appendix to Hearne, *Chronicles of John of Glastonbury*, p. 501.

on either side, and these were conventionally accepted as leading to the forum and abroad. While the scene (in modern parlance) could be changed by the turning of a three-sided machine, a scene, once set, remained unchanged during the acting of a given play, "columns, piedmonts, and statues" being accepted as the setting suitable to the dignity of tragedy, "private dwellings with balconies and views representing rows of windows," as fit for the familiarity of comedy, and "mountains, caves, trees and other rustic objects" for the satyric play.[1] We do not know where these pivoted triangular machines were set, nor the size, the use, or the appearance of them.[2] But early Italian attempts to stage classical plays or plays imitating them appear to have been influenced by the efforts of scholars to carry out some such conception of an appropriate and temporary embellishment of a permanent architectural *scena* wall, with an adaptation and combination into a more or less harmonious whole, for individual plays, of the several "houses" which, with the open space between them, marked the mediæval manner of staging. Out of these efforts was realized the perspective setting of the sixteenth century, so fully described by Serlio, a method which came at last profoundly to affect the staging of plays wherever learning and culture flourished.[3] Serlio's

Serlio's stage

stage is set with a combination of "houses" constructed of canvas stretched on frames and of at least two sides, with flat canvases painted in perspective. These are arranged on a stage which slopes slightly upward towards the back so as to produce the effect of an harmonious scene, disclosing, through a central opening, a landscape or group

[1] See Vitruvius, *de Architectura,* bk. v, chap. vi, and the translation of M. H. Morgan, 1914, p. 150.

[2] On this, see A. Choisy, *Vitruve,* 1909, especially i, 199; ii, 244; and iv, plates 50 and 51. Also on the vexed question of the περίακτοι, F. W. Kelsey in Archæological Institute of America, Second Series, 1902, vi, 396; and M. Bieber, *Die Denkmäler zum Theaterwesen im Alterthum,* 1920, p. 54.

[3] Sebastiano Serlio, *Architettura* 1537-47, anonymously translated as *The Five Books of Architecture,* London, 1611. See also L. B. Campbell, *Scenes and Machines on the English Stage,* 1923; Thorndike, *The Shakesperean Stage,* 1916, p. 16, and Chambers, *Elizabethan Stage,* chap. xix.

of buildings beyond by way of vista. The usual entrances are from either side; but the "houses"—at least those nearest the front—are frequently constructed with practicable doors and windows; and even the central opening may be, to some extent, employed for entrances and exits. Italian comedy of Roman extraction followed the rule which demanded that all the action take place on the street in front of two adjacent houses. And this became in principle, if somewhat modified by mediæval recollections, the customary method of staging English plays at court and in the universities up to the time of the building of the theater and the upgrowth of popular drama.

But there were other things that English drama learned from the revival of a study of the ancients; and important among them was a sense of form, design, and purpose. Older plays, especially the morals, often straggle aimlessly, the idea lost in more or less irrelevant detail. "Regular" applied to a play, then, means a recognition on the part of the author of the general principles of construction, design, and formal divisions into scenes and acts, the conduct of dialogue, and the conception of personage, which had come to characterize ancient drama; and the chief effect of all this was regulative. It was a happy departure when Nicholas Udall, variously master of Eton and Westminster, conceived the idea of having his boys act an English play on Plautine lines in place of the usual Latin one. Engaged in teaching from his Oxford days until his death in 1556, Udall had prepared verses for the pageantry of the coronation of Anne Boleyn and wrote a play, now lost, recorded as acted at Braintree, Essex, in 1534, while Udall was vicar there. So whether we date it in the 'thirties or later, *Ralph Roister Doister* was the work of an experienced hand. The story concerns the pretenses of Ralph, a rich and presumptious fool, who persists in pressing his attentions on Dame Custance, by help of a faithless parasite Matthew Merrygreek, until worsted by the Dame and her maids in a merry and vig-

Udall and Ralph Roister

orous repulse, happily reinforced by the timely arrival of the lady's betrothed, Gawain Goodluck. The braggart, the parasite, and other personages are Plautine, the plot—which is not ill conceived—is Udall's. The dialogue is lively, the action incessant, and didactic intention has wholly evaporated. In Udall's comedy, despite all the old influences upon it, we step into modern drama; its importance historically can scarcely be exaggerated. The other comedy which is sometimes claimed as the "first" is

Gammer Gurton

Gammer Gurton's Needle, at earliest to be dated a year or so after 1550. The authorship still remains in dispute, assignment successively to two bishops, John Still and John Bridges, having been now superseded by that to William Stevenson, a fellow of Christ's College, Oxford, where *Gammer Gurton* was acted and where Stevenson was in charge, by the records, of plays at that time. Though as unquestionably inspired by Latin comedy as *Ralph Roister Doister*, *Gammer Gurton* throws over imitation of classical personage and atmosphere, giving us a realistic picture of contemporary village life, conceived in the spirit of broad, if somewhat protracted, fun, and thus taking a further step forward. The fiber of *Gammer Gurton* is that of the interludes of Heywood, free, however, of any direct influences from France. In its droll and vigorous realism, this famous comedy has become the parent of a long dramatic progeny.

Sources of modern tragedy

In tragedy the way was longer preparing. The Senecan revival began in Italy, soon after the opening of the fourteenth century. It took the form of learned discussion of the Roman tragic poet, performance of his tragedies, translations of them, and, most important of all, the imitation of their conduct, situations, and dialogue by Italian writers in plays of their own, Latin and Italian. Seneca thus became the accepted model for modern tragedy, not because of intrinsic superiority, but because his are the only specimens of Roman tragedy extant, and because his Greek originals were less accessible and readable. Besides

this, the hard, brilliant rhetorical style of Seneca's tragedies, their blood and terror, fell in well with renaissance
taste and spirit.   In Italy, between 1515 and 1540, Trissino evolved a vernacular classical tragedy out of Seneca
with a leaning towards the purer spirit of Greece.   After
that Cinthio Italianated even Seneca in horror and variety;
and, combining both, at times, with the happy ending and
the pastoral atmosphere, inaugurated the long career of
tragicomedy in Europe.[1]   These new tragedies were at
first read aloud; when they came to be acted, it was not in
schools like the imitations of Plautus, but in the courts of
princes, especially of the Church, and by learned acade-
mies.   Among other Italian Senecans, Giraldi and Dolci
are important from their touch with English drama to
come.   Seneca soon spread to France, where the models of
the Roman poet were enriched by examples from Italy.
In France, Senecan tragedy was, from the first, "the
product of a small exclusive group, appealing to a narrow
circle of scholars, without the safeguards of public will
or traditional experience to hold it from the extremes of
academic taste.[2]   Jodelle and Garnier are two of the most
important among early French Senecans.   The former's
Cléopâtre, 1552, is memorable as the first tragedy of modern type in the French language.   Garnier later became
the model for a group of English courtly writers.   Indeed,
so far as tragedy is concerned, the cleavage between the
scholars' drama and the popular stage at one time bade
fair to become as complete in England as it actually became in France.   But this was averted in the former country by the growth of a popular tragedy beside it.   The
attitude of the popular writer on the general question is
well set forth by Lope de Vega in an often quoted passage
where, after professing the greatest respect for Aristotle
and all the precepts of the classical school, the dramatist
concludes: "But when I have to write a comedy for the

[1] Kastner and Charlton, *Works of Sir William Alexander,* as above, i.
p. lxiv-lxv, lxix.
[2] *Ibid.,* ciii.

Gorboduc

popular stage, I lock up the precepts with six keys and
turn Terence and Plautus out of my study for fear of
their outcries." [1]

The first Senecan tragedy in English is *Gorboduc;* and
it reproduces the essential characteristics of this literary
fashion abroad, although we can scarcely assume of its
performance classicality in staging.[2] *Gorboduc* was "acted
at the Christmas revels of the Inner Temple in 1561-62"
and repeated soon after before Queen Elizabeth at Whitehall; it was in print surreptitiously in 1565, in authorized
form five years later. The story resembles that of the
internecine feud of Seneca's *Thebais,* but for a fratricidal
feud of ancient Greece is substituted the civil war of two
brothers, supposedly English princes, derived from that
mythical British history which was later to furnish
Shakespeare material for *King Lear* and *Cymbeline.* But
not only was the subject novel, its treatment while preserving the gravity, the dignity, and the rhetoric of
Seneca, was freer, wider in range of subjects, and less trammeled as to that strict observance of the unities which
characterized continental followings of the Roman tragedian. Moreover, *Gorboduc* is memorable as the earliest
English play to be written throughout in blank verse, in
this leading in a departure momentous in what was to
come. In authorship, as in performance, *Gorboduc* fulfilled the sources of its inspiration. The two authors were
Thomas Norton and Thomas Sackville, the latter to rise
to great title and dignity in the state. Sackville was
already known as the author of the most poetic contribution to *The Mirror for Magistrates,* that lengthy collection of tragical narratives in verse, so popular throughout the Elizabethan age and so interesting as a parallel
to the long series of chronicle plays depicting English

[1] "The New Art of Making Comedies," 1609, quoted by J. W. Cunliffe in
his *Early English Classical Tragedies,* 1912, p. ix.
[2] Kastner and Charlton, as above, i. p. clxvii, assume multiple decorative
mediæval setting for *Gorboduc, Jocasta,* and their like; but see Chambers,
Elizabethan Stage, iii, 29.

HUMANISM AND THE DRAMA

history, of which, in a sense, *Gorboduc* is the first. It
is scarcely to be questioned that the two young authors,
who were both in parliament, had in mind much more than
the academic following of a classical model. At this
period in Elizabeth's reign the succession to the crown
was a subject of much discussion, and the example of a
state, overwhelmed by feud, was no accidental choice of
subject for a tragedy sumptuously acted by gentlemen
amateurs before the queen. Read in the blaze of light
that illuminates the drama which followed, *Gorboduc*
seems but a stiff and stilted affair; but compared with
the abstractions of the moral plays and the jingle and
inconsequence of the interlude, our first tragedy deserves
the enthusiastic welcome accorded it by Sir Philip
Sidney, who desired that for "stately speeches and well-
sounding phrases, climbing the heights of Seneca his
style," *Gorboduc* might remain "an exact model for all
tragedies."

Gorboduc was followed in the 'sixties by two other tragedies, *Jocasta* and *Tancred and Gismund* which, with *The
Misfortunes of Arthur* (possibly to be thrust back in
point of writing to 1572), constitute the four strictly
Senecan plays of this period.[1] They have much in common. All are the work of young men of station, students in the Inns of Court, all are the products of collaboration, and all were written for acting and for the attendant spectacle, presented in part in the form of dumb
shows. Gascoigne's *Jocasta* is a translation from the
Italian Senecan, Dolce, whose source was ultimately
Euripides. The subject, like *Gorboduc*, is one of fratricidal feud. *The Misfortunes of Arthur*, by Thomas
Hughes and others, again resembles *Gorboduc;* but here
the resemblance is in source, the fabulous history of England. In *Tancred* the Senecan manner is extended to romantic material, giving us the earliest English tragedy

Other early Senecan tragedies

[1] *Ibid.*, clx. *Tancred and Gismund* was known in original form as *Gismond of Salerne* and, the work of five collaborators, was "revived and
polished" by the chief of them, Robert Wilmot, and printed in 1591.

page37

founded on the love interest as well as the first to draw
on an Italian *novella* for its story; however, a now lost
Romeo and Juliet may have preceded it on the stage. Nor
were the universities less interested in Seneca. There the
technicalities of dramatic art were argued, and Latin
maintained as the only fit medium for the learned, whether
the source of their dramatic efforts were Italian, classical
story, or the novelty of the national history presented
classically as by Thomas Legge in his *Richardus Tertius*.[1]
But none of these tragedies was without admixture with
popular elements in such classically entitled interludes as
Edwards's *Damon and Pythias* or Preston's *Cambyses*,
both of the 'sixties. Without enumerating further examples, the absorption of Senecan influences into the popular
drama through the extravagances of such a production as
Locrine,[2] was reached in Kyd's *Spanish Tragedy*, on the
stage by 1586; and through *The Spanish Tragedy* Sen-
ecanism fertilized later Elizabethan tragedy at large.

Devices of Senecan tragedy

The typical English Senecan play discloses several devices characteristic of its kind. One is the dumb show, a
species of tableau, preceding each act and setting forth
symbolically what is to follow. This is an English practice, not, however, without Italian precedent.[3] A more
permanent and influential device is that of the chorus,
which needs no description here either in its classical original or in its use in later drama. Shakespeare's *Henry V*
illustrates not only one of the uses of the chorus, but likewise the employment of the "intermean," as Jonson calls
it, an intercalary narrative passage carrying forward the
action. This is also illustrated between the third and
the fourth act of *The Winter's Tale*, and is once more
referable to Italian example. Still another of these devices is the Induction, a species of dramatic setting of

---

[1] Examples of Italian source are Calfhill's *Progne*, 1594, and Alabaster's
Roxana, 1592. Two of Gager's Latin plays are *Meleager* and *Ulysses*.
[2] It seems impossible to place *Locrine* as late as 1591, unless, indeed,
it is to be regarded as a deliberate satire of the whole Senecan species.
[3] J. W. Cunliffe, *Early English Classical Tragedies*, p. xl; and F. A.
Foster in *English Studien*, xliv, 8.

the picture, of which the opening scenes of Sly the Tinker are an example in *The Taming of the Shrew*. All of these things, as extraneous to the action, fell more or less into disuse in later drama. But to Senecan influences are due some more permanent things, among them a certain sense of design and dignity, together with much moralizing, the formal divisions into act and scene, and much of the Elizabethan conduct of the supernatural, its ghosts, its revenge, its horror, and its foreboding.

In this chapter we have left not only the church performance of the miracle play and its subsequent transformation into a spectacle of the streets and the market-place; but the field and the jousting-place for outdoor performances of the moral play are likewise behind us. The farces of Heywood suggest performance at court; and, with the earliest comedies and *Gorboduc*, we add the refectory of the college and the spacious halls of the Inns of Court to the places in which drama was acted. As to actors, we note a change from the clergy, the craftsman, first to the scholar at school, lastly to the courtier who, in his Inns of Court, was still half a student. Bale utilized his scholars for the propaganda of his Protestant plays. *Roister Doister* was acted by students either of Eton or of Westminster; *Jocasta* and *The Misfortunes of Arthur* by the gentlemen of Gray's Inn and *Tancred and Gismund* and *Gorboduc* by those of the Inner Temple. It was as a student of Gray's Inn, that young Francis Bacon prepared, in 1588, the elaborate dumb shows of *The Misfortunes of Arthur*; and later he wrote speeches for the *Gesta Grayorum*. All this school and courtiers' acting and preparation of plays is as yet strictly amateur. To what extent, if any, professional assistance entered into it, as it did later, is uncertain. In Heywood we have clearly a professional, and also in his obscurer elder fellow entertainer, William Cornish, both of whom received payments at the hands of Henry VIII for disguisings and entertainments, seldom designated by name or clearly de-

Amateur and professional

scribed.[1] The distinction between young men of birth,
such as Sackville and Bacon, later to become notable in
the state, and "merry Heywood," holding out an eager
hand for the royal largess, is great. There is no such
line of demarcation between a group of schoolboys called
to court to repeat a comedy and the performance by men
and boys of one of Her Majesty's choirs under super-
intendence of their choirmaster. And thus it was that
the choirmaster and the schoolmaster became the first professional playwrights and managers, and the schoolboy
and the choir-boy the earliest professional actor.

Romantic material

Miracle plays continued to be acted, or substitutes of
one kind and another for them, by craft guilds here and
there throughout the reign of Queen Elizabeth; and moral
plays held the popular stage with interludes of various
kinds long after the regular drama had established itself
in the inn-yards of London and by means of traveling
professional troupes in the provinces. The score or so
of plays which were printed in the first five or six years
of Elizabeth's reign were "of a retrospective character,"
a miracle play of Bale, morals mostly of a controversial
nature, interludes on biblical as well as popular subjects,
and translations. But there were also things which pointed
forward. A dramatized version of the popular Spanish
story of *Celestina* by Rojas, called *Calisto and Melibea*,
printed as far back as 1530, tells a tale of two mutually
infatuated lovers and a subtle go-between; and in the recently recovered *Fulgens and Lucres*, written by Henry
Medwall between 1490 and 1500, we have the later familiar
situation of a maid wooed by two lovers, a gentleman of
great estate and a scholar, "right busy and laborious in
his books." [2] It was romantic material such as this (to

[1] The efforts of C. W. Wallace, *Evolution of the English Drama*, 1912,
pp. 31-60, to make Cornish out what he calls "an Octavian Shakespeare,"
are peculiarly unhappy. See the complete refutation of them by A. W.
Reed in *Beginnings of English . . . Drama*, and *John Heywood and his
Friends*, pp. 4-6 and 40-46, respectively.
[2] Facsimile is edited by S. de Ricci; see also A. W. Reed, *The Beginnings of Secular Drama*, as above, 6-10.

which we must add the romantically tragic story of Gismunda, already mentioned) which was later to prove dramatically fruitful; and it adds to our interest to know that both of these comedies belonged to the circle interested in drama which clustered about Sir Thomas More. Medwall wrote *Fulgens and Lucres;* Rastell printed *Calisto and Melibea* if he may not actually have written it. Strange to say, not one of these pre-Elizabethan productions can be referred to the repertory of any troupe of professional players. The university, the Inns of Court, or the "children," in school, choir, or at court, claim all which were not controversial or written to be read rather than to be acted.

CHAPTER III

The Court and Its Entertainment

The queen and the royal progress

IN THE admirable continuance of his studies of the origins and growth of English drama, Dr. E. K. Chambers lays peculiar emphasis on the influence of the court, declaring that "the palace was the point of vantage from which the stage won its way against the linked opposition of an alienated pulpit and an alienated municipality." [1] The Tudors maintained a mediæval taste for splendor, pageantry, and ceremonial. Elizabeth was crowned with pomp, proceeding through the city under a dozen temporary arches, hung with devices and inscriptions of welcome. At half as many stations, there were pauses for music and addresses, and the royal train, from the queen, crowned and in regal attire, to her scores of nobles, gentlemen, pensioners, and yeomen, glittered in gold and scarlet. While the queen resided at Whitehall when in London, she maintained, besides, many lesser places, Richmond and Hampton Court up the Thames, and Greenwich downstream; and there was constant movement of the court to and fro. The court was entertained not only at home, but likewise when abroad; for Elizabeth was a devoted lover of every form of the ceremonies of homage, hospitality, and compliment. The queen fell, early in her reign, into the custom of "going on progress," as the royal tour, accompanied by her court, into the provinces, was called. At such times it was her pleasure to visit, by prearrangement, her nobles and gentlemen at their country seats and to receive on the way the loyal welcome of the intervening towns. The progress was marked by pro-

[1] *The Elizabethan Stage*, 1923, 4 vols.

tracted speeches, elaborate decorative pageantry, allegorical masking and entertainment of a more or less dramatic
cast. The three weeks' stay of Her Majesty with the
Earl of Leicester in 1575 at his castle of Kenilworth, for
example, was productive of almost every device of this
kind, from the giant porter, welcoming the guest at the
bridge, a savage man appearing out of a bush at a pause
in the chase to utter studied compliments, to set allegories
of courtship, fireworks and music on the lake, and a mock
fight, popular pageantry in action, revived for the royal
pleasure.[1] These devices were the contrivances of many
hands, chief among them George Gascoigne, the leading
poet of the moment, and William Hunnis, Master of the
Chapel Royal; and the range of their invention with all
its incongruity of classic and romantic material, mixed
with pastoral and folk-lore, remains characteristic of the
progress on other occasions. Only rarely does coherency
emerge, as in the lively little pastoral interlude of Sidney,
The Lady of May, at Wanstead, two years later. Elizabeth visited the universities in progress—Cambridge in
1564, Oxford in 1566, and again in 1592. There, besides
addresses of welcome, disputations and dramas were much
in order, at times in Latin, a compliment to the learning
of the queen. To the Cambridge visit Nicholas Udall contributed a play, *Ezechias*, in English, and Thomas Legge,
later to write a Latin tragedy on Richard III, assisted
in the general direction. Thomas Preston, to become notorious for the bombast of his tragedy, *Cambyses*, was, for
his acting in a play of Dido, highly commended by the
queen, as his contemporary, Richard Edwards, at Oxford, was similarly approved for his dramatized version
of Chaucer's *Knight's Tale*.

Coming back to the court at home, certain seasons in
the court calendar were set apart for festivity: the return

Court
festivals

---

[1] This last was the Hock-Tuesday play, for Robert Laneham's contemporary account of which see *The Mediæval Stage*, ii, 264. On the progress
in general, see J. Nichols, *Progresses and Public Processions of Queen
Elizabeth*, 1823, 3 vols.

of Her Majesty to London in November, the Christmas
revels, New-Year's day and the like; and some of these
were habitually celebrated with masking and plays, with
tilting and mock tournaments. The extent to which the
Tudors preserved many of the outward forms of chivalry
is sometimes forgotten. There were all but annual tilts
during Elizabeth's reign; and the anniversary of the
queen's accession was signalized by the appearance in the
lists of a challenger in armor to uphold Her Majesty's
title. In 1590 the royal champion, Sir Henry Lee, now
grown old, transferred his office to a successor, the Earl
of Cumberland, with appropriate song and ceremony, and
the poet Peele was responsible for the devices.[1] Indoor
entertainments at court were various and the mask held
the first place among them. Originally, as we have seen,
a visit in disguise by a party of gentlemen, attended with
torchbearers and musicians, bearing gifts, dancing and
then inviting the guests to join in the dance, the mask took
to itself in time the presenter, from whose words of welcome
or explanation the dialogue later developed; it developed,
too, a spectacular element which afforded a background
either by way of movable pageantry or other decoration.
It will be seen at once that the mask may exist without
drama, though drama may add to the effectiveness of this
"episode in an indoor revel of dancing." An example of
the length to which these solemn amusements of the court
were at times carried is the *Gesta Grayorum* of 1594, in
which the law students of Gray's Inn constituted themselves an elaborate court, a "prince" at their head, and,
sedately parodying their sovereign's establishment at
Whitehall, welcomed and entertained that royal lady with
a profusion of masking, speech, and other entertainment.[2]

It was on this occasion that, a difficulty arising in the
process of events, "a cry of common players," kept waiting

[1] *Polyhymnia* describing "the Honorable Triumph at Tilt," 1590, a
blank-verse account of this ceremony.
[2] Edited for the Malone Society by W. W. Greg, 1914; and by B.
Brown, 1921.

for such a contingency, was called in to act "a comedy
of *Errors* like to Plautus his *Menechmus*," thus offering us
a Shakespearean touch with court entertainment.[1] The
artistic, scenic, and dramatic development of masking was
yet to come with Jonson in the reign of James. Save
for Lyly, in these earlier years it was only at the universities that Elizabeth was regaled with authentic drama;
and that was either tragedy of classical type or comedy
after the Italian-Roman manner at best.

Among the documents relating to the Office of the
Revels,[2] the generic word *play* appears with *device, inven-*
tion, show, moral, and even *pastime.* "A moral of the Marriage of Mind and Measure" is clear enough; and so is
the "pastoral of *Phillida and Corydon*"; but the nature of
the "Tragedy of *The King of Scots*," however some have
guessed the former to be *Calisto and Melibea* and the
latter a contemporary dramatization of the murder of
Darnley, must remain undetermined. It is clear that classical subjects abounded: *Agamemnon and Ulysses, Scipio*
Africanus, Pompey, Narcissus, and the like. Enigmatic
titles there are, like *Error,* which may well stand for the
Menœchmi, or Toolie, despite a Hibernian smack, for no
more than Tully or Cicero. But *story,* or *history,* appears to extend to other times: the "history of the *Duke*
of Milan," the "history of the *Cruelty of a Stepmother.*"
Plain as Can Be, Jack and Jill, and *Six Fools* suggest
comedy, *Effigenia* and *Orestes,* severely classical tragedy.
A novelty is the "comedy or moral on a *Game of Cards*";
"inventions" of "three plays" and "five plays" occur; and
"fighting at barriers"—the cloth-covered fence down the
middle of the jousting-field at mock tournaments. "Feats
of activity and tumbling" are recorded as well. To what
extent material, later employed in extant drama, appears
in these "accounts" is purely matter for guesswork. *Felix*

The
repertory
of the
revels

---

[1] This was on Innocent's day, 1593-94. Similarly, *Twelfth Night* was
acted before students of the Inner Temple, in February, 1602.

[2] Edited by A. Feuillerat, in *Materialien,* those of Elizabeth in 1908;
those of Edward VI and Mary in 1914, vols. xxi and xliv.

45

and Philiomena, an episode in Montemayor's *Diana,* is the topic of *The Two Gentlemen of Verona; Ariodante and Genevora* has been thought to have relation to *Much Ado about Nothing.* In *Murderous Michael* some have seen a reference to the popular murder play, *Arden of Feversham;* while *Timoclea* (fellow captive with Lyly's Campaspe at the Siege of Rhodes) would suggest a closer contact with Lyly's well-known play were it not for the circumstance that apparently *Timoclea* proved so tedious that there was no time or temper for the accompanying mask.

Italian comedy And now this confusion of entertainment at court and without began to feel a new and harmonizing influence, the spirit of Italy. It was natural that England should look to Italy in Tudor times, not only for the inspiration of learning, but for all the things that go to mark the amenities of life. For out of Italy had come the glory of the renaissance and men still cherished not 'the Italy of reality, but the Italy of a golden and inspiring dream. More widely famed as the author of the fantastic epic, *Orlando Furioso,* Lodovico Ariosto wrote five comedies between 1508 and 1531, variously acted at Ferara and elsewhere, and in them laid the foundation of modern European drama. Among the many who followed him were Macchiavelli, Dolce and Grazzini; and all, with some others, were translated or imitated in English. Like the school drama, this new Italian comedy is an offshoot of Terence and Plautus; but it took a different turn. In the first place, it exists in a free artistic atmosphere, frankly for entertainment, and for entertainment alone. Again, it took to itself, not infrequently, material drawn from popular fiction, and in so doing represented more or less truly a picture of contemporary Italian life. And still again, it was not unaffected, this *commedia erudita,* as it was called, by the *commedia dell' arte,* an extemporaneous and popular drama which links back perhaps with minstrel and mime. The spirit of the classics rules in

Italian comedy, and despite much sameness and conventionality we may agree that "the idea of cinquecento comedy as a mere lifeless reproduction cannot survive a study of the actual plays." [1]

Certain things are outstanding in this Italian drama, and some of them are important—far more so than mere borrowings of story—in their influence on the English stage. Italian comedy is neither historical nor concerned with the doings of people of rank. It is a burgher, or citizens', drama, using the relations of the family for its basis, the prosperous and often outraged merchant, his spendthrift son, the clever intriguing servant, a clandestine love affair, mistake, disguise, surprise, deception; on the romantic side, separated and reunited parents and children, a background of war, piracy, and accident. These things are the universal stuff of later drama. Out of this evolve certain typical personages, the braggart, already well known to Latin comedy (for political reasons in Italy, a Spaniard), repeated in Shakespeare's "Fantastical Monarcho," Fletcher's Pharamond, and many others. Other figures, with an illustrative Shakesperean example for each—there being, of course, many besides—are the pedant (Holophernes), the faithful, grumbling servant (Grumio), the friar confessor (Friar Laurence), the sorcerer (glorified in Prospero), the Innkeeper (of *The Merry Wives*); equally common in Elizabethan drama at large, if not in Shakespeare, are the familiar parasites, the doctors of law or medicine, treated more or less with ridicule, ·and the like. Among female figures the nurse, garrulous and coarse of speech, is mother of a long progeny, chief among them Juliet's Nurse; and the pert waiting-maid, or soubrette, seems equally derivative as Julia's Lucetta, and Hero's Margaret sufficiently show. The Italian heroine was limited by the conditions of Italian life. She is often represented, after ancient comedy, as an innocent girl in the clutches of a brothel-keeper, as

[1] R. W. Bond, *Early Plays from the Italian*, 1912, xxi.

47

is Marina in *Pericles;* and when she goes abroad she masquerades in doublet and hose, as do Julia, Viola, and Rosalind. The employment of prose or at least of unrhymed verse, a consciousness of the unities of time and place, if not a respect for them, and innumerable smaller matters, among them the aside overheard, the soliloquy, and the like—all these things come more or less directly into English comedy by way of Italian practice.

Gascoigne's Supposes
Let us take an English example in its roots backward and its branches upward. In 1566, Gascoigne presented at Gray's Inn his *Supposes,* a vigorous and successful adaptation of Ariosto's historically important comedy, *I Suppositi.* It was acted, like his *Jocasta,* a similar adaptation of a tragedy of Dolce's, by Gascoigne's fellow students, and was a deliberate step in the development of dramatic composition and presentation. *I Suppositi* is confessedly based on both Terence and Plautus; and Roman comedy was less a mirror of the Roman life of any period than a following of earlier Greek representation in comedy of contemporary Greek life. Wherefore with origins Greek and a growth which gains Roman accretions, Ariosto adds further to the process, giving to his comedy an Italian atmosphere, that of his own time. Gascoigne appears to have been an excellent Italianist; and his changes were chiefly made with a view to English colloquialism, force and vivacity, although he sacrificed in the process some of the polish and gayety of his original.[1] Some twenty years after *Supposes,* the story was once more employed in *The Taming of a Shrew,* somewhat cut down, as it serves only for the sentimental foil of an underplot; and it was from this that Shakespeare transferred this much-transmuted material to his rewriting of *The Taming of the Shrew.* A feature of Gascoigne's comedy, not to be forgotten, is his following of his original, in one of its versions, in the use of prose. This is the

[1] Gascoigne has been ably edited by J. W. Cunliffe, *Complete Works,* 1910-13, 2 vols.

first extended use of prose in English comedy. Of Gascoigne personally it is enough here to say that he was a
gentleman, well trained at Cambridge and Gray's Inn,
proud of his sword as of his pen, having wielded the
former in the Netherland wars. Impoverished, perhaps
by riotous living, he sought to recoup his fortunes with
his pen, displaying considerable ingenuity in seeking out
new ways in fiction, satire, and dramatic experiment. *The
Glass of Government, Jocasta,* and *Supposes,* his three
plays, mark, respectively, the most elaborate following of
Dutch humanist drama in England, the earliest steps after
the lead of *Gorboduc,* and the first notable adaptation of
Italian comedy; and Gascoigne bore, too, his part, as we
have seen, in the royal entertainment, notably at Kenilworth, in 1575. Two years later the poet was dead. Other
adaptations from Italian comedy are *Fidelio and Fortunio,*
a translation of Pasqualio's *Il Fedele,* and *The Bugbears,*
by John Jeffere, similarly derived from Grazzini's all but
contemporary *La Spiritata.* Into this latter the mock
supernatural enters in a diverting situation. Even Whetstone's *Promos and Cassandra,* the more genuinely romantic spirit of which later furnished Shakespeare the theme
for *Measure for Measure,* belongs strictly to this group.[1] Other
Whetstone's source here was not a play, but that usual comedies
quarry of later times, Cinthio's *Hecatommithi,* one of the inspiration
novels of which he had already translated into English
prose. Whetstone's life was one of adventure—service as
a soldier in the Low Countries, a voyage to Newfoundland,
and it is even possible that he was for a time an actor.
Like Gosson, he turned against the stage and attacked it
for its abuses. He survived his friend Gascoigne, whom
he eulogized in an epitaph, dying in 1587.

In the time of Henry VIII, the entertainment of the

---

[1] *Fidele and Fortunio* (c. 1584) has been edited for the Malone Society
by P. Simpson, 1909; *The Bugbears* (1563) is accessible in Bond's collection, as above. Whetstone's play, which was first printed in 1578, has
been most recently reprinted by J. S. Farmer, 1910. On the staging of
these plays in the Italian manner, see *Elizabethan Stage,* iii, 28.

court had been mainly in the hands of men like Heywood and Cornish. There was as yet but little organization or direction, although it had long been customary to appoint a Master for a given revel or entertainment and a temporary Lord of Misrule at the Christmas season. In 1545 Sir Thomas Cawarden was put in charge of the Revels; and the office grew in importance with increasing interest in the drama, until in the hands of aggressive and capable Sir Edmund Tylney, whose mastership ranged from 1579 to his death in 1610, its prerogatives were extended to a general supervision of the drama not only at court, but at large.[1] In Elizabeth's earlier days, however, all this was yet to come and men like Cawarden could muster not much more than the schoolmaster's, or at best the choirmaster's, help in the device of theatricals; and even the choir-boys, chosen first to sing, and only as an afterthought to act, were scarcely professionals. The organization of the students of schools, like Westminster and the Merchant Taylors, could have been for little more than occasional performances. The Children of Her Majesty's Chapel and the choiristers of St. Paul's Cathedral, however, soon developed into practically professional actors; and a group of master-manager-playwrights was evolved in the 'sixties and 'seventies, among whom Richard Farrant, Richard Edwards, and William Hunnis are the more important. Edwards and Hunnis were successive masters of the Queen's Chapel, and dramatic writers of note in their day. Edwards was the author of other plays besides his extant and avowed *Damon and Pythias*, chief among them *Palamon and Arcite*, acted at Oxford before the queen in 1566. While the activity of Hunnis, largely to be gleaned from the accounts of payments to him as manager and deviser of court entertainments, has been en-

The Revels
and the
Choir-
master

[1] On the Revels' Office, see *ibid.*, i, 71-105; Tylney was succeeded by Sir George Buck, who, in 1623, was followed by Sir Henry Herbert. As to Tylney's grant of authority over plays, see Feuillerat, *Revels, Elizabeth*, 326.

larged to extraordinary and surely unwarrantable proportions.[1]

Richard Farrant, as Master of Windsor Chapel, had
been active in devising plays for the entertainment of the
queen. In 1576, James Burbage was projecting a structure to house popular professional plays, now beginning to
attract public attention; and Farrant conceived the idea of
a similar organization by which the boy actors of the royal
choirs might also have a playing place of their own and,
under guise of better preparation for the entertainment of
the queen, give public performances to the enrichment of
all concerned. To build a new theater was beyond his
power, so he contrived to obtain the lease of a property,
sometime occupied by the Office of the Revels and forming
part of the priory buildings of the Dominicans or Blackfriars, and converted it into a playhouse, "commodious for
his purpose." His model was doubtless no more than "the
halls at court in which the children had been accustomed to
act," at one end a platform, an auditorium furnished with
benches or chairs, and necessary lighting for both, as these
performances were planned for night.[2] This was the first
Blackfriars Theater, situated in a precinct still so called,
without the walls of the city and not far from the court at
Westminster. His theater ready, Farrant combined his
own children of Windsor with those of the Royal Chapel,
whose Master was Hunnis, apparently contriving to supersede the latter's control, and for three or four years ran his
theater with success, but died in 1580. Hunnis with others
arranged to carry on the venture, although the owner of
the ground sought again and again by law to terminate
the lease. At length the Earl of Oxford, a patron of the
drama and a playwright himself, acquired the lease and
presented it to his secretary, John Lyly, who retained

Farrant and
first
Blackfriars

[1] Mrs. C. C. Stopes, *William Hunnis and the Revels of the Chapel
Royal*, 1910. As to Edwards, see J. Nichols, *Progresses of Queen Elizabeth*, ed. 1823, i, 212.
[2] J. W. Lawrence, *The Elizabethan Playhouse*, 1913, ii, 12, notes the
smaller size of the first Blackfriars, as contrasted with Burbage's, and
that it was on the second floor and therefore not so lofty.

Hunnis for the training of the young actors; and a combination was arranged with Hunnis's own Chapel Children and the Children of St. Paul's Cathedral, already organized under Thomas Giles.

John Lyly It was doubtless this gift of a theatrical lease, this opportunity of theater and company made to his hand, that confirmed Lyly in his purpose to write plays and gave us the first important name in the list of Elizabethan dramatists. John Lyly was a Kentish man, born in 1554, and grandson of William Lyly, the noted grammarian, who, after a due sojourn at Oxford, sought to make his way at court. In 1580, Lyly found himself suddenly famous on the publication of *Euphues*, the most successful piece of fiction which had appeared in England up to that date. And he followed this up with a second part, reinforcing in it his appeal to the cultivated tastes and refinement of his readers, and creating, as it was said, "a new English" in which to express, with elegancy and conscious attention to many artifices and niceties of style, not only idle thoughts of gallantry and courtship, but more serious discussions of conduct, manners, and education. Lyly was at all times the courtier, and his quest was preferment in the queen's service. This he never attained beyond the post of "esquire of the body," which made him a member of the royal household. He was a more or less perpetual candidate for the office of Master of the Revels, a post for which he was eminently fitted; but he never gained it. He appears to have been in charge, at one time, of the boy company of his patron, the Earl of Oxford. But though most of his plays were acted by Paul's boys, he was apparently never their Vice-Master, nor did he hold any post in the Revels.[1] Lyly's station in life was that of Gascoigne, not that of Edwards or Hunnis. He sat in several

---

[1] Lyly's earliest petition for the Mastership dates December, 1597: Feuillerat, *Revels, Elizabeth*, 440; and the same author's *John Lyly*, 1910, p. 196. But the allusion to "these ten years" in a letter to the queen, 1598, and another to "thirteen years," point to the likelihood that Lyly was "encouraged" in his ambition because of his first successes.

Parliaments. In 1580, Lyly transferred the cultivated dialogue of his fiction to the stage in *Campaspe*, and it was acted before the queen in December, 1581, having been previously performed at Blackfriars. Thus launched, *Sapho and Phao* soon followed, and these were the two comedies with which Lyly signalized his control of the boy players acting at Blackfriars. But Lyly's moment of opportunity was brief. In 1584, the owner of the property obtained a judgment in his favor, the lease was forfeited, Lyly, Hunnis, and their young charges ousted, and their theater converted into tenements.

This, however, was not the end of Lyly's connection with the stage. In the next year, 1585, *Endimion*, the most famous of his plays, was acted before the queen by Paul's boys alone, and to this company he adhered for the rest of his plays. It has been cited as a proof of the unusual interest which the queen was now taking in the drama that, about this time, she issued a special commission to Thomas Giles, the Master of Paul's, "to take up apt and meet children" and impress—or draft them, as we should say— into this new service. Such commissions had previously been confined to the masters of royal chapels. This extension of privilege Giles notoriously abused.[1] In 1590 Paul's boys were "dissolved," probably for some misdemeanor in connection with the Marprelate controversy in which we know that Lyly had taken a part, even to the writing of abusive comedies, now lost; and Lyly's dramatic career was cut short at its height. In his last play, *The Woman in the Moon*, 1595, the old courtier, exasperated by neglect, dared to turn from the drama of flattery to the drama of satire, and suffered a temporary disgrace in consequence at the hands of his imperious Pandora, Elizabeth. When, in 1599, the inhibition of Paul's boys was removed, it was too late. A new drama had superseded Lyly's and he was out of the race.

Lyly and the stage

---

[1] Feuillerat, *Revels, Elizabeth*, 470; E. K. Chambers, *Modern Language Review*, ii, 1906.

Lyly's
court plays

The eight extant plays of Lyly mark a departure in English drama which it is as easy to overestimate as to decry. All are comedies, and all save one are written more or less in the elegant and conscious prose to which attaches the term euphuistic. All were deliberately prepared for the personal entertainment of Elizabeth and her court. Certain definite limitations attach to work of this kind; but if we are to judge Lyly by the degree of success with which he achieved exactly what it was that he set out to do, we must give him high praise. *Campaspe* is an episode in the life of Alexander the Great, amplified, refined, and dramatized, apparently without ulterior purpose. *Galathea* and *Love's Metamorphosis*, are both pastoral in tone, but of much independence of treatment. *Mother Bombie* turns back to a free adaptation of Plautine comedy; *The Woman in the Moon*, with all its allegory, is clearly satirical. But the distinctively Lylyan contribution to English comedy is the politico-allegorical drama, which touches, in the personages presented and in the relations of the fable, upon certain contemporary events, or rumors of events, and turns them to a deft and telling flattery of the queen. Thus *Sapho and Phao* times with the negotiations for a marriage between Her Majesty and the Duc d' Alençon; *Endimion* with the complications which involved Elizabeth with her prisoner, Mary Queen of Scots, and James, Mary's son, in his ambition to become Elizabeth's successor; while *Midas* is a species of contemptuous song of triumph over Philip of Spain upon the failure of the Armada.[1] Obvious enough is the allegory which makes the Spanish monarch that Phrygian king, at whose touch, by at once the gift and the curse of the gods, everything turned to gold and whose folly cost him the growth of his ears into those of an ass. Not less clear, despite much ingenuity on the part of scholars hith-

[1] A. Feuillerat, *John Lyly*, and R. W. Bond in his edition of the poet, 1902. Feuillerat's interpretation of *Endimion* has been seriously impugned by P. W. Long in *Modern Philology*, viii, 1911; Chambers, i, 327, approves Long's doubts.

erto, would seem the major figures of *Endimion*: Cynthia, celestial queen of heaven, devoted to chastity, beyond the range or reach of earthly desires; her foil, Tellus (Mary Stuart), the earth, beautiful, fascinating, dangerous, aided and abetted by the wicked sorceress, Dipsas (perhaps the Roman Church); and Endimion (King James) cast into a long sleep until restored by the kiss of favor bestowed upon him by the peerless Cynthia (Elizabeth). To him who reads only of these old artifices of flattery, all this will seem crass enough. But an actual perusal of Lyly's comedies, their graceful elaborate prose, their atmosphere of elegance and refinement, and their undertone of that genuine loyalty, fervor, and pride which Elizabeth appears so often to have inspired—all this abundantly justifies his contemporary success and gives to his work an abiding interest.

The facts do not warrant the assumption that Lyly was any great innovator in drama. There is scarcely a feature of his art that is not exampled in his immediate predecessors; his lack of constructiveness, thinness of characterization, and absence of action are all characteristic of his lesser fellows. Yet, none the less, Lyly marks a startling advance on stilted *Gorboduc* and hybrid *Damon and Pythias*, as his work surpasses *Appius and Virginia* with its limping didactic tone and *Horestes*, so crude that we may well marvel the toleration of it at court. The bombast even and high "Ercles vein" of Preston's famed *Cambyses* could have been received by Lyly's cultivated auditors only in a spirit akin to that of the court of Theseus and Hippolyta towards the efforts of Bottom's scratch company. Lyly's comedy is a protest against all this. He deals neither with horror nor with romance; he disdains the schoolmaster's moralizing and didacticism, and is tempted into neither vulgarity, coarseness, nor horseplay. Neither Plautus, Seneca, nor Italian comedy does he accept as authority; however, he reverts to the first under stress, in *Mother Bombie*, perhaps to keep up with

His sources and originality

55

popular drama. Italian pastoral he uses in a manner his own. Lyly found his inspiration in the masks and devices allegorical which preceded him, and in a certain idealization of the manners, conversation, and social etiquette accepted in the court of the time.

Staging
of court
plays

From the evidences of these same "accounts" it appears that the preparations, staging and costumes in particular, of court plays were often elaborate and costly. Appropriateness of scene was as little known, as in the following age of Shakespeare. In Lyly's own comedies there is nothing of what we call local coloring, although his scene is Athens, Rochester, Arcadia, or Utopia. There was plenty of costume in character—hunters, seamen, Irish kerns, Turkish archers, knights, nymphs of Diana, and the like. But all was anticipated and conventional. As contrasted with the public theaters even at this early date, the staging of these performances at court was "a variable quantity" to be "altered, augmented, or rearranged to omit special requirements." [1] It is even possible that while it was the duty of the Master of the Revels to select beforehand "out of many plays . . . the best that there were to be had," the theatrical bill of fare, so to speak, presented by his court chamberlain to Theseus in *Midsummer Night's Dream* may be no more than the exaggeration of a possible condition of readiness for several alternative performances. As to setting, *The Accounts of the Revels* abound in the mention of "houses," "made of canvas, formed, fashioned, and painted such as most highly to express the effect of the histories played." [2] We hear of "long boards" "for the steer of a cloud" and of these and other properties as handled with cord and pulley. We hear, too, of "great cloths" which must have been of a considerable size; a castle for *Sarpedon*, a city and battlements for *Scipio Africanus*, a senate house for *Pompey*

---

[1] Plays at court were given in the great hall, occasionally in the Banqueting House when it was not occupied by masks. *Ibid.*, i, 216.
[2] Feuillerat, *Revels*, 129, 175, 197, 201, and elsewhere, and Chambers, i, 229.

with a curtain before it, and a prison for the *Four Sons of Fabius*. The rock for *The Knight of the Burning Rock* was so large that it required a ladder to reach the chair within it.[1] It is difficult to see how such objects could have been represented except by means of perspective either in the painting of a single cloth or in the setting of several "houses" variously sized upon the stage. Where the play involved several places, there was undoubtedly a survival, at times, of the mediæval method of multiple setting. To anticipate somewhat, naïve to a degree almost ridiculous are the amateurish plays prepared for Paul's boys by William Percy (a son of the Duke of Northumberland) about 1601, if not really a decade earlier.[2] These plays are furnished with elaborate stage directions, and exhibit several features, such as the designation of the stage into three definite localities, the employment of signs for the title of the play, hung "aloft," if not also for the localities on it, with the use of the term "canopy," apparently at Paul's meaning the alcove, all of which has been applied in hasty generalization to the Elizabethan stage at large.[3] But, to return, the tendency in general was towards a greater simplicity and a smaller number of structures or "houses." Unlocalized scenes were acted either in oblivion of the "houses" or before the more appropriate one. *Campaspe* demands three places or edifices, the market-place, designated by Diogenes's tub, the palace and the studio of Apelles. And the action moves easily from place to place, the locality being unimportant except where emphasized. Other plays of Lyly, and notably Peele's *Arraignment of Paris*, were obviously staged wholly by means of the pastoral setting suggested as fitting to satiric or country drama: in *Love's Metamorphosis*, a

---

[1] Feuillerat, 320, 336, and 306; in this last case the "burning" was effected by aqua vitæ.

[2] Percy's plays are *Arabia Sitiens*, *The Aphrodysial*, *Cupid's Sacrifice* and *Necromantes*, as yet unprinted; and *The Cuckqueans and Cuckolds Errant* and *The Faery Pastoral*, edited for the Roxburghe Club by J. Haslewood, 1824. Also, G. T. Reynolds in *Modern Philology*, xii, 1914.

[3] Below, chap. x.

wood with several glades, a house in each of them; in Peele's play, a dominating tree and the bower of Diana.[1] Chambers finds in the exorbitant requirements of romantic narrative literature the staging of which soon became a popular demand, the breaking down of Italian staging and with it of the methods of the Lylyan school.[2] When a drama, such as *Common Conditions*, begins in Arabia, wanders into Phrygia and back again, with intermittent trips to the Isle of Marofus, the pretty certainties of unity of place go by the board and the celebrated strictures of Sidney become justified: "Where you shall have Asia of the one side, and Affrick of the other, and so many other under-kingdoms that the player, when he cometh in, must ever begin with telling where he is, or else the tale will not be conceived."

George Peele

If the criterion of successful art is not alone the degree to which it fulfills a specific purpose, but that wider power that keeps it vital, then the palm of superiority, in the restricted field of the court drama, must be conceded to George Peele and not to Lyly, although we have but one production of the former to determine the matter. Peele was born in the year of Elizabeth's accession, the son of a trusted clerk of Christ's Hospital who had been in his day a maker of pageants. George was educated at Oxford, where he made a reputation for poetry and the writing and staging of plays. *The Arraignment of Paris*, his one extant court play, was acted before the queen by the Chapel children in 1584 and published in the same year, thus appearing in print as early as Lyly's earliest comedies.[3] *The Arraignment of Paris* repeats with dramatic and lyric elaboration the old story of the golden apple of dissension cast among the godesses Juno, Minerva, and Venus, and of the decision of Paris in favor of Venus. At this point

---

[1] On the setting of Lyly's plays, see J. W. Lawrence, *The Elizabethan Playhouse*, i, 242, and Chambers, iii, 33. Bond, editor of *Lyly*, ii, 369, quite misconceives the subject.

[2] Chambers, iii, 37.

[3] *Campaspe* appeared in three quartos in 1584; *Sapho and Phao* in one.

the ancient myth is given a new twist by the arrival of Mercury, who arraigns the decision at the command of Jupiter, because the award has been hastily made within precincts sacred to Diana, a deity even higher than any of these, whereupon Diana in person takes the golden apple in hand, crosses the hall to the steps of the throne, and there, kneeling, presents the prize to her own vice-regent of chastity on earth, the peerless "nymph Eliza." There is a directness, simplicity, and beauty about this somewhat naïve dramatic compliment to Elizabeth, wanting to the more studied rhetorical eloquence of Lyly's comedies, and, besides, in Peele's drama we breathe the air of veritable poetry.[1] Judged by its very early date, the blank verse of the prologue preceding Marlowe's, its charming lyrics presaging a whole tuneful age, *The Arraignment of Paris* is a very important play. A fragment by Peele, *The Hunting of Cupid*, is all that remains of his only other effort at actual court drama.[2] Before long he went over to the popular stage, and became notorious in his day for a species of jocular roguery which has attached to his name a number of anecdotes little to his credit. An experimenter in his subsequent work, Peele imitated Marlowe, wrote a biblical drama, *David and Bethsabe*, and maintained, in his pleasing comedy of popular fairy-lore, *The Old Wives' Tale*, a quizzically critical attitude towards the very thing he was trying to do.[3] Recent scholarship is inclined to assign an important place to Peele in the beginnings of historical drama, and the assignment of many other authorless plays to him crowds his short and supposedly idle days with an assiduous and diversified activity.

A consideration of the extant plays, subsequent to Lyly, performed at court and before the queen elsewhere, would

Other plays at court

---

[1] V. M. Jeffery, *Modern Language Review*, xix, 1924, finds the source of Peele's play in *Il Giuditio di Paride*, by Anello Paulili, printed in 1566.
[2] Edited by W. W. Greg, for the Malone Society, *Collections*, i, 307.
[3] The view of the late F. B. Gummere, in *Representative Comedies*, 1903, i, 341.

take us into the popular drama. Plays continued to be
written primarily for court acting; but more frequently,
perhaps, popular successes were adapted or revived for
court. Of the former class is the masque-like *Summer's
Last Will and Testament* by Thomas Nash, which was
acted at Croydon in 1592. Nash had become notorious for
his vituperative pamphlet controversy with Spenser's prag-
matical friend, the Cambridge don, Gabriel Harvey, besides writing an effective picaresque novel, *Jack Wilton*.
A tragedy on Dido, in which Nash had a hand, too, with
Marlowe, was acted by Children of the Chapel Royal much
about this time. An interesting example of the "trimming"
of a popular play, somewhat later, to prepare it for court
may be found in Dekker's poetic comedy, *Old Fortunatus*,
revived for performance before the queen in 1599. In
the prologue cognizance of the presence and glory of her
august Majesty becomes the topic of a conversation between "Two Old Men," who correspondingly conclude the
play with a prayer for her continued prosperity. It is
possible to find in these passages of devotion to a great
sovereign more admiration for a genuine and creditable
loyalty than criticism of a form of flattery the conventionality of which was quite as well understood then as now.

Lastly of this topic, it has been thought that two comedies of Shakespeare were written particularly for occasional performance by boy companies before the queen.
Those are *Love's Labor's Lost* and *Midsummer Night's
Dream*. An interesting suggestion as to the former refers
it to the progress of Elizabeth into Sussex in 1591, finding
a parody of certain features of the queen's entertainment
on the previous days in the play itself and placing the
performance of it at Titchfield, the seat of the young Earl
of Southampton, on September 2d of that year. At Caw-
dray House the queen and her maids were entertained at
a royal hunt and later listened to speeches of the common
people headed by a curate and a schoolmaster. In the
interval they had ridden to Oseburn Priory to be received

by a group of gentlemen arrayed as hermits "in Batchelors' Hall"; and these trifles furnish much of the subject matter of *Love's Labor's Lost*. But, more important, may not the motif of the young men, sought out in their seclusion and determination to study by a bevy of ladies, refer none too covertly to the efforts of Burleigh to marry his three granddaughters, daughters of the bankrupt Earl of Oxford, to three wealthy royal wards, Southampton chief among them; and may not the postponement at the conclusion of the comedy of the union of the three pairs until the princess marry the King of Navarre (if ever it happen) veil Southampton's efforts at least to escape this marriage, in which he finally succeeded? This interpretation would represent Shakespeare as engaged by Southampton to stage allusively contemporary court happenings in a manner in which, at this date, Lyly could not but stand as his inevitable model. That Shakespeare should have laid the scene of his comedy in France with personages named after the leaders in an existing war, was an apt and timely tribute to what the court was thinking about; for the queen, on this same progress, reviewed troops at Portsmouth destined to reinforce Henry of Navarre. Could we accept all this, this dramatic improvisation, by Shakespeare, of contemporary matters (for no literary source for *Love's Labor's Lost* has been found) assumes a new interest, and Southampton's relations of patronage to Shakespeare (to whom Shakespeare was to dedicate his *Venus and Adonis* and his *Lucrece*) are more fully explained.[1]

As to *Midsummer Night's Dream*, that diverting comedy has long been referred to the celebration of some noble marriage at court, possibly that of the Earl of Derby, himself the reputed author of plays, to Elizabeth, daugh- *Midsummer Night's Dream*

---

[1] See A. K. Gray, "The Secret of Love's Labor's Lost," *Publications of the Modern Language Association*, xxxix, 581, 1924; and A. Acheson, *Shakespeare's Last Years*, 1920, p. 165, where the suggestion connecting this comedy with the Cawdray-Titchfield progress is made and the subject matter of much of the play referred to incidents in the progress.

ter of Lyly's patron, the Earl of Oxford, the very lady whom Burleigh had sought to marry to Southampton; or that of Anne Russell to Lord Herbert, as more recently suggested.[1] It is interesting to notice that in these two comedies, above all his others, have critics discovered the immediate example of Lyly on Shakespeare's conception of personage and conduct of dialogue. In both, too, there is a play presented by humbler folk to a court with the attitude of noble ladies and gentlemen towards these humble histrionic efforts. We need not doubt that Shakespeare had, himself, witnessed a brutality the equal of that with which poor Holophernes is cried down in the former play; and Theseus, in the latter, speaks in admiration of the ideal when he says:

> Our sport shall be, to take what they [the players] mistake:
> And what poor duty cannot do, noble respect
> Takes it in might, not merit.

[1] W. J. Lawrence, "A Plummet for Bottom's *Dream*," *Fortnightly Review*, cxi; n. s., p. 833.

CHAPTER IV

The Playhouse and the Companies

ELIZABETHAN London was still a mediæval walled town; although, much to the apprehension of the authorities, houses were stretching out beyond its ancient gates—Aldgate, Ludgate, Cripplegate and the rest—on every side. The city lay along the Thames, in Middlesex, from the Tower to Temple Bar, extending half a mile or more back from the river, over which London Bridge alone gave access to the Surrey side. The jurisdiction of the Lord Mayor practically stopped at the several gates of the city and at the middle point of the bridge, a circumstance which had much to do with the history of the stage; for when civil attack was made on the abuses incident to the crowding of London inns, where performances were commonly given, those interested in theatrical ventures took their playhouses to the liberties, as the precincts without the walls were called, there to be free from civic interference. The axes of London's thoroughfares ran north from the bridge through New Fish Street, Gracechurch Street, and Bishopsgate Street to the gate of that name, and west from the Tower through East Cheap and Cheapside to St. Paul's, through Fleet Street and the Strand to Temple Bar, the limit of the city towards Westminster. To the north beyond Bishopsgate lay the commons and pleasure grounds of Finsbury Fields; and, on its edge, in St. Leonard's parish, Shorditch, on ground which had formerly been the property of the Priory of Holywell, was erected, in 1576, the Theater, earliest structure specifically built for theatrical purposes in England. The Curtain followed in the next year within a stone's throw to

63

the south, Holywell Lane dividing the two. Later, in 1600, came the Fortune in St. Giles, Cripplegate, also without the city's precincts and further to the west. Following back our axis southward and across London Bridge into Surrey, we reach the Bankside, as the low marshy part of Southwark lying along the river is called. This region, which included the precincts of Paris Garden and the Clink, was variously subject to the crown and the Bishop of Winchester, and had been from time immemorial a place of license and refuge. Here from early days had flourished two "gardens" or amphitheaters, in use for bear-baiting and bull-fighting; and here, too, were maintained, among the butchers and their slaughter-houses, the mastiffs trained to worry these unhappy beasts for the amusement of the people. To this neighborhood likewise belonged the stews, taverns, gambling-places, resorts of thieves and sharpers, thriving impudently just beyond the reach of the law. In this unsavory region flourished, within the reigns of Elizabeth and her successor, four playhouses, the Rose, the Swan, the Globe, and the Hope, with a fifth at Newington Butts, about a mile back across St. George's Fields from the river. The Bankside was accessible not only by way of the Bridge, but by means of wherry, as the small boats plying the river by hundreds were called; and after a play, towards twilight, lively must have been the scene, say at Falcon Stairs, near which we have reason to believe that Shakespeare once lived, with the crowding of a merry audience dismissed from a play, the incessant cry of the boatmen ringing, "Eastward Ho!" if your way lay towards the Bridge and deeper into the city, or, "Westward Ho!" if your journey was towards the politer precincts of Westminster.

The Inn-yards Before the playhouses popular theatrical performances were staged in barns, schoolrooms, churches, in the streets or other open places, best of all in inns or inn-yards. The structure of the Elizabeth inn, built as it was about a yard and galleried within, lent itself peculiarly to such a pur-

pose. In consideration of the outdoor habit of mediæval
popular drama, I feel that we may still accept the inn-
yard, rather than any conversion of the room of the inn
itself, as the original of Elizabethan playhouse structure.[1]
The arrangement of the stage, in the middle of the yard
or at one side of it, was simple enough, and the auditors
must have been divided almost from the first, as the old
moral puts it, between "the sovereigns that sit and the
brothers that stand right up," the latter on the stones of
the yard, the former seated in the surrounding balconies
and later even on the stage itself. The annals tell of five
Elizabethan inn-yards converted temporarily or perma-
nently into playhouses. It was to the Cross Keys in Gracechurch Street that Lord Strange's players "went," reports
the Lord Mayor of 1589, "in very contemptuous manner
departing from me . . . and played that afternoon to
the great offense of the better sort"; and there, too, Bank's
marvelous trained horse, alluded to by Shakespeare, performed. Tarlton, the famous clown, who died in the year
of the Armada, acted at the Bell and the Bull. Both of
these inns were on the line of thoroughfare, running
north through Bishopsgate. It would seem that a Boar's
Head of theatrical history was not Falstaff's immortal
hostelry in Eastcheap, but another inn of that no unusual
sign "in Whitechapel just outside of Aldgate." There
was likewise the Bel Savage on Ludgate Hill.[2] Plays at
this last wrung from even so notorious an objector as
Stephen Gosson the admission that, in two at least of its
prose books, "there was never a letter placed in vain"; but
the conceited old Puritan was thinking of work of his own
in his unregenerate days.[3] Inn-yards continued to be used
for theatrical purposes throughout the reign of Elizabeth

[1] On the general subject see J. Q. Adams, *Shakespearean Playhouses*,
1917; Chambers, ii, 353-379, and G. F. Reynolds, "What We Know of the
Elizabethan Stage," *Modern Philology*, ix, 1911.
[2] Adams, p. 7; *Revels*, 102, Chambers, ii, 443.
[3] *The School of Abuse*, ed. Arber, 40.

and even into the time of the Stuarts; but only the Bull survived the Great Fire.

James Burbage

In 1576 James Burbage conceived the idea of building a structure specifically for the acting of plays. Burbage was a joiner by trade; but since 1572, he had been a member of the Earl of Leicester's company of players. That he was encouraged in his project by Farrant's contemporary venture at Blackfriars seems likely, although encouragement may have worked the other way. Burbage was a business man, as we should call him, who saw and took his opportunity.[1] It is groundless to attribute to him disinterested motives or any considerable acquaintance with the nature of theatrical structures rearing in foreign countries.[2] The immediately impelling force as to the selection of site especially came from the incessant efforts of the city to restrain, if not totally to abolish, the acting of plays within the walls.

Opposition to the stage

This hostility of the city was the outcome of complex conditions; for the regulation of the stage, as it developed into an increasingly popular amusement, became a matter of serious solicitude both to the crown and to the authorities of London. Into the origins of this hostility and the degree of the acuteness to which a long quarrel had arrived, it is impossible here to enter.[3] It is sufficient to recall that even among the humanists there had been qualms as to the degree of acceptance to be accorded to the acting of plays; while Puritanism, recalling the infamy of the Roman *histriones*, biblical injunction against masquerade in habiliments of the other sex, and the tirades of the early Christian Fathers, set itself resolutely against the stage, dwelling in fulminations both written and spoken on its vanities and scurrility, its temptations and ungodliness. In the 'eighties an animated and protracted con-

---

[1] Mrs. C. C. Stopes, *Burbage and Shakespeare's Stage*, 1913.

[2] See especially L. B. Campbell, *Scenes and Machines*, p. 118, who refers the building of modern theaters to classical influences.

[3] On the general subject, see V. C. Gildersleeve, *Government Regulations of Elizabethan Drama*, 1908; and E. N. S. Thompson, *The Controversy between the Puritans and the Stage*, 1903.

troversy raged at Oxford in which John Rainolds, later
president of Corpus Christi, attacked the whole practice
of plays in the university, and William Gager, of Christ
Church, the author of several academic Latin tragedies,
championed the defense. But even earlier, the clergy and
Puritan satirists had opened their batteries on the more
serious menace to religion, morality, and the public peace
which they found in the popularity of the London playhouses. The pamphlets of Northbrooke, Stubbs, Gosson,
and Munday, the latter two recusant players, called forth
several replies, among them the *Honest Excuses* of Thomas
Lodge, the dramatist. Sidney's *Defense of Poesie* was the
most important literary outcome of this controversy, although Sidney's thesis was a wider one and his own views
of the popular stage were obviously, in 1583, conservative
and critical.[1] As to the abstract merits of the case, there
can be no question that there were abuses on the Elizabethan stage; but the arguments of the two parties
scarcely ever really join issue. In one thing alone were
both agreed, and that was the reference of the drama to
a standard wholly ethical; for the conception of an æs-
thetic valuation of art was unknown to Elizabethan criticism.[2]

To the queen and her Council the abuses of the playhouse presented a twofold aspect: there was danger of
sedition, and there was danger of heresy; and the distinction was narrow between them. To the city fathers there
was the more immediate practical problem of preserving
the public peace, of preventing the spread of contagion
in the frequent recurrences of plague, and of censoring, so
far as possible, public morals. In earlier days of religious

The fight against the theaters

---

[1] *Dicing, Dancing, Vain Plays or Enterludes*, by John Northbrooke,
1577; *The School of Abuse*, 1579, *Plays Confuted*, 1582, both by Stephen
Gosson; *The Second and Third Blast of Retreat from Plays*, 1580, by
Anthony Munday; *The Anatomy of Abuses*, 1583. Lodge's *Honest Ex-
cuses*, dates about 1579; Sidney's famous tract was not printed until 1595.
[2] Chambers, i, 260; and compare the attitude of later critics of poetry,
William Webbe, *Discourse of Poetry*, 1586; George Puttenham, *Art of
English Poetry*, 1589; and Sir John Harington, *Defense of Poetry*, 1591.

revival and controversy we find regulations of Parliament against "players' intermeddling in their plays with matters religious." Later interventions on the part of the Privy Council or the Master of the Revels, who in time became the recognized dramatic censor, are confined almost wholly to allusions seditious or at least impudently critical of authority. These subjects untouched, the court favored the drama and protected the players, when duly organized under noble patronage; and the players habitually justified their own existence and public performances by declaring that they must have opportunity to practice their art, if they were to play before the queen. The attacks of the city authorities on the stage ranged from the regulation of performances on Sunday or the discouragement of profanity to the suppression of acting in seasons of plague, and attempts (usually when exasperated by special disturbances or accident) at the total abolition of playhouses within the city and in the liberties as well. The times were turbulent and we hear of "riots" at the Curtain, of the falling of scaffolds at Paris Garden, of defiance of the Lord Mayor and his orders, and of the arrest and indictment of Burbage himself, on one occasion, for encouraging unlawful assemblies at the Theater. In the earlier years of the reign there was continual conflict between the Corporation of London and the Privy Council as to the regulation and licensing of players. It ended in a victory for the latter. In 1581, the Master of the Revels, who was subject to the Lord Chamberlain, was commissioned to license all plays; and the Lord Mayor was compelled to be content thereafter with efforts to influence the Council to his way of thinking. But Puritanism continued the fight against the theaters, and the exchange of orders, messages, petitions, and decisions continued. Nor were the players silent. Aside from answers, rejoinders, and petitions in their own behalf, when the Martin Marprelate controversy was at its height, in 1589, their friends, the playwrights, came eagerly to their aid; and Martin was

vigorously satirized, under figure of a grotesque ape, let
blood for his evil humors, and otherwise lampooned on the
public stages.

The protection of players by noblemen and princes is
traceable to the immemorial patronage of the minstrel.
The custom was the outcome of mediæval conditions that
could find no place in the organization of society for the
masterless man; and it was confirmed by various statutes
which gave the player a legal status only when organized
and attached, by way of service, to a baron or "other
honorable person of greater rank." The annals of Elizabethan theatrical companies are attended with extraordinary difficulties, as the material, while abundant, is dependent on records of many different kinds, often scattered
and incomplete. The same patron does not always mean
the same company, and only at times can we trace the
progress of a given company from one patron to another.
The organization of the players was subject to continual
change in personnel, to union, disbanding, reconstruction;
and the frequent travels of the companies in the provinces,
whither they journeyed especially in times of plague, together with the disjointed nature of provincial records,
further complicate the subject. Up to the time of the
building of the first theaters, the boy companies, maintaining a humanist tradition, literally dominated the
stage.[1] After 1576, there was a sudden increase in the
number of adult companies and important officers of the
crown, such as the Lord Chamberlain, the Lord Admiral,
and royal favorites assumed the patronage of players.
As early as 1578, we hear of "eight ordinary places in the
city occupied by players," although only six companies
were allowed to appear at court: those of the Earls of
Leicester, Warwick, Sussex, Essex, the Children of the
Royal Chapel, and Paul's boys. Among these companies,
Leicester's men received, in 1574, the unusual favor of a

The theatrical companies

[1] Chambers, ii, 3, very properly refers the popularity of the companies
to their acceptance at court, giving figures which show their relative
positions.

royal patent. By the year 1583 the adult companies had gained a definite lead over the boys in the favor of the court, and this despite the efforts and the talents of Lyly, which now began to be pitted against new popular writers such as Marlowe and Kyd. The success of the men was likewise due, at least in part, to an effort to bring the profession into better control by the formation of a single company under the patronage of Queen Elizabeth herself, made up of the twelve best actors available from other companies. These were chosen by Tilney, approved by Secretary Walsingham, and given the status of grooms of the chamber; and among them appear Robert Wilson, famed for his extemporal wit, and Tarlton, the popular comedian, as well as others whose names recur later among the fellows of Shakespeare.[1] But the Queen's players had their rivals, especially in the Admiral's men, who, in the late 'eighties and earlier 'nineties, achieved signal success, especially in combination, first with Lord Hunsdon's men and afterward with the company of Lord Strange.[2] This latter amalgamation brought together the two important names of Edward Alleyn, the leader of the Admiral's men and the creator of several rôles of Marlowe, and James Burbage, builder of the Theater. There the two companies were acting in 1591 when possibly a quarrel with Burbage over financial matters caused their migration to the Rose, where we hear of them from Henslowe as still acting together.

During the greater part of 1592 and 1594 the plague shut all the playhouses, and it has been surmised that it was the confusion among the companies at this time which led to "the ephemeral existence of Lord Pembroke's men" and their extraordinary success with Marlowe's *Edward II* and other plays. However, in the autumn of 1593

[1] Wilson is usually accredited with the authorship of *The Three Ladies of London* and the *Three Lords of London*, 1584 and 1590, printed with the initials "R. W.," and with being the "Robert Wilson, Gent.," of *The Cobbler's Prophecy*, 1594, and of Meres' mention in 1598.

[2] Leicester's players are mentioned in the year of Shakespeare's birth; Lord Strange's are first heard of as exhibiting feats of agility, in 1580.

Henslowe wrote to Alleyn of Pembroke's players that they were "fain to pawn their apparel for their charge"; and, soon after, their "books" began to come into print, sure sign of the disruption of the company.

It is customary in biographies of Shakespeare to trace back the pedigree of the company with which he is supposed to have been connected from the Chamberlain's men, in which we find him a full sharer in 1594, to the players of Lord Strange and even to those of the Earl of Leicester.[1] But if Shakespeare was associated from the first with Strange's men, then long prior to this we should have some word of him among the actors in that company, of which we have an unusually full list; or we should have at least some traces of plays, certainly of his writing for this company.[2] Such traces only two plays appear to afford, *Titus Andronicus* and *1 Henry VI*, the first a Strange-Sussex-Pembroke play, as the title of the quartos declare; the second a play of Strange's men, but no more than the other generally believed by present scholarship to be wholly Shakespeare's. It is argued, then, as more reasonable to assume that the great poet began with Pembroke's men, exercising his earliest talents in revision of Marlowe's old *Contentions* into *2* and *3 Henry VI*, and Peele's older, now lost, play on that topic into what is now *1 Henry VI*. It was to Pembroke's company, after his earlier successes in *Tamburlaine* and *The Jew of Malta* with the Admiral's men, that Marlowe had transferred about 1590. This rivalry of Peele in the one case and rewriting of Marlowe in the other would sufficiently account for Greene's famous gibe at "the new upstart crow beautified with our feathers," addressed more particularly to Peele and Marlowe,[3] and the

The companies of Shakespeare

---

[1] See S. Lee, *Life of Shakespeare*, ed. 1922, pp. 54, 55; A. H. Thorndike, *Shakespeare's Theater*, 1916, p. 292.

[2] Adams, *Life*, 134, 136; and C. F. Tucker Brooke, ed. of "1 Henry VI," *The Yale Shakespeare*, 1918, p. 138, who, however, regards this play as a late revision of Peele's of 1592, remodeled to precede Marlowe's *1* and *2 Contentions*, already transformed into *2* and *3 Henry VI*. He conjectures that *1 Henry VI* may have followed *Henry V* in 1599 and refuses to accept Shakespeare's possible connections with Pembroke's men.

[3] See the same critic's *The Authorship of King Henry VI*, 1912, p. 188.

failure of Pembroke's men soon after would leave Shakespeare free, after a period of non-dramatic composition, represented by the narrative poems and perhaps the *Sonnets*, to make a new dramatic alliance with the Lord Chamberlain's company in 1594.[1] Certain it is that with this company Shakespeare remained associated, becoming with Richard Burbage its leading spirit. The Chamberlain's men are first recorded as acting with the Admiral's company in June, 1594, at Newington Butts. To the end of the reign these were the chief rivals, a status almost approaching a joint monopoly and one recognized by the action of the Privy Council as such in 1597. Only once was their leadership threatened, and that was by the passing vogue in 1599 and 1600 of Paul's boys and the Children of the Chapel, when certain satirical poets took upon themselves to assert the writer against the actor. With a mention of the emergence into repute, about this time, of another adult company, the Earl of Worcester's, this sketch of an intricate topic comes to a close for Elizabeth's reign. When all the companies passed, with the accession of James, under the royal patronage, the Chamberlain's men maintained their primacy as the King's, the Admiral's following as the Queen's players.

Henslowe's Diary   Our chief authority for the details of the theatrical business of Elizabethan days is the document known as *Henslowe's Diary*.[2] This manuscript is really a book of accounts, written almost wholly in Henslowe's own hand and containing, besides much irrelevant to our purpose, more or less complete memoranda of his transactions with half a dozen companies, nearly thirty playwrights, with actors and others connected with the stage. These accounts include lists of daily performances from February, 1592, to November, 1597; entries of outlays and expenditures for the companies from October of that year to March, 1603, and a mass of miscellaneous matter as to

[1] Adams, *Shakespeare*, 129.
[2] Edited by W. W. Greg, 1904-08, with a valuable commentary.

theatrical undertakings. Henslowe is first heard of as the servant of a man of property in Southwark whose widow he married, thus laying the foundations of his fortunes. But his success as a backer of theatrical enterprises came more definitely through association with Edward Alleyn, the famous actor, who married Henslowe's daughter in 1592. Henslowe thrived not only in the building of playhouses and in financing companies, but he acquired likewise a place as groom of the chamber to Queen Elizabeth, and later as gentleman sewer (or cup-bearer) to King James. He purchased for himself and Alleyn the posts of Masters of the Royal Games of bulls and bears and contrived to die a respected burgher of Southwark, leaving a considerable fortune which came into the hands of Alleyn. It is of interest to know that this money, through bequest by Alleyn for the foundation of the College of God's Gift in Dulwich, is still fulfilling in enlarged usefulness the charitable intent of the donor.

In the conduct of his theatrical business, the most important person with whom Henslowe had to deal was the Master of the Revels, during Henslowe's lifetime Sir Edmund Tylney. To him Henslowe paid for the license of his playhouse and for the specific licensing of individual plays. The weekly payment of 5s. for an acting license rose under the steady pressure of the Masters to 40s. a month and a claim, in the time of Charles, of two "benefits" and a share of £100. As to Henslowe's closer dealings with players and writers, there is every reason to believe that few of his accounts are personal—"laid out for the company's reckoning with my Lord Nottingham's men," and the like, being familiar phrases. An interesting series of entries is that which records payments made to writers in earnest of promised work or in payment for completed plays. The usual sum for a play in the earlier 'nineties was £6; but the price steadily rose to eight and ten, until we find a minor playwright like Robert Daborne, in James's reign, receiving three times as much and de-

Henslowe's theatrical business

manding more. Henslowe's relations to the companies which he financed seem to have varied from simple landlordship, like that of Alleyn, who rented the Fortune theater outright to the Palsgrave's men for £200 per annum, to a share in the daily receipts, regulated by varying conditions. Henslowe had likewise dealings in the wardrobe, purchasing of properties, accepting costumes as pledges for loans and selling apparel and jewels to the players in payment by installments. That he developed a somewhat rough and ready finance in his dealings with the carelessness and improvidence, which seem in all ages to characterize the actor's profession, is not to be wondered. But a close study of the *Diary* hardly bears out the picture of a grinding usurer that is sometimes drawn of "the theatrical banker of the Bankside." The greatest interest of *Henslowe's Diary* lies in his mention by name of most of the dramatists of his day with the titles, and often the date of first and other performance of some 280 plays. When we learn that 217 of these are not otherwise known, we can appreciate what the loss of such a document would mean to the history of the drama.[1]

The Globe playhouse and the second Blackfriars In 1597 James Burbage died, harassed and involved in lawsuits. One of his last efforts, in despair of continuing at the Theater, was to purchase the old refectory of the Blackfriars and convert several rooms of it into a theater. But before it was ready for occupancy, a petition to the crown blocked the plan, and the sons of Burbage, Cuthbert and Richard—later the great actor—succeeded to his projects. Thus balked of removal to Blackfriars, and under threat from the owner of the ground of the Theater to take possession, the Burbages sent workmen by night and, pulling down the old playhouse, carted it away to the Bankside, where it was used to erect a new theater, com-

---

[1] Greg suggests that "but for the accident of the preservation of *Henslowe's Diary* the number of plays which we should be in a position to assign to the Admiral's men would be hardly greater than that which we habitually can assign to the King's (*i.e.,* Shakespeare's) company." *Henslowe,* ii, 146.

pleted in 1599, and called the Globe.[1] As to the new
Blackfriars, while the prohibition against its occupancy
by a professional company appears to have held, the
Burbages succeeded in finding a tenant in Henry Evans,
who had managed the old Blackfriars for Lyly and Hunnis,
and saw here an opportunity of employing the queen's
commission for the taking up of children to serve the
Royal Chapel for the further purpose of providing a dramatic company for the royal entertainment.[2] Accordingly,
he formed a partnership with Nathaniel Giles, Master of
the Royal Chapel (1597-1634), to whom officially belonged this right, and the two proceeded at once to recruit
their company, but with so high a hand that, having kidnapped, as he was returning from school, the son of a
gentleman named Clifton, they so exasperated the father
that Evans became the subject of an inquiry by Star
Chamber, and his rights in Blackfriars were taken away
from him.[3] The Children of the Chapel were alike a
histrionic and a financial success in their day, and they
contrived to continue under other management into the
next reign. They were famous for satirical plays and
noted likewise for their skill in music, which they appear
to have exercised at times by way of concert before the
play.[4] The idea of Wallace that this establishment of
the Chapel Children at Blackfriars was maintained at the
cost of the crown and officially by Queen Elizabeth has not
been accepted as proved by the evidence cited.[5] There
seems, too, to have been, as we have seen, a revival during
the latter years of the queen among the boy actors of St.
Paul's under their master, Edward Pierce, some of the

[1] A succinct account of the modern controversy respecting the precise
site of the Globe will be found in Chambers, ii, 427-432. A late word on
it is that of W. W. Braines, *The Site of the Globe Theater in Southwark,* 1921.
[2] Adams, *Shakespearean Playhouses,* 201.
[3] C. W. Wallace, *The Children of the Chapel at Blackfriars,* p. 84, and
especially Chambers's resumé of the whole subject, ii, 43-45, and note
as to the lawsuits involved, *ibid.,* 23.
[4] The Duke of Stettin in his "Diary," *Transactions of the Royal Historical Society,* 1890, vi, 26, declared the skill of these children unequaled.
[5] Wallace, as above, 126; Chambers, *ibid.,* ii, 46, 47.

most important dramatists, for the time being, writing for them. The relation of this revival of the boy companies to their adult rivals must be deferred.

Private playhouses

There is no subject related to early English drama which has attracted more persistent scrutiny than that which concerns the construction of the Shakespearean theater, its stage, appointments, and methods of presentation. Moreover, considerable new material on the general subject has been turned up, adding to our information and modifying at least some of our preconceptions. Clearly the two theaters at Blackfriars, of which we have heard, Farrant's and Burbage's, were rooms converted into an auditorium. The opinion has been expressed that Farrant's must have been at best a small room, "not over 25 feet in width." As to Burbage's theater in Blackfriars, Wallace makes out its dimensions to have been 66 feet by 46, and supposes it provided with galleries.[1] Those and subsequent ones like them—the playing-place or singing-school of St. Paul's boys[2] and that of Whitefriars—were called private houses. They appear to have differed little from the public playhouses except that performances were commonly by candle-light, before a somewhat better class of auditors and at higher charges for admission. The theory of their existence was that of places of practice for the preparation of the royal entertainment. But some of their characteristics came in time to modify the simpler methods of the popular playhouses.

Public playhouses; the Theater

The Theater, like most of the public playhouses which followed it, was circular or octagonal in form, constructed of wood and plaster, galleries running about a yard within which was called the pit, and open to the sky. Stockwood, an indignant preacher, speaks of "the gorgeous playing-

---

[1] Chambers, ii, 522, suggests that in private theaters "admission was paid for in advance and in money taken at the door." The distinction appears on title pages: *e.g., Satiromastix* was acted publicly by the Chamberlain's men, privately at Paul's.
[2] Paul's singing-school had a circular auditorium, Chambers, ii, 554.

place erected in the fields." But spaciousness and gorgeousness are comparative. The Curtain, so called from the title of the estate on which it was built and not with reference to the familiar drapery of the stage, must have been of much the shape, if not of quite the size, of the Theater. Both were built on leased ground. There seems to have been a close relation between these two old playhouses; and they shared many vicissitudes such as riots, lawsuits, earthquakes, and threats of demolition. Many of the earlier plays of the Chamberlain's men, after 1594, were acted at the Theater; *Romeo and Juliet* won "Curtain plaudities." [1] A more or less circular structure was maintained in the playhouses of the Bankside, perhaps originally suggested by the amphitheaters there. In 1587, Henslowe erected a playhouse, the Rose, on property of his own, in the Clink, near to the Bear Garden, and slightly farther from the river. The Swan, remotest of the Bankside theaters from London Bridge, lay to the west in Paris Garden, not far from Falcon Stairs. It was built in 1595 by Francis Langley, a goldsmith, and is pictured, as to the interior, in a sketch by John De Witt, purporting to have been originally made in the following year by a German traveler and, since its discovery in the Library of the University of Utrecht in 1888, reproduced in every schoolbook. Here recur most of the familiar features of the Elizabethan playhouse; but several of the details of this sketch—which, after all, is not at first hand—have been questioned, and it would be unwise to accept it in full as representative and typical.

But at a time somewhat after this, in 1600, Alleyn had built his playhouse, the Fortune, in St. Giles, Cripplegate. As the contracts for this building are extant among Henslowe's papers, we know more of it than of any other. A striking feature is the departure from the circular form prevalent, the outside measurements being 80 feet each way. The interior was a square of 55 feet by the same,

The Fortune Playhouse

---

[1] Marston's *Scourge of Villainy,* Bk. iii, Satire xi.

the difference from the outer lines making the requisite allowance for wide galleries. Of these there were three, 12, 11, and 9 feet, respectively, in height, and 12 feet 6 inches in depth. There was provision for four "gentlemen's rooms," although their actual position in the house, like that of the "twopenny boxes," is uncertain. These rooms were sealed, and the general material of construction was lath and plaster on brick foundations. Galleries and stage were roofed in tile and a "shadow" or "heaven" over the stage was provided, just how or in what position is not clear. The width of the stage is named as 43 feet, and it extended into the yard 40 feet. Wherever anything is left unspecified in Henslowe's contract, the Globe is referred to as the model, a point as interesting as it is tantalizing; for we can get at the Globe only by the specifications of the Fortune. The total cost of the Fortune, lease, freehold, building, and outbuildings has been estimated at from £1,320 to £1,380; the second Globe at £1,680; the old Theater at 1,000 marks, or £666. It has been suggested that the improvements on the second Blackfriars cost Burbage about £900.[1] The Globe and the Fortune were the last theaters to be built during the lifetime of Elizabeth; the Red Bull in Clerkenwell and the Bankside Hope both came later. The Theater, as we have seen, was pulled down to use in part as material for the Globe; and Newington Butts and the Rose scarcely lasted into the reign of James. The Curtain was standing in 1627, the Swan into the 'thirties. Of the older playhouses, the Globe and the Fortune alone remained to be closed with later houses by the Puritans in 1642. The old playhouses, of which there seem always to have been at least three in simultaneous use, differed in the character of their performances as those of any other time. The better houses were given over solely to drama which was varied in inferior ones with puppet shows, bull- and bear-baiting,

[1] These estimates are those of Chambers, ii, 391, 423, 436; and Thorndike, *Shakespeare's Theater*, 57, substantially agrees.

cock-fighting, and fencing bouts. Lying open to the sky as did the yard at least, performance was dependent on the weather. It was undoubtedly as nearly daily as the recurrence of the plague and the interference of the authorities would permit.

The Elizabethan company of players involved the shareholders and the housekeepers, or owners. There were likewise hired men and servants. The shareholders owned the costumes, properties, and playbooks and bore the expenses of the performance, taking in return, usually, at least, the proceeds at the door. The housekeepers, or owners of the building, received the extra charges of the galleries, or a part of them, charges later commuted into a regular rental. In the case of the Globe, and the Blackfriars when the Burbages resumed their lease, the two Burbage brothers, Cuthbert and Richard, were the householders, while Richard as an actor, with Shakespeare, Heminge, Condell, and the rest, constituted the sharers. This plan of a joint stock company sharing in profits and expenses worked exceedingly well to the closing of the theaters. In contrast Henslowe exploited his several companies as a capitalist confessing ingenuously: "Should these fellows come out of my debt, I should have no rule over them." There were many modifications in these arrangements, but it is obvious that a man in the theatrical business of the time might derive income from his investments in playhouse property, for negotiation as to the writing of plays, for the use of properties and costumes, and for the advance of money, all of which things did Henslowe. Or he might be at once an owner, a sharer, and an actor, as was Richard Burbage, and add to all this, theatrical authorship, as did Shakespeare.

Organization of the company

We have outlined in these paragraphs the externals of the stage up to the close of the old queen's reign. The much-mooted topic, the staging of an Elizabethan play, must be deferred to a future chapter. There are many details as to the history of the stage which, in the limita-

The companies, abroad

79

tions of a picture on this scale, we cannot but rigorously exclude. London was then, even more than now, the center of the English theatrical world. But in times of plague or for other reasons, the companies often traveled, usually reduced in numbers; and an intricate chapter traces their movements in the English provinces and even overseas.[1] Notable among journeys abroad was that of Leicester's company under leadership of William Kempe, successor to the fame of Tarlton and later a fellow player of Shakespeare. This was in 1585 when Leicester assumed command of the English troops in the Low Countries and onward a couple of years. The company traveled on this tour first into Denmark and then to the court of the Elector of Saxony. Nor was this by any means the only continental tour of Elizabethan players whose popularity, especially in Germany, is attested in a well-known passage of *The Itinerary* of Fynes Moryson, who witnessed the acting of such a troupe at Frankford in 1592, and criticized it as compared with what he remembered of contemporary acting in London.[2] An interesting foreign relation of English actors was that of Lawrence Fletcher, who was well received by James in Scotland on at least one trip thither with an English troupe and entertained as "comedian to His Majesty," before the royal coming to England. Fletcher heads the list of the new patent to the king's men in 1603, although the better opinion seems to be that he was never an actor in Shakespeare's company nor really in business relations with it.[3] There is no reason for thinking that Shakespeare was among the players who traveled either to Scotland or elsewhere abroad.

[1] The extent to which the companies traveled in England has only been appreciated in recent years. Some troupes seem to have been purely provincial. On the subject see J. T. Murray, *English Dramatic Companies*, 1910, vol. ii; and Chambers, i, 341-347, which contains a summary of the subject. Also *ibid.*, ii, 269-294.
[2] C. Hughes, *Shakespeare's Europe*, 1903, pp. 304-373.
[3] Chambers, ii, 270, 318.

CHAPTER V

THE NEW DRAMA OF PASSION

IN turning to a consideration of the succession of plays which held the boards of Elizabethan playhouses in bewildering profusion from Marlowe to Shirley, we are struck with their exceeding variety in kind and with the further difficulty that a single play commonly combines in itself characteristics often very contrasted. To take familiar Shakespearean examples: *Henry IV* is a chronicle play, its subject English history, but the scenes of Falstaff and his rout are realistic comedy of contemporary tavern life, and the product is the better for the combination. So, too, *Othello* is a drama of domestic type, cast, however, in a romantic atmosphere, in conclusion a tragedy; as *Antony and Cleopatra* is Roman history, and alike the most consummate study in two commanding personalities and the greatest of romantic love stories. Rare is the playwright who, like Lyly or Marlowe, confined his art to one variety of the drama; and if one author seem wholly this or another devoted merely to another mode, it is perhaps because we cannot recover the completeness of either's work. Of few Elizabethan dramatists can we feel sure that we have all that he wrote; and some that we have is certainly wrongly attributed as to authorship. Not only was work often printed without name to give it parentage, but plays were frequently penned in collaboration by two, three, or even a greater number of writers; and whatever the playhouses held was subject to alteration, revision, excision by the original author at times, but quite as often by others. The age, in a word, was eclectic and experi-

Complexity of Elizabethan drama

81

mental; the relations and the limitations of authorship were as yet little understood.

For the understanding, then, of this amazing variety and diversity in the plays of Elizabethan times, some means of guidance seems imperative. Accurate chronology of the plays, either when written or when acted, is unascertainable. With almost every playwright writing in several modes, authorship alone is misleading. The larger dimensions of tragedy and comedy, as they exist simultaneously, simply cleave the subject. More vital, it would appear, than distinctions founded on happy or tragic endings, are those which inhere in the writer's bias in his art, that of simple representation, that which heightens picturesque and emotional possibilities, or that which in laughter at absurdity involves the moral sense: the realist's, the romantic, the ironic view of life, if we are to employ the old abraided coinage of the schools. Besides, smaller groups of plays are distinguishable—a passing fashion, a manner of writing, preference for a topic of momentary interest—things which arise, have their vogue and decline; and these follow one the other in a species of irregular succession; for example, the conqueror play, thrust into popularity by *Tamburlaine*, the tragedy of revenge, referable to the vogue of *The Spanish Tragedy* of Kyd, naïve romance of adventure, followed by comedy, domestic, romantic, or both in combination, to be succeeded by Ben Jonson's famous comedy of humors; and later, tragicomedy, Fletcher's contribution to the complexity of the drama. Such groupings seem not unnatural, if, with the warning of Polonius, we pursue them not to the absurdities of "tragical-comical-historical-pastoral, scene individable or poem unlimited." The application of "scientific" terms and "scientific" classifications to subjects to which such terminologies and classifications are only applicable by way of figures of speech, will be remembered as the prime obsession of our generation. It is, therefore, with a lively sense of the dangers of such

A way through the labyrinth

methods that any grouping of subject-matter is offered in
this book. For all aids and appliances such as these are
in the nature of a provisional scaffolding, essential to the
construction of the building, but to be demolished, if we
are to know the structure in its completed beauty.

The phrase which heads this chapter may be applied, *The
romantic
pronuncia-
mento* in no sense of any novelty, to the plays which, beginning
about 1586, mark the sudden change wrought in the very
nature of English drama by the tragedies of Marlowe and
those who shared or imitated his daring and poetic spirit.
In tragedies of the previous generation we have much of
the ranting "*Cambyses* vein," but little real emotion; and
we have discordant scenes of foolery, not above the average
of the interlude; and as a more or less universal vehicle
of dramatic dialogue, the long line of tumbling measure
with the incongruous chime of inevitable rhyme. It was
with such stuff as this in mind that Marlowe blew the
clarion notes of his famous prologue of *Tamburlaine the
Great*:

> From jigging veins of rhyming mother wits,
> And such conceits as clownage keeps in pay,
> We'll lead you to the stately tent of war,
> Where you shall hear the Scythian Tamburlaine
> Threatening the world with high astounding terms,
> And scourging kingdoms with his conquering sword.

Here was to be life, action, and passion, and a new and
elevated tragic style suitable, in the majestic tread of
blank verse, to a great and spacious subject. Seldom
has there been so assured a pronunciamento of radical
change; far more rarely has such a pronouncement been
fulfilled with a success so complete and immediate. Marlowe literally leaped into fame. And his tragedies struck
a lead which few of his successors dared not more or less
openly to follow.

Of Christopher Marlowe's actual life and dramatic activ- *Christopher
Marlowe* ity much less is known than of Shakespeare's. Born at

Canterbury in February, 1564, the year of Shakespeare's birth and but a month earlier, Marlowe's station in life was not dissimilar. However, better opportunities and a certain precocity, we may assume, took him to Cambridge, there to be quickened by the study of classical poetry and the unorthodoxy of Francis Kett, and confirmed in that insolent and rebellious spirit which informs his work from the first. Marlowe was an independent thinker rather than the reputed atheist which tradition makes him. And he was likewise ambitious, imaginative, and a poet of almost unlimited possibilities. He came too early, or was of too free a spirit, to fall into the slavery of Henslowe's mart of theatrical trade; but most of his plays drifted sooner or later into the repertory of the Admiral's men, and the tradition is that Alleyn was the chief actor in them. There is a willfulness about Marlowe that makes it unlikely that he long endured the yoke of collaboration with anybody; and whatever may have been his possible association with others—in chronicles, if not in other plays —he must have broken away from it early to independent venture.

Marlowe's plays and following Marlowe's six or seven recognized plays are crowded into as many years at most, from *Tamburlaine*, the first part on the stage by 1587, to the poet's tragic death— killed in a tavern broil is the tradition—in May, 1593. In quick succession followed *Doctor Faustus*, *The Jew of Malta*, *Edward II*, *The Massacre at Paris*, and *The Tragedy of Dido*, the last written with Thomas Nash and least in point of merit.[1] With Marlowe the conception of the superman comes first prominently into English litera- ture. Through everything that he wrote runs an inspiring dominant motive, perhaps somewhat expressed in the words, poetry, passion, exorbitancy. Tamburlaine, ruthless con- queror, lashing the world with "high astounding terms,"

---

[1] On Marlowe's plays see especially Professor C. F. Tucker Brooke, "The Marlowe Canon," *Publication Modern Language Association*, xxxvii, 1922; as to Marlowe's reputation, the same author in *Trans. Conn. Acad- emy*, xv, 347, also 1922; and his ed. of Marlowe, 1910.

no less than with the victor's sword; Faustus, selling his
soul to the devil in an avid eagerness to know all, to enjoy
all; the Jew, extravagant in his revenge as in his avarice,
ingeniously wicked and daring in all his scheming—each of
these is sustained through scenes, instinct with the engaging improbabilities of true romance, on the strong wings
of magnificent verse and with the verve of that genuine
passion, that high artistic seriousness which can carry
anything in its splendid flight. It is no wonder that Marlowe swept his auditors off their feet and that his *Tamburlaine* should have held the stage for the generation
which knew Shakespeare. This exorbitant tragedy, indeed,
begot a numerous progeny of imitation: Greene with his
Alphonsus of Arragon, Peele with *The Battle of Alcazar,*
others anonymously with *Wars of Cyrus* and *Selimus, Emperor of the Turks,* by some thought Greene's, by others
even Marlowe's own.[1] *Doctor Faustus,* too, world story
that it is of him who sold his soul and hope of salvation
for the brief joys that the world can give, a tragedy frag-
mentary and corrupt in text, as handed down to us, and
disfigured with inconsequent foolery, must have been a
drama of overpowering effectiveness with Alleyn in the
title rôle and an implicit belief in the supernatural on the
part of auditors such as our unbelieving age knows not.
There is an excellent old story extant of how, once when
Faustus was acted in the provinces with a small troupe
and the scene of the seven deadly sins was on, in wild
orgy circling Faust and Mephistophiles within their magic
circle; suddenly some one counted, and behold, there were
eight devils, not seven. The troupe was all accounted for,
Jack here, Will there, and Harry at the door. Wherefore
with one accord the actors fell on their knees in contrition
for their wickedness and folly, and their auditors stam-

---

[1] See Grosart, *Temple Dramatists,* "Selimus," 1898, Introduction; and C.
Crawford, *Collectanea,* 1906, i, 46ff., where this play is not only declared
Marlowe's, but the predecessor of *Tamburlaine.* The further matter of
this paper which makes Spenser Marlowe's master is striking and worthy
of attention.

peded home with a lesson administered by superstition, rather than art. There is a group of plays suggested by *Doctor Faustus*, likewise, notable among them Greene's pleasing comedy of *Friar Bacon and Friar Bungay* with its emphasis on "white" or harmless magic over against the "black magic" of unhappy Faustus. And later, in 1607, there is the application of the theme by Barnabe Barnes, sonneteer and friend of Gabriel Harvey and Percy, to the wicked life of Pope Alexander VI, called *The Devil's Charter*, a tragedy of much theatrical effectiveness. Like the other two, *The Jew of Malta* was also fruitful. In the story of Barabas, mad in the ingenuity and exorbitancy of his revenge—the murder of his own daughter, the poisoning of a whole nunnery, the betrayal of Malta—we have the seed-play, so to speak, of one of the two important species of the tragedy of blood, that which, followed out by others, begot the hideous enormities of *Titus Andronicus* and degenerated into the even grosser sensuality of *Lust's Dominion*, which it is difficult to believe Marlowe's.[1] It is not accidental that Macchiavelli, the personage who, in Elizabethan literature, became the accepted parent of politic and godless intriguing, should have been chosen by Marlowe to speak a prologue justifying villainous craft. On mention of Barabas, Marlowe's monster Jew, the mind reverts to Shylock, who, however humanized by a hand which could reach human nature as never could Marlowe, owes much to that earlier striking stage realization of a popular misconception of the Jew.

The dramatic promise of Marlowe

An accepted canon of criticism as to Marlowe deplores the poet forced into the dramatic mould; as if poetry and drama must be ever things repugnant. *Tamburlaine*, it is true, is as epic and disjointed as any contemporary chronicle play; and *Doctor Faustus* is a string of episodes, harking back to the moral play in its introduction of abstract figures with the alternate promptings of the hero by

[1] On this topic, see the discussion of E. E. Stoll, *John Webster,* 1905, pp. 94 ff. *Alphonsus of Germany,* attributed to Chapman, registered in 1653 as by John Poole, and *Revenge for Honor* belong to this category.

the spirits of evil and of good. But as a matter of fact both *The Jew* and *Edward II* are well-wrought dramas for their period and disclose a constructive capability which Shakespeare himself scarcely surpassed at Marlowe's years. It is always to be remembered that, if we have in Marlowe extraordinary achievement, there was in him even more extraordinary promise. Save for comedy, of which the comic scenes of *Doctor Faustus* (that may not be Marlowe's) offer but a sorry example, almost anything might have been predicted for a genius such as his; but "cut" was now

> the branch that might have grown full straight
> And burned is Apollo's laurel bough.

Marlowe was dead before he arrived at thirty. Shakespeare dying at a corresponding age, we should have had from his hand, barring *Titus Andronicus* (which few believe wholly his), no tragedy except *Romeo and Juliet;* and this in a version by no means that which we now possess. We may set against this Shakespeare's earlier comedies; but be it remembered that even *Midsummer Night's Dream,* at the date of Marlowe's death, was as yet unwritten.

In the few years of Marlowe's heyday there was only one tragic writer who could hold his own against him in the popular estimation, and this was Thomas Kyd, and in only one of his plays, the famous *Spanish Tragedy,* on the stage about the time of *Tamburlaine,* whether before or after, it is quite impossible to say.[1] It speaks much for the literary integrity of these two youths—for they were little more—that, writing in the same room, even, it would appear, at the same table, we can discover little appreciable influence of the one on the other. Kyd's tragedy is of an older type than Marlowe's, preserving much of

Thomas Kyd

---

[1] Adams, *Shakespeare,* 119, boldly assigns to Kyd the leadership in the new school of professional playwrights. The date of *The Spanish Tragedy* has been variously set between 1584 and 1589.

Seneca, though popularized, infused with a new vigor, and disclosing a certain cleverness in dramatic situation which is equally novel. As romantic in plot as *Tancred and Gismund, The Spanish Tragedy* is founded, in the manner of the moment, on imaginary relations between Portugal and Spain which are given the guise of veritable history. And little effort to poetize sustains the rhetorically heightened dialogue and the orderly conduct of its prevailingly somber scenes. Of Thomas Kyd we learn that he was the son of a scrivener, born in London as early as 1558, and apparently not college bred. He appears to have revolved in the outer circles of the literary influences of the Countess of Pembroke, under which he transcribed into English one of the tragedies of Garnier in his *Cornelia*. To Kyd has been attributed, besides several other plays, *Soliman and Perseda*, which dramatizes the play within *The Spanish Tragedy* and reads like an imitation of it. An earlier and now lost version of the story of Hamlet seems Kyd's on the more convincing grounds of several allusions to a play of that title earlier than Shakespeare's and because of the coupling of Kyd's name with a *Hamlet* in Nash's *Epistle to Menaphon*, 1589, in terms very difficult to interpret otherwise. How far Kyd may have been a party, also, to the older plays which underlie the *Henry VI* trilogy is as problematic as his alleged authorship of *Titus Andronicus*. But the present writer feels that he must accept the strikingly effective murder play, *Arden of Feversham*, as probable work of Kyd's hand. The reasoning, based on solid evidence, of Crawford on this subject seems quite convincing.[1] *Arden* is alike the first and the best of several domestic dramas, based on more or less recent English crimes, the sort of stuff that begets sensational headlines in a modern newspaper; and its peculiar excellence lies in the transformation of this sordid material into a tragedy of such inherent worth that creditable critical opinion has

---

[1] *Collectanea*, i. 101; *Arden* has been variously dated between 1586 and 1592, in which latter year it was first printed. See also the corroboration of Sykes, *Sidelights on Shakespeare*, 1919, pp. 48-76.

again and again referred it to Shakespeare.[1] It adds to our appreciation of the versatility of Kyd that he should thus have vitalized both romantic tragedy and the homely circumstantial murder play. *Arden* inspired a number of like productions, among them *A Warning for Fair Women*, 1599, and *A Yorkshire Tragedy*, 1608. The brief effectiveness of this last little drama in ten scenes has placed it, too, in the category of *Shakespeare Apocrypha*. It has been referred, with better reason, to the authorship of George Wilkins, who derived his *Miseries of Enforced Marriage* from the same unhappy realities, and was Shakespeare's coadjutor in the writing of *Pericles, Prince of Tyre*.[2]

Between 1590 and 1593, Kyd and Marlowe were both in the service of a certain lord (Pembroke, Strange, or Sussex) for whose players the latter was writing. As the two poets shared the same room and perhaps the same table, their papers became mixed; and when Kyd was arrested on suspicion of being a party to the posting of certain "mutinous libels" on walls of the Dutch church, papers were found that led to an order for the arrest of Marlowe likewise. Marlowe had already given bail, in 1588, to appear at the next Middlesex sessions, on what charge we do not know; and at the time of Kyd's arrest, in 1593, Marlowe was the subject of a "Note" by an informer alleging atheism and blasphemy. But his death intervened before the service of the order. It was while Kyd was in prison and under torture that he wrote letters to Sir John Pickering, the Lord Keeper, seeking to explain his relations to Marlowe and to repudiate any share in his opinions. Marlowe's paper, found under these circumstances, turns out to be a speculative discourse addressed to a bishop on the Trinity, tainted with what we should now call Unitarian leanings. It is not a piece of blasphemy. Kyd was released later in this same year, 1593, but died before the

Personal relations of Kyd and Marlowe

---

[1] Swinburne especially advocated Shakespeare's authorship.
[2] See especially Sykes, as above, 77, 143.

expiration of 1594, still in disgrace, for his parents refused to administer his goods.[1]

Robert Greene

There remain of "the predecessors" two, Robert Greene and Thomas Lodge. Both, like Nash, were pamphleteers, those unstable forerunners of journalism, and only incidentally playwrights. Greene was a Norwich man and born in 1558. He was boastful of his acquirements at two universities and enjoyed an extraordinary popularity in his brief day for his prose fiction, romantic and realistic. His period of dramatic authorship falls between 1587 and 1591, and comprises some five or six plays. In *Alphonsus of Arragon* Greene frankly imitated *Tamburlaine* and matched the black magic of *Doctor Faustus* with the "white" or harmless magic of *Friar Bacon and Friar Bungay*. With Lodge he reverted to the obsolete mode of the moral play in their satirical *Looking Glass for London and England;* and in *Orlando Furioso* he attempted to stage the romantic extravagance of Ariosto. But the forte of Greene lay in less extravagant comedy such as that of *Friar Bacon* and *James IV of Scotland*, which latter is not history, but a tale of love and intrigue out of Cinthio. Industrious scholarship has striven to enlarge Greene's dramatic authorship by considering him, with Lodge, Peele, and Marlowe, among the writers of pre-Shakespearean chronicle histories as well as of several other plays. But Greene's extraordinary activity as a pamphleteer may reasonably be urged against assigning too much to his dramatic pen. He was much at enmity with his fellows, especially Marlowe, whom he attacked in his pamphlets as he attacked the players in general.[2] When Greene wrote exposing "conycatching," as sharp practice and cheating was called, he was taken to task for a like piece of roguery in selling his *Orlando* first to the Queen's

[1] F. S. Boas, "New Light on Marlowe," *Fortnightly Review,* 1899, ii, 467; his ed. of Kyd, 1901; and T. K. Brown, "Marlowe and Kyd," *Times Supplement,* June 2, 1921, who adds a letter to those previously discovered by Professor Boas.

[2] See especially the preface to "Perimedes the Blacksmith," Grosart, *Works of Greene,* vii, 7; and the preface to "Menaphon," *ibid.,* vi, 86, 119.

players and again to the Admiral's men.[1] Just before his death Greene became involved in a literary squabble with Gabriel Harvey, a learned and crusty Cambridge don, the friend of Spenser; and the quarrel continued, Greene dying, with Nash as his champion, until the world became disgusted with the whole affair and the books of both antagonists were ordered burned wherever found. Greene's life was ungoverned, and he died miserably, bequeathing to the wife whom he had deserted the charges of his funeral. The most memorable thing about Greene is his notorious pamphlet, *A Groatsworth of Wit Purchased with a Million of Repentance*, which, the story goes, was written on his deathbed. To a bit of autobiography—for Greene is always autobiographical—in this book, is added an address, "To those gentlemen, his quondam acquaintance, that spend their wits in making plays," in which occurs all but a direct mention of Peele, Marlowe, and Nash, and likewise, the first printed allusion to Shakespeare, under the nickname "Shakescene," with an unmistakable grudge at his success.[2] But Greene was dead, in 1592, before Marlowe, "of a surfeit of pickled herring and rhenish." The sweet and wholesome comedies of this strangely contradictory man will claim attention in another place.

Thomas Lodge, of much the age of Greene and son of a Lord Mayor of London, was sent to Oxford, in 1573, where he made an early reputation as a poet. A traveler, a writer of fiction, a playwright ashamed of his craft (for he printed only one play, *The Wounds of Civil War*, 1594, under his name), at length a translator, Lodge contrived to live down the wild days of a Bohemian past and to die a respected physician, ten years after his junior, Shake-

Thomas Lodge

---

[1] "Defence of Conycatching," *ibid.*, xi, 75.
[2] Professor Tucker Brooke, *The Authorship of King Henry VI*, p. 191, objects to this time-honored interpretation, finding in Greene's famous words merely a protest against "one of the cruelest injustices of Elizabethan life, the pauperizing subservience of the dramatic poets to the managers of theatrical companies," and "not the voicing of literary spite and unfounded charges of plagiarism."

speare. The range of Lodge's alleged dramatic authorship is likewise doubtful; including, besides his part in
A Looking Glass for London and the Roman history just
mentioned, little of which we can feel certain. To Lodge
has been assigned, too, a part in the early chronicle histories and in several other masterless plays. Whatever his
actual range of authorship in the drama, he must remain
memorable as the author of the charming story, *Rosalynde, Euphues' Golden Legacy* on which Shakespeare
founded his *As You Like It*. It was later that Shakespeare
similarly utilized a story of Greene, *Pandosto*, for *The
Winter's Tale*. In summary of the group just considered,
it is perhaps worth repeating that in the early 'nineties,
when Shakespeare was coming into his own, his possible
competitors fell, one after the other, out of his way:
Greene in 1592, Marlowe in 1593, Kyd in 1594 and Peele
in 1597. Nash, after this latter date, was given over to
his pamphlets, dying in 1601; Lyly lived on to 1606, but
the age had passed beyond him. Lodge, alone, survived
to 1625, in other fields of activity; to him the drama had
been merely an episode.

"The predecessors of Shakespeare" With Kyd and Marlowe we have before us two of the
more important members of the group of dramatic writers
which has been dubbed *par excellence* "the predecessors of
Shakespeare"—as if he had no others—"the pleiades"—
although it is somewhat difficult to count them just seven—
or "the university wits"—however some of them, as Kyd
himself, for example, frequented neither Oxford nor Cambridge. Lyly, a third of the group, has been treated above
as belonging solely to the court; and Peele also another,
who commenced a competitor, if not a follower, of Lyly.
Peele was an experimentalist in drama and an imitator, as
we have seen, of Marlowe. His range of authorship, like
others of the group, has been enlarged by wise and unwise
inclusion to embrace several other plays of various kinds,
among them even the *Titus Andronicus* in our current

editions of Shakespeare.[1] This, with his *Battle of Alcazar* and his chronicle-like biblical tragedy, *David and Bethsabe*, should give Peele his place among writers in the drama of passion. Thomas Nash, the fifth of our pleiades, was a notorious pamphleteer and controversialist; except for a single masque-like effort, *Summer's Last Will and Testament*, the scandal of a lost comedy, and his slight collaboration with Marlowe, Nash scarcely touches drama at all.[2]

Leaving for the nonce the part which some of these men **Romance** took in other kinds of drama, let us follow tragedy, which **and Italy** Marlowe had infused with this new equality of passion, into some of its later manifestations. Tragedy from the first appeared in many forms and chose almost any subject. The romantic way of looking at things is dependent little on topic, and its potency is not so much in the novelty or even the difference of the figures of its choice as in the atmosphere with which it surrounds them. However, there is scarcely a convention so imbedded in Elizabethan literature as that which beholds everything Italian through a species of luminous mist, half imagination, half enchantment. Old English balladry had long since imaged "the banks of Italy" as flowering under sunlit skies and filled with happy, care-free inhabitants. And the Elizabethan imagination accepted this convention with the added recognition, even more thrillingly romantic, of the unbridled passions, the unimaginable crimes, and the hideous labyrinthine intrigues, the home of which, too, was that beautiful, unregenerate land.

Earlier romantic influences in English drama take us **Romantic** at least as far back as *Calisto and Melibea* (1530), in- **influences** teresting as a sporadic example of a contact between English and Spanish literature not to become frequent until generations later. Traces of Chaucerian romantic story dramatized are to be found at court, at the universities, and

[1] As Chambers puts it, iii, 462, "Peele's hand has been sought in nearly every masterless play of his epoch."
[2] *Summer's Last Will* was acted in 1592 before Archbishop Whitgift at Croydon. R. B. McKerrow, *Works of Nashe*, 1910, iv, 418; *ibid.*, iv, 416.

later in popular drama; and a series of plays, now lost, of heroic-sounding titles, *Herpetulus the Blue Knight* and *Perobia the Knight of the Burning Rock, Philemon and Philecia,* are to be gleaned from the *Accounts of the Revels* in the 'seventies, which are not improbably well represented in such contemporary extant productions as *Common Conditions and Sir Clyomon and Sir Clamydes,* with their impossible adventures and their general air of romantic unreality only paralleled in *The Faery Queen* itself. Greene in his *Orlando Furioso* tried to outdo his source, Ariosto; Peele in *The Old Wives' Tale,* attempted good-humoredly the ridicule of this sort of thing (both date soon after 1590); while some years later, Dekker turned romantic extravagance into a species of controversial political allegory in *The Whore of Babylon* (1605), in which, dealing with Romanists' plots against the queen, he took for model Lyly as well as Spenser, and borrowed names from Shakespeare to figure forth Elizabeth as Titania and, even more absurdly, her father, Henry VIII, as Oberon. Extravagant in another way is Heywood's *Four Prentices of London,* dating before this, in 1592; for here heroic impossibilities are adapted to the tastes of the city's groundling playgoers and with Geoffrey of Bulloigne and the siege of Jerusalem for climax, and English trades-folk for heroes, the London citizen is glorified in pre-posterous adventure and eulogy. When, years after, Heywood's play was revived and Beaumont turned these absurdities to the ridicule which they deserved, we learn that the devotees of the London playhouses did not approve. It was Beaumont's *Knight of the Burning Pestle* (1607), with its clever mockery, that failed, not the exploits of the prentices in carving out for themselves un-historical kingdoms or the successes of Dick Whittington and his miraculous cat, the actual topic of a play of perhaps not dissimilar type now lost.

English drama and the *novella* But we have wandered from the drama of veritable passion which disappears in inventive extravagances such as these. To return, the inspiration, which was to develop romantic tragedy (and romantic comedy as well) to its height, came from a source less akin to Marlowe's exuberant tragedy of the superman than to the more human intrigue, the more humanly emotional tragedy of Kyd. This source was found in the wealth of Italian fiction, *novelle* or short tales of love, revenge, adventure, and intrigue, by Boccaccio, Cinthio, Bandello, and their like, early gathered into English collections such as Fenton's *Tragical Discourses* and Painter's *Palace of Pleasure,* the latter in print two years after the birth of Shakespeare.[1] Painter especially became a quarry as frequently resorted to for tales of passion and intrigue as was Holinshed for British history. In Painter, as also elsewhere, will be found the story of Gismund, of the Countess of Salisbury, so effectively employed in the anonymous *Edward III* that Shakespeare has been thought by some to be the author of part of it; and there, too, will be found the stories of Romeo and Juliet, Giletta of Narbonne (source of *All's Well that Ends Well*), and The Duchess of Malfi, original of Webster's master tragedy. Indeed, Painter's liberal pages hold likewise Timon of Athens and Lucrece, and even more strictly historical personages—Cyrus, Alexander, Hannibal and Coriolanus —but viewed, for the most part, in the light of romantic anecdote, not in any veritable sense as history. It is much to our purpose to realize that tales such as these were the accepted fiction of readers in Shakespeare's childhood, and that a credible witness, the translator of the story of Romeo and Juliet, declares that he had seen "the same argument lately set forth on stage" two years before the great dramatist's birth.[2]

If we discard *Titus* and exclude *Romeo and Juliet*, up to 1600 Shakespeare's ventures into tragedy had been only

Romeo and Juliet

[1] On the general subject see the well-known study of J. J. Jusserand, *The English Novel in the Time of Shakespeare,* 1890.
[2] Arthur Brooke, "Address to the Reader," *Romeus and Juliet,* 1562. Hazlitt, *Shakespeare's Library,* part I, vol. i, 72.

those incidental to the chronicle play; and *King John* and the two *Richards* had marked the height of his achievement. To these we shall recur in the next chapter. *Romeo and Juliet* is of the very essence of romantic tragedy, cleared of outworn example and freed, especially when we contrast it with productions like the story of Gismund or that of Belimperia (in *The Spanish Tragedy*), of that stain of illicit intrigue which gives so sinister an aspect to much old drama. In the creation of this lovely picture of adolescent passion Shakespeare's originality is deeper than that of theme. Not only has he given to the personages of his source a truer reality and that universal significance which is the mark of the highest art, but, in the invention of new characters, such as Mercutio, and in the development of suggestion in others, such as Friar Laurence, Old Capulet, and the Nurse, he has surrounded his major personages with touch after touch to make for atmosphere and artistic effect. *Romeo and Juliet* was on the stage, we may well believe, in a less perfected text than we now have it, by 1592, and was later revised and improved, five or six quarto editions, up to the date of the publication of the folio of 1623, attesting its continuous popularity. In it the poet reached that sureness of touch, that competency in his art, that compelling power over emotions and clarity in the drawing of his figures, which remained his ever after.

The tragedy of revenge

A striking manifestation of the new romantic spirit is the tragedy of revenge, the designation which has been applied specifically to a series of dramas of extraordinary vigor which, inspired by a revival of Kyd's *Spanish Tragedy* about 1597, came to include some of the most remarkable works of the age.[1] In the type of plays represented by *The Jew of Malta* and *Titus Andronicus*, the revenge is personal and in retaliation for contempt or

---

[1] On the tragedy of revenge, see the excellent thesis of A. C. Thorndike, *The Relations of Hamlet to Contemporary Revenge Plays*, 1902; his volume, *Tragedy*, 1908; and E. E. Stoll, *John Webster*, who calls this type somewhat cumberously "the Kydian tragedy of blood."

other wrong. Revenge is secondary to ambition, lust, or mere murderousness, and the protagonist is a self-conscious, energetic, and capable schemer who bustles his way to the end. In revenge plays of Kyd's inspiration in contrast, the wrong is, so to speak, a derivative or inherited one, some crime perpetrated on one beloved, a son (as in *The Spanish Tragedy*), a father (as in *Hamlet*), a wife (in *The Second Maiden's Tragedy*); and vengeance becomes a thing, not only sanctified by the affections, but a duty the fulfillment of which is urged by supernatural incitement. This transforms the protagonist, normally, into a righteous man with a wrong to redress, open to supernatural influences, full of doubt, hesitancy, and presentiment, but stoical and fatalistic in his philosophy of life, if not reticent in the delivery of it. Features of these plays are madness, or pretended madness, in the protagonist, the apparatus of horror in certain scenes by night, and a ghost which has been taken out of the induction or the prologue where the Senecans left him, to become a vital element in the plot. To which we may add the motive of incest in the villain, as illustrated in the marriage of Hamlet's mother with his uncle, and a love interest, suggested in the undefined relations of Hamlet and Ophelia or vigorously developed in those of Horatio and Belimperia in *The Spanish Tragedy*. The action proceeds by the method of intrigue and counter-intrigue and employs either for the discovery of crime or for bringing about the catastrophe, a play within a play. Obviously, all this is the formula of both *The Spanish Tragedy* and of *Hamlet*, to an older version of which, we have seen, attaches likewise the name of Kyd. This formula remained to become that of many tragedies to follow.

The Spanish Tragedy held the stage more constantly and was revived more frequently than any play until the heyday of Shakespeare. Henslowe notes performances in 1592 and in 1597, and no less a person than Ben Jonson was put to work on "additions" to this famous tragedy in

Shakespeare and Jonson in rivalry over the tragedy of Kyd

97

1601 and 1602. The usually accepted date assigned for Shakespeare's first writing of *Hamlet* has formerly been put just about this time; for the first and imperfect quarto bears date 1603. And we have thus the suggestion that these two great poets were simultaneously at work in revising these two old successes of Kyd, Jonson interpolating heightened scenes in *The Spanish Tragedy*, Shakespeare rewriting Kyd's old *Hamlet* into his own vital tragedy. But the rediscovery, a few years since, of a mention of "Shakespeare's Hamlet" by Gabriel Harvey on the margin of a book, printed and commented on somewhat as if the book was new, thrusts back Shakespeare's work to a period "at least as early as 1600, if not as early as the end of 1598." [1] The later date would still leave Jonson's revisions for the Admiral's men not so far from Shakespeare's rewritings for the Chamberlain's company. Or perhaps Jonson had something to do with the earlier revival of Kyd's *Hamlet* in 1597. Dekker declares that Jonson once acted the part of Hieronimo in *The Spanish Tragedy* when he was young and success had not yet come to him. I am reluctant to give up this conception of Shakespeare, already assured in his art, and Jonson, ten years his junior, but bold and confident to a fault, entered one against the other in a dramatic rivalry over the spoils of the most popular of their tragic predecessors.

John Marston

These matters aside, in the revival of the tragedy of revenge John Marston played an important part; for his plays on Antonio and Mellida were both of them on the stage before the conclusion of 1599, and in them most of the devices of the species appear, exaggerated with a self-conscious extravagance of diction and vocabulary that called forth the reprobation of the purist in Jonson. John Marston was born about 1575, the son of a lawyer of Coventry, and educated at Oxford. Though destined for the law and a member of the Middle Temple, after a dozen

---

[1] *Henslowe's Diary*, i, 17; G. C. Moore Smith, *Harvey's Marginalia*, 1917, p. viii. M. Castelain, *Ben Jonson*, questions Jonson's authorship of the "additions" to *The Spanish Tragedy*.

or more years' venture in the drama, he ended in the
church. In youth, Marston was of a daring, satirical,
and salacious spirit. This last caused him to write a poem
in perversion of the type to which Marlowe's *Hero and
Leander* and Shakespeare's *Venus and Adonis* belong; the
other characteristics made him an avowed and impertinent
satirist, after the truculent manner of Juvenal, in his
Scourge of Villainy, printed in 1598. As Chambers puts
it, "the setting up of Paul's boys in 1599 saved Marston
from Henslowe." During Elizabeth's reign, he wrote for
them only; and after 1604, for the Queen's Revels, in
which he had an interest. This he abruptly disposed of
in 1608, giving up all converse with the stage. Marston
died in orders in 1634. *Antonio and Mellida* is the earliest tragedy of note consciously to employ the material *Antonio
and*
to be found in the intrigues and crimes of petty Italian *Mellida*
courts; and *Antonio's Revenge,* the second play, adapts
the accepted recipe for the tragedy of revenge to this
manner of play. The Hamlet-like melancholy of Antonio,
who is also a scholar and in like manner is pretendedly
mad, his vengeance for his father's murder in which his
mother joins him, the appearance of the ghost to incite
revenge, the passion of the murderer for Antonio's mother
—these and other details point to the certain writing of
the second of these plays with special reference to *Hamlet.*
Other features are as palpably derived from *The Spanish
Tragedy:* the Macchiavellian Piero, who uses a lesser
villain much as Lorenzo uses Pandulfo in Kyd's play, and
rids himself of him by a grim joke, fatal to his victim,
and the final deadly masque. The night scenes of *The
Spanish Tragedy* are imitated with melodramatic intensi-
fication in the murder of the innocent young son of his
enemy by Antonio, in a churchyard among grewsome horrors. Marston's is the dubious credit of having first deliberately played, not only on the popular appetite for
the stimulus of horror, but on a no less prevalent human
penchant for the piquantly risqué in speech.

Marston's plays were soon followed by Henry Chettle
with *The Tragedy of Hoffman or Revenge for a Father*,
for which Henslowe paid him five shillings in part in December, 1602. Here, although most of the features, save
the ghost, are preserved, the hero accomplishes his revenge
at the beginning of the play and degenerates into a mere
villain. Chettle, who was a printer by trade, turned to
the stage about 1592, writing chiefly for the Admiral's
men and Worcester's. His hand has been recorded, usually
writing with others, in nearly fifty plays, all of them lost
except a scant half dozen, *Hoffman* being the only one
that is the work of his unaided pen. Chettle is chiefly
memorable as the editor of *A Groatsworth of Wit* and for
his apology, in the preface of his own *Kindheart's Dream*,
for having published this notorious attack of Greene on
Shakespeare. Chettle was always in need and often in
prison. His work discloses a competent and uninspired
hack writer for the stage, not a distinguished and perverse
one as was Marston, whose eccentric personality and Italian
extraction, on his mother's side, give to the plotting, the
characterization and the diction of his dramas, especially
these earlier ones, a strange originality and a frequently
disappointing inequality.

The tragedy of revenge thus relaunched and enthusi-
astically accepted by the public, Shakespeare now gave
to a thorough revision and development of the theme of
Hamlet the exertion of his highest genius, and in the
process strained to the breaking point the possibilities of
his stage. There are four versions of *Hamlet*, the quartos
of 1603 and 1604, the latter almost doubled in rewriting,
the version of the folio which contains some passages in
neither quarto and omits others; and lastly, *Der Bestrafte
Brudermord*, an old German translation, from a manuscript of 1710, but dating as to contents much further
back, which has been taken by most critics to be based
at least on a pre-Shakespearean drama and probably
founded on an old play by Kyd. One reason for the diffi-

culties which beset any consideration of this famous tragedy lies perhaps in the circumstance that we have not
really in all these versions one Hamlet, but a composite
picture of the immortal and thus vexatious Dane. The
earlier quarto scarcely seems a mere piracy. With all its
defects, it is the better acting play, and only appears to
us imperfect because we know so well the later text.
Indeed, *Hamlet* with everything that the Prince says, as
nearly anyone will admit who has tried to sit it out, is
beyond pleasurable endurance. And yet the best of the
play is not in the earlier quarto, in which Polonius appears as Corambis, Reynaldo is Montano (as in the German version), and Osric is no more than "a Braggart
Gentleman"; here, too, the queen is less unmistakably not
a party to her husband's murder, and Hamlet is less
pretendedly mad.

The popularity of *Hamlet* stands unparalleled among
dramatic creations. No character was so frequently alluded to in the poet's own time, nor has any one personage
in fiction given rise to more comment or greater conflict
of opinion.[1] That Shakespeare should have wrapped up
an enigma with wanton forethought of mischief in writing
Hamlet is only a little more unthinkable than that he should
have lavished his dramatic art and the wealth of his poetry
on a covert allegory of momentary allusiveness to contemporary events.[2] Even Shakespeare could not escape the
influences of those every-day happenings which bulk large
to us because they are near. But this is very different
from harnessing the Pegasus of poetry to furrow the fields
of history. Such interpretations verily reduce the Eliza-

*Interpre-
tations of
Hamlet*

[1] See among many other discussions that of F. G. Hubbard, *The First
Quarto of Hamlet,* 1920, where most of the important previous bibliography finds mention; J. M. Robertson, *The Problem of Hamlet,* also 1920;
and especially Clutton Brock's critique of this latter and like disintegrating scholarship, *Shakespeare's Hamlet,* 1922. H. D. Gray refers the first
quarto to the recollection of the actor who took the part of Marcellus,
Modern Language Review, x, 1915.
[2] See the thesis of Miss L. Winstanley, *Hamlet and the Scottish Succession,* 1921, and her later *Macbeth, King Lear, and Contemporary History,*
1922.

bethan stage to "a platform for the exposition of current political history disguised to meet a repressive censorship." [1] In a sense *Hamlet* marks the crown of the biographic drama, going beyond the biography of event into the biography of the spirit and the emotions, and thus anticipating by generations a species of literature, the since exaggerated intellectuality and forced analysis of which has come to be the ruling literary mania of our time. As to interpretation, *Hamlet* will be interpreted in the terms of the spirit of each successive generation, as historical personages and great events are interpreted again and again. Wherefore we feel no surprise that a recent critic finds, as others before him, a contemporary solution of the "mystery" of Hamlet's indecision as to the killing of the King in "the application of a current psychological formula" that the nervous shock caused by the ghost's revelations generates in Hamlet's mind two discordant resolves—"a conscious resolve to obey his father's injunction and an unconscious resolve to escape its horror." [2]

George Chapman

It must have been while *Hamlet* was still on the stage that Chapman turned his attention to tragedy of this type. *Bussy D'Ambois* is the dramatized biography of a bravo, with the deservedly tragic fate that overtook his adventurous life. But a second part, entitled *The Revenge of Bussy D'Ambois*, concerns Clermont, his brother, a hesitant moralizing scholar, forced to a revenge to the completeness of which he reluctantly dedicates himself, an unmistakably Hamlet-like figure.[3] George Chapman, who was older than Shakespeare by some four or five years, was born in Hertfordshire and trained to scholarship in both universities.[4] He has been thought, but only by a few, to have been the "rival poet" of Shakespeare's *Sonnets* and

[1] *The Year's Work in English*, p. 68.
[2] Ibid., 70, and A. Clutton Brock's essay, "Why Hamlet Delayed," *Shakespeare's Hamlet*, 1922, p. 45.
[3] *Bussy D'Ambois* has been variously dated between 1598 and 1604; *The Revenge* between 1608 and 1610.
[4] For Chapman and his plays, see the scholarly edition of T. M. Parrott, *Plays and Poems of Chapman*, 1910-14.

to have suffered, the victim of Shakespearean satire, early as absurd Holophernes, late as disgusting Thersites.[1] Chapman's work as a playwright began, as early as 1596, at least, in Henslowe's workshop; but although he reached a recognized success in both tragedy and comedy, his most purposeful work was his famous translation of Homer, which, failing of its promised patron on the death of Prince Henry, left the poet in struggle and indigence for the remainder of a long life. Chapman died in 1634. Chapman's distinctive contribution to tragedy consists of five historical plays which derive their material in common from the history of all but contemporary France. Besides the two involving D'Ambois, there are two more concerning Charles Duke of Byron, the arrogant field-marshal of Henry of Navarre, overwhelmed by his own contumacy and self-righteousness. This was on the stage before 1608. Lastly, there is *Chabot, Admiral of France*, the pathetic story of an honorable man, maligned and ruined before his king to the breaking of his heart.[2] This last, in its superior clarity and reserve, owes much to the revising hand, in the next generation, of James Shirley; for the art of Chapman, though often rising to eloquence and authentic poetry, is, in tragedy at least, prevailingly turgid and irregular. In thus extending tragedy to historical topics derived from France, Chapman may perhaps have been only following the suggestions contained implicitly in many scenes of the chronicle plays and more particularly in the work of his friend, Marlowe, whose *Massacre at Paris* preceded by several years Chapman's efforts in this kind.[3] Chapman's interest in French court intrigue is less historical, to be sure, than romantic. His associa-

Chapman's dramas on French history

[1] A. Acheson, *Shakespeare and the Rival Poet*, 1903; and *Shakespeare's Sonnet Story*, 1922.
[2] *Chabot* is dated by Parrott at about 1613 in an earlier form.
[3] To these French tragedies of Chapman is now to be added *Charlemagne or the Distracted Emperor*, first printed from manuscript by Bullen in his *Old English Plays*, 1882-85, and recently critically re-edited by F. L. Schoell, 1920. Less effective than those on more modern subjects, this play may be accepted as Chapman's; with contemporary criticism, too, we may reject Chapman's alleged authorship of *Alphonsus of Germany*.

tion with Marlowe, whose beautiful narrative poem, *Hero and Leander*, he had the temerity to complete, seems one of the irrecoverable chapters in the history of literature. That the elder and longer-lived scholar owed much to the precocious young innovator in his literary ideals as in his diction, is easily recognizable to a reader acquainted with both.

Tourneur's contribution to the tragedy of revenge

But revenge as a dramatic motive was not yet exhausted. Cyril Tourneur, the reputed author of two plays ambitiously of the type, belongs here, although his name in print only attaches to one of them, *The Atheist's Tragedy* (1607). Of Tourneur, except that he spent many years in the Low Countries in the service of the state, was temporarily secretary of the council of war on the expedition against Cadiz in 1625, and died in Ireland, we know nothing. His *Atheist's Tragedy* is an ambitious effort to outdo the horrors and iniquities of its kind. D'Amville, the hero, is an active, plotting villain, uniting in his person the madness of Hieronimo and the Hamlet of the older version with the lust of Piero (in *Antonio and Mellida*) and *Hoffman*, the whole monstrously strained to attempted incest. There is, however, none the less, a moral earnestness about Tourneur's play and an evident attempt, as Thorndike expresses it, "to embody a philosophical conception in a revenge play." [1] It is the contrast suggested by this especially which has led to a general doubt as to Tourneur's authorship of *The Revenger's Tragedy*, 1606, with its extraordinary cynicism, its pruriency and the hideous picture which it presents, however powerfully conceived and executed, of the lasciviousness, the hypocrisy and persistent wickedness of the petty renaissance Italian court. This, more than *The Atheist's Tragedy*, seems deliberately modeled on Marston in its bitter cynicism of tone, its "humorous" method of drawing character, its delights in uncleanliness of thought, sardonic wit and eccentric gloomy moralizing. Inventive in plot (again like Mar-

[1] *The Relations,* as above, 196.

ston), potently at times, ghoulishly realistic, this play may be accepted as the *ne plus ultra* of the tragedy of revenge, as it is likewise the leading example of that long and forbidding series of tragedies which represent the fascinated horror of the English imagination for the Italy of the Cencis and the Borgias.

As the larger groups just mentioned would carry us far into the next reign, and there is still much to discuss that is earlier, let us leave this topic of the drama of romantic passion for the nonce, recognizing that, in a volume of this scope, it is impracticable even to mention many a play, much less do justice to the frequent merits of productions, little read, as the world now wags, save under the lamp of scrutinizing scholarship.

CHAPTER VI

THE VOGUE OF HISTORY

National spirit and history

IN the last chapter we chose from among the many varieties of plays which come into popularity in the fifteen eighties the new romantic drama of passion, more especially in that high and insolent vein which distinguished it in tragedy. And this choice was referable less to any ascertained chronological priority than to a feeling that, when all is said, Marlowe's is the first dominant personality in popular Elizabethan drama. Existent simultaneously with this and far from unaffected by its passionate impulses is a large class of plays which, laying the scene in England, or in Britain, at least, attempt to portray events as they have been chronicled in the annals of the race, their deeds in war, the intricacies of state, above all, the intrigues, the glories, the vicissitudes, and the tragical falls of princes. "What has happened" is a simple definition of history, and curiosity as to the past comes inevitably to a nation when success in the present awakens the national consciousness. Splendid was the spirit of Elizabethan England as it blazed up to the repulse of the Spanish Armada, sustaining the queen with that superlative combination, gallantry for womanhood and loyalty to a queen. And it was in the very nature of things that an important mass of writing, devoted to the history of England, should spring up and that that interest should broaden to a curiosity as to the history and the conditions of other lands and other ages.

Elizabethan patriotic literature

The amount and variety of this Elizabethan literature bearing the national and patriotic stamp are extraordinary. Its range is from legendary Brute, founder and name-giver to Britain, through Arthurian and Saxon

106

story to Elizabeth herself and happenings within the memories of living men. It took every event, every story or rumor, into account circumstantially or imaginatively; the doings of princes, their wars and intrigues, record of plague or report of unusual weather or petty private crime. It was moral and tragic in the verse narratives of *The Mirror for Magistrates*, controversial in Foxe's stupendous *Book of Martyrs*, biographical in Cavendish's *Life of Cardinal Wolsey*, poetic in verse of Daniel and Drayton, and written, for the most part, by way of annals in the prose chronicles of Halle, Holinshed, and Stow. Thus it was that the soil was not unprepared when the immediate predecessors of Shakespeare turned to the national history for subject-matter for drama; and it is always to be remembered that the Elizabethan chronicle play was only one form, however the most striking, of an extensive and varied literature expressing the national spirit.

A chronicle history, or chronicle play, is a piece out of the story of England, dramatized and set on the stage. It is sometimes made to center about the personality of a king or other hero, and, as such, becomes essentially his story; but the scene is commonly filled with a multiplicity of personages, and proceeds from event to event much as a panorama moves from picture to picture. It is obvious that to demand of the chronicle play the unity and concreteness which we demand of tragedy—or even of comedy —would be to mistake its nature. Ordinarily the scenes straggle forward with little but the consecutiveness of time to control their order; and it is not to be denied that the slovenly technique of the chronicle history reacted on contemporary dramas of other type, to their disadvantage from the point of view of dramatic construction. That a spirit of patriotism inspired the writing of many of these plays is not to be denied; but their leading impetus was love of story, and everything was staged, whether the prowess and glory or the incompetence and mishap of English kings and heroes. The steps which led to the

The chronicle play

vogue and flourishing of the chronicle play have been often recounted.[1] They include the folk-plays of St. George and Robin Hood, and that curious conversion in process, so to speak, of a polemical moral play into an historical one, the *King Johan* of Bishop Bale. *Gorboduc* tells the story of a British king, as acceptably such to the historic imagination of Tudor days as the late King Henry himself, but clearly of a classical impulse. No less such must have been the inspiration of *Richardus Tertius*, by Thomas Legge, acted at St. John's College, Cambridge, in 1579, and conspicuous as "the first history play that can be truly so called," though written, not in the vernacular, but in Latin. There is no English king the tradition of whose life so lends itself to neo-Senecan dramatic treatment; but the story invoked likewise a contemporary interest in that it told of the overthrow at Bosworth Field which had settled the stable Tudor dynasty on the throne. Boas, who has treated this tragedy most fully, tells how its crowded incidents stretch the narrow Senecan rules, noting—especially of interest to us in this place—that the dramatists, Greene and Nash, were both of St. John's, as Marlowe was soon to be of Bene't College.[2] Legge became the respected head of Caius College, and, as Vice-Chancellor, was party to negotiations between the university and the Privy Council to restrain common players in their visits to Cambridge. It was Legge's Oxford contemporary, William Gager, highly reputed for his Latin verses, who, despite a vigorously avowed hostility likewise to the professional stage, left behind him several Latin tragedies.[3] But Gager's adherence to an older tradition as well as a dead tongue left him without influence on the public stage, save perhaps indirectly through Peele.

[1] See the present writer's *English Chronicle Play*, 1902; and, as to Shakespeare and his sources, W. G. Boswell-Stone, *Shakspere's Holinshed*, 1896.

[2] F. S. Boas, *University Drama in the Age of the Tudors*, 1914, p. 113.

[3] *Meleager, Dido, Ulysses Redux, Œdipus* between 1582 and 1592. Gager and Peele were associated at Oxford, in 1583, in the theatrical entertainments offered to Albertus Prince Palatine of Poland on his visit to the university. Boas, as above, 179.

THE VOGUE OF HISTORY

Turning to the popular drama, *The Famous Victories* *of Henry V* is the earliest extant specimen of an actual chronicle play. This curious hodge-podge of popular report as to the wild life of that king when a prince, with the humors of the tavern, its suggestion of Falstaff in the character of Oldcastle, and its rude delineation of the difficult relations between Prince Henry and his father, was acted by the Queen's men when they were most popular, and therefore well before the Armada. It is interesting as a primitive of its type, and likewise because in its scenes of comedy we have a transcript, however crude, of contemporary every-day life, a kind of drama which continued a feature of many subsequent chronicle plays and was represented as well in independent comedy. An even slighter production is *Jack Straw*, which treats the episode, Wat Tyler's insurrection: but it marks an advance in spirit and especially in style. Among pre-Shakespearean chronicle histories, there are several interesting plays: Peele's avowed *Edward I*, the two dramas known as *The Troublesome Reign of King John* (basis of Shakespeare's *Life and Death of King John*), the two parts of *The Contention of the Two Famous Houses of York and Lancaster* (later rewritten into *2* and *3 Henry VI*), and *The True Tragedy of Richard III* (not wholly unrelated to Shakespeare's *Richard III*). To these may be added *1 Henry VI*, although we now have it only in the later form which Shakespeare gave to it when he made it a part of the trilogy on that unhappy monarch. The whole group was in print by 1595; and some of these plays must have been first written well before the Armada. In accordance with the practice of this earlier time, in none of the early quartos is there any mention of the author. As to Shakespeare's relations to this group of plays, of late the older theory which assigned to him a part in the original plays on Henry VI, if not in the two on King John, has been almost wholly abandoned; and the notion that these plays were written in various combinations by Marlowe, Greene,

109

Peele, and even Kyd, has been succeeded by an effort to refer certain of them to individual, or at least fewer, authors. In this endeavor Marlowe has been given more than ever an important place, being held by some all but alone responsible not only for the earlier versions of *2* and *3 Henry VI*, but for much of *Richard III* as we have it in current editions of Shakespeare. Peele, too, assumes an important rôle, as to him is assigned (with Greene or even alone) the authorship of *1 Henry VI*, which Shakespeare later interpolated with a few new scenes and placed in his trilogy. This measurably frees Shakespeare from the obloquy attaching to the monstrous perversion of the figure of Joan of Arc in the last play, although it deprives him of Nash's eloquent attestation as to the popularity of certain scenes concerning Talbot's prowess against the French. "Jingoistic national pride" is otherwise than in the perversion of Joan a characteristic of Peele, as exampled in a similar distortion of the "good Queen Eleanor of Castile," in his *Edward I*, into one conversant with witch-lore and evil. Peele's activity has been further extended in this group to include the two old plays on King John. This is a work of very considerable merit, and considering its probable date, may be justly described as the earliest vital representative of national historical events on the English stage.[1] Whatever scholarship may definitely make of these conditions of promiscuous and unstable author-ship, certain it is that in this early group of chronicle plays Shakespeare found his quarry, feeling it worth his while to connect the old dramas on Henry VI and Richard III into a sequence by means of newly written scenes, pointing their relation, and imitating the tetralogy, so combined, in one of his own, that of *Richard II, 1* and *2 Henry IV* and *Henry V*.

[1] Tucker Brooke, Introduction to "1 Henry VI"; *The Yale Shake-speare*, 1917; and "The Second and Third Parts of Henry VI," by the same, in Proceedings of the Connecticut Academy, xvii, 1912. Also A. W. Pollard, in *The Times Literary Supplement*, Sept. 20 and 26, 1918; and H. O. Sykes, *Sidelights on Shakespeare*, as to *The Troublesome Reign*.

THE VOGUE OF HISTORY

The enumeration of some of these earlier chronicle plays has brought several things before us: the crudeness of the type, its want of constructiveness, its frequent anonymity, and its mingled classical and popular origin. There are likewise its confusion of comedy with serious matter, or perhaps rather its alternation of the two, and its acceptance of anything in the way of myth or tradition for history. As to source, Holinshed's *Chronicles of England, Scotland and Ireland* is by far the most usual quarry. From the second edition, that of 1587, Shakespeare took practically all the material for his British historical plays, with much for other plays besides.[1] For the "historical" matter of Holinshed includes not only the deeds of the august line of English and Scottish kings, but extends liberally the idea of the "historic" to embrace legends of Leir, "tenth king of Britain," "Macbeth, a valiant Scottish gentleman," Rosamund, "fair concubine of Henry II," and "Shore's wife, spoiled of all she had and put to open penance."The vogue of chronicle history lies between 1590 and the end of the reign, prolonged a little by a small group of obituary plays, as they have been called, in which the recent death of Elizabeth quickened a demand to learn more of the queen and her youth.[2] During these years the chronicle play led all others in popularity, extending its methods to plays of other kinds. Taking the 280 titles of plays, extant and non-extant, recorded in *Henslowe's Diary*, 80 of which are indeterminable as to their precise nature, we find that considerably more than a third of the remaining 200 are English in scene, more than half of them "historical," and nearly half of these, or approximately 50, are founded on "British history," the rest being*Characteristics of the chronicle play*

Range and vogue of the chronicle play

[1] W. G. Boswell-Stone, *Shakspere's Holinshed*, 1896. Preface. The possibility of the intervention of earlier plays must always be borne in mind.
[2] Plays of this type are *Sir Thomas Wyatt*, by Dekker and Webster, which concerns Northumberland's effort to settle the succession on Lady Jane Grey; Heywood's *If You Know Not Me You Know Nobody*, the first part on the "troubles of Queen Elizabeth," the second on her "victory," the Armada. Samuel Rowley's *When You See Me, You Know Me* and Dekker's *Whore of Babylon* detail events in the reign of Henry VIII.

111

variously foreign, classical, or biblical. Or to take an individual author: during the years 1598-1602, Dekker wrote thirty plays with other authors, and ten of them "draw their material from British history." [1] Henslowe is not the whole drama, but these are indications. During these years—if we include the many mentions of non-extant plays with those which we may read—we find a range of subject-matter that includes incidents in the lives of every English sovereign from Edward the Confessor to Elizabeth herself, including mythical British princes and minor heroes of all ages, presented in a great variety of ways but of a quality prevailingly epic.

The biographical chronicle But from the first there was a frequent biographical emphasis in these plays and their subject-matter was soon extended to heroes less than royal, some of them all but contemporary: Cardinal Wolsey and Thomas Lord Cromwell, powerful implements in the tyranny of Henry VIII and victims of it as well, the younger Sir Thomas Wyatt, who precipitately attempted an anticipation of Elizabeth's accession to her crown, or Sir Thomas Gresham, financier of the queen and the founder of the Royal Exchange. [2] In this particular group there is none so interesting as the play on Sir Thomas More, recently the subject of renewed attention by reason of the effort to identify one of the six handwritings in which the manuscript is preserved as Shakespeare's. Rambling in construction and the work of perhaps as many authors as there are copyists, the grave jocularity of the traditional More is happily preserved in this rough and ready example of its kind, and anecdotes recited of him are bodily conveyed from Halle's *Chronicle* and Roper's *Life*. As to the animated mob-scene, which has been attributed to Shakespeare, I confess myself half

[1] M. L. Hunt, *Thomas Dekker,* 1911, p. 48.

[2] Besides Shakespeare's *Henry VIII* and Samuel Rowleys *When You See Me You Know Me,* Wolsey figures in three lost plays by Chettle and others of Henslowe's mention. There is *Thomas Lord Cromwell* by "W. S.," 1592; *Sir Thomas Wyatt,* by Dekker, 1602; Gresham figures in Heywood's *If You Know Not Me,* 1607. The dates here refer to probable year of acting.

a convert to the belief that it may be his; and this less because of the technical arguments concerning Shakespeare's handwriting and the bibliographical and other analogies, cogent although these are, than because of the strong case, made out by Professor R. W. Chambers, as to the expression of political ideas in this scene in their comparison with Shakespeare's known opinions expressed elsewhere.[1] The concentration of biography on a single tragic motive opened possibilities of the highest dramatic importance; and this concentration we find for the first time in plays of this type, in Marlowe's *Edward II*, on the stage in the earliest 'nineties. This tragedy, regarded as a drama, is altogether the best work of Marlowe, and it must have created a sensation on first acting. For Marlowe himself the theme was a new one, for King Edward at least is no superman. The overpowering pathos of the concluding scenes reaches a poignancy that few of Marlowe's successors ever approached, suggesting new possibilities in the author, had he but lived. Present opinion as to Marlowe's part in other chronicle plays has been indicated above. That he was concerned in other productions of the type seems undeniable; but so shining a mark must he have been from the first for imitation, that, when all is said, his own inferior work is not readily separable from successful copying by his lesser fellows.

Several departures from the biographic as well as the epic type of the chronicle play are discoverable almost from the first. There is first the group of mythical histories dealing with King Arthur, King Lear, Vortigern and other such themes. *Locrine*, which borrows historical material from *The Faery Queen* and phrases and lines from Spenser's *Complaints*, belongs here, with the elder *King Leir*, which ends in reconciliation.[2] Both were staged

Mythical histories

[1] *Shakespeare's Hand in the Play of Sir Thomas More*, W. W. Greg, and other contributors, 1923; but see also the strong counter-argument by Professor L. L. Schuecking, *The Review of English Studies*, 1925, i, 40.
[2] C. Crawford, "Edmund Spenser, Locrine, and Selimus," *Collectanea*, i, 47; and C. A. Harper in *Modern Language Review*, viii, 369.

in the early 'nineties and have been variously assigned as
to authorship among "the predecessors" or their school,
Peele, as usual, attracting most of the guesses. It was on
foundations such as these that the superstructures of
King Lear, Macbeth, and *Cymbeline* were subsequently
reared. Equally pseudo-historical but smacking more of
popular legend and folk-lore are plays such as the two on
Robert Earl of Huntingdon (otherwise Robin Hood) by
Chettle and Munday, or *The Birth of Merlin,* later revised
by William Rowley, both of the later 'nineties; while earlier
came comedies preserving an historical British atmosphere
in which romance rules, however veiled or frankly. Thus
Fair Em, the Miller's Daughter of Manchester contains
in the main plot an extravagant distortion of William the
Conqueror into a knight of pseudo-chivalric romance, and
Greene's very unhistorical *James IV of Scotland,* like the
anonymous *Edward III,* despite historic titles, finds origin
in romantic fiction. Not less certainly has the historical
interest been shifted, by Greene once more, in his *Friar
Bacon,* to a similar test of womanly constancy mixed with
trade in necromancy; while in minor productions like Munday's *John a Kent and John a Cumber* and the anonymous
Look About You, historical personages are subordinated
to the surprises of disguise and the supernatural.[1]

The common man in old drama

Before we leave these derivatives of the chronicle play,
if we dare so call them, two or three must claim a further
word. The assignment of *George a Greene, the Pinner
of Wakefield,*[2] to Robert Greene has been questioned, though

[1] The plays mentioned in this paragraph lie between 1589 and 1599,
Friar Bacon the earliest, *Look About You* the latest. I accept with C. W.
Stork, *William Rowley,* 1910, the identification of *The Birth of Merlin*
with the *Uter Pendragon* of Henslowe's mention in 1597, howsoever it may
have been subsequently rewritten. See W. Wells, in *Modern Language
Review,* xvii, 129, who assigns this play to Beaumont and Fletcher.
[2] This play was registered in 1595 and printed 1599, as acted by Sussex
men which places the performance at 1593. Greg, *Henslowe,* ii, 158. A
MS. note in the Chatsworth copy assigns it to Greene on the authority of
Juby, a contemporary. This has been interpreted to relate to a certain
adventure of Greene's, transferred to the play, and not to authorship. See
R. B. McKerrow, *Malone Society, Collections,* i, 289.

its likeness in romantic realism to *Friar Bacon* and *James IV* should seem sufficient to set such questionings at rest. The story is that of a brave and simple yeoman who holds his own and maintains the duties of his office valiantly, confounding the king's enemies in the process. Bidden by his sovereign to name his recompense, he asks for the royal influence with Old Grimes to gain for him in marriage the girl he loves; and, bidden kneel, he anxiously inquires:

> What will your majesty do?
>
> *Edward* Dub thee a knight, George.
>
> *George* I beseech your grace, grant me one thing.
>
> *Edward* What is it?
>
> *George* Then let me live and die a yeoman still:
> So was my father, so must live his son.
> For 'tis more credit to men of base degree
> To do great deeds than men of dignity.

Here was an appeal to the common man, the man in the street, as we call him, which cannot but have met with a hearty popular response. Nor is this old drama void of other like instances, none the least among them the interview of King Henry V by night with soldiers of the rank and file of his army on the eve of Agincourt. The tendency to speak of Elizabethan drama as wholly an aristocratic institution, worshiping kings, disdaining the common man and libeling him, especially when congregated in crowds, is not borne out by an acquaintance with Shakespeare or his fellow dramatists. The age was one in which rank and station were recognized, only a little more frankly than today; and, forming, as did these things, the basis of society, they were represented in drama like any other fact. As to the crowd, it is its humor which chiefly strikes the old dramatists and its fickleness which all the apologists who have written cannot gainsay. Man in masses (save in a limited sense), man unwashed and subject to the passions of the herd, is not interesting to the dramatist who individualizes his people and groups them not in categories. The common man as an individual is as honestly treated in this old art as his place in the life which surrounded him demanded. The concern of the dramatists was with the world in which they lived and not prophetically with what we have contrived to make it out four hundred years after. Indeed, the concern of the dramatist lies in the making of a play, a process wholly within the domain of art and not in the representation of a political position or the exploitation of a theory in economics.

The normality of Shake-speare

In a book demanding the rigorous concentration of this it would be folly to repeat the well-known "facts" as to the life and dramas of Shakespeare. It is more to our purpose to note how normal the great dramatist was and how naturally he lived and worked among his fellows. It cannot have escaped the reader that we know rather less of any of these predecessors of Shakespeare than we know of Shakespeare himself, and that the actual range of their authorship is less determinable. Shakespeare's years were all but precisely those of Marlowe, and his birth and station in life were much the same; except that Canterbury, where Marlowe was born, was more a center than outlying Stratford, and Marlowe's forwardness as a boy attained for him, in all likelihood, his Cambridge exhibition or scholarship; wherefore his speedier career and wherefore, likewise, perhaps the speedier end to it. His most recent biographer makes much of the probable excellence of Shakespeare's schooling, so far as it went, under masters of Oxford training in the local free grammar school at Stratford, and gives renewed emphasis to Beeston's well-known report to Aubrey that Shakespeare "understood Latin pretty well, for he had been in his younger years a schoolmaster in the country." That Shakespeare first joined Pembroke's rather than Strange's men, as has been usually accepted, we have had reason to explain as probable.[1] With the enforced idleness of all the companies, by reason of the

[1] Adams, *Shakespeare*, 90-94, and above MS., p. 90.

plague in 1593 and the earlier part of 1594, Shakespeare turned his attention to non-dramatic poetry, publishing *Venus and Adonis* in the former year, quickened, we may well believe, by the example of Marlowe's *Hero and Leander*. *Lucrece* followed soon after. These works not only confirmed for their author the friendship as well as the patronage of the young Earl of Southampton, to whom both were dedicated; they gave Shakespeare almost immediately a repute among poets, as opposed to playmakers, a fame not only grateful in itself, but admirable stock in trade with which to take up the drama anew. It is not impossible that this, quite as much as his previous short record with the stage, may account for our finding Shakespeare a principal sharer with men like Burbage and Kempe at the age of thirty.

Whatever the circumstances, the stage once chosen, Shakespeare had before him the example of Lyly's court dramas, with all the classical experiments behind them; he had, too, the realism, the humor of Greene at his best, and, most salient of all, the tragic vigor, the romance and poetry, the acclaimed success of Marlowe. With such music ringing in his ears, Shakespeare could have learned little from buffoons like Tarlton or plodders in moral plays like Wilson. Shakespeare's schoolroom was the theater; but there was the world outside. Less than any man did he need schools of any kind, for his was what Bagehot so happily called "the experiencing nature." It is deeply interesting to notice, as we look at his career of authorship in large, that Shakespeare tried his hand at nearly every kind of drama that was known to the contemporary stage, but that he led the way to no new form hitherto untried. So likewise, in subject-matter, Shakespeare took that which was already tried—*Romeo, Richard II, Lear, Hamlet*, to name no more—and invented only where it was imperative. That he, best of all, could invent at need a perfection into a superior form of whatever he touched, a more informing significance, an expansion into a truer picture

Shakespeare's models and his success

117

of life, and a sounder and wider outlook—all this is sufficient to attest. But just as the highest art is that of the greatest economy of stroke, so we may say of the craft of Shakespeare that it achieved its best results with the smallest necessary effort. Despite all that may be said of a certain elaborateness, especially in his earlier work, an elaboration and exuberance that was, after all, characteristic of Elizabethan literature as a whole, it may be declared of Shakespeare that his was an artistic thrift as well as a worldly one. Assuredly nothing could present a more vivid contrast than the shiftless lives of Greene, Peele, and Marlowe with their untimely and disgraceful ends, and the steady industry and progress in fortune of Shakespeare, honored in "the quality he professed," respected, appreciated, and beloved, retiring substantially rich for his station before he was fifty.

Experimental comedies That Shakespeare's traffic with the stage began in deliberate experiment seems as certain as anything not documented. If *Titus* be his, its horrors are only the logic of its terrible species carried out with the determination to try out that sort of thing in full.[1] It needs but a reading to declare *Loves Labor's Lost* a faithful following of Lylyan court drama in its conceptions of personage, its dialogue of persiflage, even, we may well believe, in its intimate allusiveness to occurrences and personages within the minor circle of Elizabeth's court. So, too, *The Comedy of Errors*, another certain early play, is a deliberate experiment to see what might be done with the old material of classical comedy, doubling the improbabilities—once more with the artist's logic—to test out the thing veritably and in full. Save for *Midsummer Night's Dream*, in which the example of Lyly still lingers, Shakespeare never re-

---

[1] A late word on *Titus* is that of T. M. Parrott, *Modern Language Review*, 1919, iv, 16, who regards it as an old pre-Shakespearean production belonging originally to Pembroke's men, acquired by Henslowe from Alleyn about 1593, a version acted at the Rose, in January, 1594, by Sussex men, superficially revised by Shakespeare. See also Greg's reference to his bibliographical theory as to this play in the same volume, 322; and Chambers, ii, 129.

turned to any of these experiments. Plainly, Seneca and Plautus were outworn, and the court drama of allusive compliment had been worked out to be discarded. Another experiment led to better results, that of romantic comedy and tragedy as exampled in *The Two Gentlemen of Verona* and the earlier version of *Romeo and Juliet;* but this lead must be followed later.

In the chronicle plays, I cannot but think that Shakespeare experimented more thoroughly than in any other form and that we may find in their august succession the steps in sequence of his apprenticeship and development in dramatic writing.[1] There is, foremost, *2* and *3 Henry VI*, in which, as compared with earlier non-Shakespearean versions, we have not much more than a copying out and reordering of previous material. Secondly comes *1 Henry IV*, in which certain interpolated scenes occur, superior to the rest of the text, although, unhappily, no older version is actually extant for comparison. It is tempting to believe that to Shakespeare's revision belong the scenes concerning Talbot which inspired in Nash, in 1592, the enthusiastic passage running: "How would it have joyed brave Talbot, the terror of the French, to think that after he had lain two hundred years in his tomb he should triumph again on the stage and have his bones new embalmed with the tears of ten thousand spectators at least (at several times) who, in the tragedian that represents his person, imagine they behold him fresh bleeding!"[2] But recent scholarship deprives Shakespeare of this honor to bestow it, as we have seen, on the inevitable Peele.[3] If we must have another illustration for this stage, then, of Shakespeare's development in authorship perhaps the

Shakespeare's growth in the chronicle play

---

[1] This notion was broached by the present writer in his *English Chronicle Play*, 1902.

[2] "Piers Penniless, his Supplication," *Works of Nashe*, ed. McKerrow, 1909, i,

[3] While acknowledging that this play not only lacks design and unity and that the Talbot scenes are far from compelling to a modern reader, these very defects make it all but impossible to accept Professor Brooke's suggestion that such a revision of older work could have followed *Henry V;* see his ed. of *1 Henry VI* as above.

Shakespearean scenes of *Sir Thomas More* may supply it, although the date of this play falls later. But to return, we have next the rewriting of two old plays in *King John* into the greater cohesion and dramatic significance of Shakespeare's tragedy of this monarch. And now, given an independent play to write, Shakespeare noted the success of his fellow, Marlowe, scarcely his senior, how he had concentrated the interest in a single protagonist, Tamburlaine or Faustus, giving to each the dilation, the grandiloquence, the self-consciousness of the superman; and Shakespeare wrote *Richard III*, a play, in all these respects, and in its lyricism, so like Marlowe that there have been those who have not hesitated to assign it in part at least

**Shake-
speare
rivaling
Marlowe**

to him. Our fourth step, then, is Shakespeare rivaling Marlowe in Marlowe's own manner; and the fifth must have followed almost immediately after, for by this date, whatever year it may have been in the earlier 'nineties, Marlowe had staged his *Edward II*, the tragedy of an unkingly king overthrown by his outraged barons. There is just one other English king whose story may be as accurately described in the very same words, and this was Richard II, uncrowned by crafty sagacious Bolingbroke and meeting a similarly tragic death. But in his play, *Richard II*, however similar its topic, Shakespeare sought to outrival Marlowe, not in Marlowe's own manner, but with a new freedom, a new poetry, a manner wholly his own. We may remain in doubt as to which of the two catastrophes of these contrasted plays is the more piteous, but there is no scene of Marlowe's the equal of Richard's abdication with its ebb and flow of emotion and the vividly conceived antithetical personalities of the two royal rivals. Shakespeare's apprenticeship was now at an end and the independent trilogy of *1* and *2 Henry IV* and *Henry V* soon followed. In a sense a reversion to the less organic methods of the earlier chronicle play, especially in the oscillations between heroic war and the low-comedy scenes of Falstaff and his rout, this trilogy marks none the less the

limitations of the possibilities of drama of this kind. In
place of criticism of the author for the crudities of his
stage warfare, for the irregular progress of the action,
with its stands and breaks, its employment of the old
"braves," excursions and single encounters, let us recall the
often quoted passages in *Henry V* in which Shakespeare **Shake-**
realizes the inadequacy of any stage to the presentation **speare
and the**
of such heroic themes, and recognize how much, after all, **chronicle
play**
he has made of them under restrictions so binding.

In these kaleidoscopic scenes of warfare, chivalry, and
political dispute, king, prince, noble, hero, warrior, traitor,
pass and repass in incessant change of incident and adventure, and personage after personage emerges, each clear
and defined with a vividness and semblance of reality that
belong not to the pages of the historian. How courteous
and well bred are Shakespeare's nobles and gentlemen, how
bravely his combatants bandy their taunts of valor; how
episode follows happily on episode and incessant is the
movement always forward. The council chamber, the lists,
the battle-field, the camp by night, the walls of a belea-
guered city, all are invoked for us, as we read with the aid
of imagination's inward eye, or suggested, whether the
scenery before us is meager or elaborate. The cruel,
cowardly John, patriotic, brusque Falconbridge, impotent
Richard, politic Bolingbroke, and that other terrible Richard the Hunchback; Hotspur, chivalrous, hasty, head-
strong; Glendower, mystic, austere, and a seer of visions;
Prince Hal, companion of wastrels in Eastcheap, a doer
of deeds at Agincourt; his saintly, hapless son, surrounded
with quarreling nobles and linked to a virago, the "she-
wolf of France"; the pathos of the little Prince Arthur
and the dignity and tragic resignation of Katherine of
Aragon—nowhere in literature is there the like of all this.
There is no such monument to the spirit of national patriotism as these chronicle histories of Shakespeare, their
theme

This blessed plot, this earth, this realm of England,
This nurse, this teeming womb of royal kings,
Feared for their breed and famous by their birth,
Renownèd for their deeds as far from home,
For Christian service and true chivalry,
As is the sepulcher, in stubborn Jewry,
Of the world's ransom, blessed Mary's Son.

Nor should we forget that the chronicle plays have given us, next to Hamlet, the most vital and popular of Shakespearean personages; for if mystery must always trail behind the fatal Dane, however that mystery is much of our own making, far greater is the enigma which Falstaff presents us. A braggart, a drunkard, foul of mouth, a coward and a lecher, these are the counts against him; and yet we receive him into our heart of hearts for his incomparable charm, his "infinite variety," and his regally triumphant wit. It has been well remarked that Shakespeare, alone of all authors, is imperturbable, impersonal, impartial before the creations of his brain. Wherefore the merciless justice of the king's denial of Falstaff. You or I would have forgiven Falstaff. You or I would not have let Cordelia die. And we boggle that *All's Well* should end well and clamor that measure be meted out for measure. Shakespeare alone is not afraid of the truth; for none of his creations has he fear and for none has he favor. In practice, too, Shakespeare realized that the logic of art is a higher logic than that of life.

Theatrical rivalry in the chronicle play

Returning to the chronicle play at large, an interesting light is cast on the active competition of the companies in the manner in which a pathetic incident or a successful comic personage is rivaled or imitated in successive plays. Heywood's *Edward IV* includes, with much more, the pitiful story of the two little sons of that king, murdered in the Tower by Tyrell at the instigation of their wicked uncle, Richard. Heywood wrote after Shakespeare, and cleverly and successfully evaded mere imitation, stirring to the depths in his scene between the two children in the

Tower—for which there is no parallel in *Richard III*—
the compassion of his hearers.[1] Falstaff became, at once,
a shining mark for imitators; and a striking, if not shameless, example is that of the play, *Sir John Oldcastle*, for
which Drayton, Hathway, Munday, and Wilson conjointly
were paid by Henslowe. First, the title was filched, for
survivals in the text of *1 Henry IV* go to show that Sir
John Oldcastle was the name under which Sir John Falstaff first figured, as suggested by a personage of the
former name in the old *Famous Victories of Henry V*.
Secondly, the character of Falstaff is grossly plagiarized
even to the name, in Sir John of Wrotham, a knavish,
drabbing priest; and scenes, such as the king's visit by
night incognito to his troops before Agincourt in Shakespeare's *Henry* V, are imitated.[2] A later similar parallel
—and a closer study will reveal many more—is suggested
in the two plays on Henry VIII, that of Samuel Rowley
called *When You See Me You Know Me* and the *Henry
VIII* with which Shakespeare had to do. This latter, we
have reason to believe from the prologue, which plainly
alludes to Rowley's play, was once known as *All is True*.
But for the explication of these niceties, the reader must
be referred to works of larger scale than this.[3]

Before leaving Shakespeare in the chronicle play, we
may look forward a moment to record a strange contemporary faith in the efficacy of such scenes displayed by
men who must have known the drama well. The praise of
Spenser, in his *Prothalamion*, and Shakespeare, in this
chronicle of *Henry V*, may well have turned the head of
the impetuous and daring young Earl of Essex, whose success in the "spectacular expeditions" against Cadiz and
the Azores had made him a popular idol. But failure
overtaking his rash campaign into Ireland, he crowned
folly with the madness of an attempt to seize the government and control the queen. It was when Essex and his

*Richard II
and the
Essex
conspiracy*

[1] Cf. *Edward IV*, iii, 5, with *Richard III*, iv, 3, 1-23.
[2] See the present author's *English Chronicle Play*, 125-133.
[3] *Ibid.*, 242-249.

123

friend, Shakespeare's patron, Southampton, were planning this *coup d'état* that some one of their party conceived the idea of a performance of *Richard II* before the conspirators and their friends, in order that these vivid scenes of the misrule and enforced abdication of an incapable sovereign might whet their courage and inspire them to action. Shakespeare's play was revived for this purpose and actually so acted, August 7, 1601, the day before Essex marched through London in arms, expecting the rally to his standard that never came. Evidently the Chamberlain's men were innocent dupes, not parties to rebellion; and although Essex came to the block and Southampton remained in prison until the death of the queen, the actors none of them suffered. Adams has lately revived the interesting suggestion that Shakespeare's silence in the choir of poetic eulogy of the dead queen may have had reference to sympathy with his imprisoned patron and a tenderness for the memory of Essex.[1]

Henry VIII

Only once more did Shakespeare revert to chronicle history after the trilogy of *Henry IV* and *V* and that was in *Henry VIII*, which has been variously referred as to date to that active period, just after the death of Elizabeth, when the chronicle history was revived for the nonce in several plays, or to a late and unseasonable recurrence to an outworn form, long out of fashion. Whatever the facts, with the story of the courtship of Anne Boleyn and the baptism of the infant Elizabeth, *Henry VIII* groups with *Sir Thomas Wyatt*, Rowley's *When You See Me You Know Me*, and Heywood's *If You Know Not Me You Know Nobody*, popular presentations of events in the recent history of the Tudors. It is Shakespeare's genius which focuses the interest of his play on the pathetic tragedy of Katherine, the discarded queen, and converts a mere chronicle of events, as he had done again and again before, into an artistic drama of human passion.

[1] Adams, *Shakespeare*, 356.

And here we reach precisely the chief element in the Contempo-
disintegration of the chronicle play, and perhaps equally raneous-
its chief merit, and that is its picturing of the immediately chronicle
known rather than the constructively imagined. Falstaff play
is the Elizabethan toper and braggart, and Prince Hal is
going the pace in Elizabethan Eastcheap. Historical
imagination was undeveloped and anachronism as yet
unknown. It has been said of Shakespeare that he is at
all times strictly contemporaneous, as indeed were most of
his fellows; but a reason for his power, above the rest, lies
in the circumstance that he possessed the creative gift to
pick out of his own surroundings not only that which was
contemporary then, but that which is contemporary
always. Scenes of mere comic diversion in the chronicle
play early developed into considerable pictures of contemporary life. We may feel sure that Thomas Heywood,
who was writing not impossibly before the death of Marlowe, wrote the two parts of his *Edward IV*, less for the
excellently repeated story of the wicked Crookback and
the boy princes murdered in the Tower, than for the
pathetic domestic scenes of Jane Shore, the king's enforced
and penitent mistress. So, too, into each of Dekker's two
very different comedies, *Old Fortunatus* and *The Shoemakers' Holiday*, an English prince enters as in so many
other plays; but the spirit of the former is romantic and
supernatural, while in the latter, with the figure of the
immortal Simon Eyre, Mayor of London, his rollicking
apprentices about him, we meet with one of the earliest,
as it is in many respects the best, comedy of contemporary
London life, its merriment, romance, and pathos.

The continuance of dramas, begotten ultimately in the Plays of
impulse of the chronicle play, into Stuart times need not adventure
here engage us. *King Lear, Macbeth*, even *Cymbeline* in
such backgrounds "historical" as are theirs, in a sense,
belong here. But these were much besides. Out of this
drama of fact and history developed, too, an interesting
group, mostly of Stuart plays, concerned with travel and

125

adventure. As early, indeed, as 1596, there is the dramatized story of Thomas Stukeley, a restless adventurer of
Devon stock, like Hawkins and Raleigh, who planned the
carving out for himself of a kingdom in Florida, but
became the inevitable enemy of his queen and died fighting the Moors. The author of *Sir Thomas Stukeley* is
unknown; but Day, Wilkins, and William Rowley combined to contrive a play, about 1607, out of the several
adventures of the three brothers Shirley in Persia, Russia,
and Italy. Following a journalistic spirit, strong in an
age of action, the stage responded to the popular interest
which several acts of piracy called forth about 1609, with
several plays in which adventure on the high seas figures.
Examples are Robert Daborne's melodramatic, *A Christian Turned Turk,* founded on the deeds of two notorious
pirates; and such, too, are the romantic dramas, *Fortune
by Land and Sea* and *The Fair Maid of the West,* in both
of which the fertile and adaptable Heywood was concerned, in the former with the aid of William Rowley.
A belated specimen of the class, dating the year 1625, of
the accession of King Charles, is *Dick of Devonshire.*
Here, as in other passages of these plays, glows once more,
if only in reminiscence, that brave, indomitable national
spirit as when

> That glory of his country and Spain's terror,
> That wonder of the land and the sea's minion,
> Drake of eternal memory, harrowed the Indies.

and English seamen dared unheard-of odds for glory and
plunder.[1]

Summary
of the
chronicle
play

If we will look back at the chronicle play as a whole, it
becomes at once manifest that its contemporary vogue and
success was chiefly due to Shakespeare. It was he alone
who devoted a third of his dramatic activity to plays of
this type, having to do with a greater number of them
than all his predecessors put together; and this pre-emi-

[1] "Dick of Devonshire," Bullen, *Old English Plays,* ii, 13, who suggested
Heywood as the author.

nence, as we know, was not quantitative alone. Shakespeare's splendid succession of English kings on the stage owe their success not so much to the mere fact that they are better plays than those of his fellows, but because they so competently make real both person and event, and thus humanize these old narratives. When all is said, the permanent worth of the chronicle play resolves itself into the terror and pity of Marlowe, the humane reality of Greene and Heywood, and Shakespeare's chivalric elevation and large humanity. In comedy it gave us Falstaff and his rout; in serious drama, Bolingbroke and Henry V; in tragedy, Marlowe's Edward and Shakespeare's Richards and Queen Katharine; nor must we forget Heywood's Jane Shore and the two little princes, pitilessly murdered in the Tower. It cannot be said that without the comic scenes of the chronicle plays English comedy would not have developed as it did; but assuredly such scenes count much in the growth of that comedy. Again, it would be claiming too much to speak of these plays on English history as the kind of drama out of which alone was to come such potent tragedy as that of *Macbeth* or *King Lear;* and yet these and even the tragedies of classical subject, *Cæsar, Coriolanus, Antony and Cleopatra,* still preserve much of the chronicle manner. The historical play was a school in which Shakespeare learned more than his fellows, because he practiced more in it. His tragedies owe, at any rate, far more to chronicle history than they ever learned of the ancients; for in a manner it was the freer movement of these epic plays on English myth and tradition which enfranchised the drama from the scholars' rule of a dead hand.

CHAPTER VII

COMEDY, DOMESTIC AND ROMANTIC

Varieties of comedy

WE turn now to the continuance of comedy, which we may distinguish in this chapter as either naïve, romantic or domestic. Naïve comedy is that which is conceived of as simply telling the story. In domestic comedy emotions evolved out of the relations of the family chiefly hold the stage. In romantic comedy the animating principle seems rather an eagerness of spirit which yearns after the new and the untried, a thirst to be slaked in several ways: by the surprising, the extravagant, the supernatural even, or by a certain charm in unfamiliarity that whets curiosity while it satisfies, none the less, the innate expectancy of beauty and moral truth. These distinctions do not involve logical classification. They are not mutually exclusive; for the naïve manner of telling a story may concern itself with fact or with impossible adventure. Domestic comedy may content itself with an amusing recital of the thing as it happened, the fun being in the occurrence and in the people concerned, as in *The Merry Wives of Windsor;* or it may tinge the plot with a glamor, strange and enticing, as in the jealousy of Leontes or the incredible wager of Posthumus as to the virtue of Imogen. For both are innately comedy, however serious their subject-matter. One kind of comedy this chapter will not touch, and that is the species in which the attitude towards life is ironic. This attitude, which involves satire, is patently antithetical alike to the romantic and the naïve way of looking at things; though, obviously enough, much domestic comedy breathes the ironic atmosphere. Ironic comedy, otherwise the comedy of marners, came into vogue

128

later than these other kinds and is best considered in the light of later developments. The critical scrutiny of life in the very act of portraying it which is called satire came to color comedy only towards the end of the reign.

As to naïveté as a characteristic of early comedy, no better example could be found than the little play of *Mucedorus*, which dramatizes an episode of Sidney's *Arcadia* with an unaffected simplicity, the story involving a princess in distress, a prince in disguise, a wild man and a bear, all of which justified an unusual popularity without the added "delectable humors of Mouse, the clown." This unsophisticated performance was reprinted a dozen times after 1598, which must have been long after its first acting. It has been attributed to Lodge with a trifle more justification than to Shakespeare. The author is really unknown. Peele's *Old Wives' Tale* presents, too, much the same atmosphere to the unwary reader; but here we may suspect the mischievous smile—we shall not call anything so pleasant the leer—of the parodist. This quality of naïveté, which accepts commonplaces and marvels as alike deserving of record and credence, is of course a salient quality of the heroical romances such as Greene's *Órlando*, and, in a less romantic manifestation, of Heywood's preposterous *Four Prentices*, both of which have been mentioned with Peele's comedy above. Indeed, it is not to be denied that this quality constitutes in large degree the charm of the comedies of Greene, especially *Friar Bacon* with its obvious necromancy of bodily transport on the backs of devils from place to place and its fresh little love story of the young lover, Earl of Lincoln, sent in disguise by his prince to court, Arden-wise, the lovely dairy-maid of Fressingfield, for his royal master. There is a grace and a delicacy about the fancy and the diction of Greene that, added to a considerable skill in plot and a sense for the minor realities which give verisimilitude to the scene, give him his primacy among writers of comedy in his earlier time. The women of Greene, his "fair maid," Ida and

129

Dorothea of *James IV* have been deservedly praised for naturalness and womanliness. We have only to compare them with the unrememberable women of Peele, Marlowe, or Kyd to recognize the justice of Greene's repute.

The Henslowe group of playwrights

With the dropping out of Greene, Kyd, and Marlowe, popular dramatic authorship fell into the hands of a new group of men of a position in life much that of their predecessors.[1] Chettle, Day, Drayton, and Munday in collaboration with Houghton, Wilson, Hathway, Smith, and Rankins, all are disclosed by Henslowe, some of them credited with a score or larger number of plays, written in collaboration and most of them lost: out of Munday's fifteen, four remaining; out of John Days's, nineteen, five at most; out of Chettle's, fifty, one alone; and out of Drayton's half as many, also but one, and this his only in part. Of Chettle we have heard as the publisher of Greene's unhappy attack on Shakespeare. Anthony Munday was an actor, general writer, and translator, as well as a maker of pageants and plays. He was often the butt of satire among his fellow playwrights and was engaged in public employment as a pursuivant and messenger. Save for Day and Drayton, of whom more below, little is known of the rest outside of the *Diary;* of Richard Hathway, nothing at all. More important than any of these are Chapman, Dekker, and Thomas Heywood, who are equally of this group and whose work begins in the middle 'nineties. Chapman's comedies, for their satiric bias, belong below. Dekker and Heywood took over earliest the work which fell from the lifeless hands of Greene and Marlowe. Dekker's activity with Henslowe is quite the most surprising of all, running to forty-four titles, mostly in collaboration, between January, 1598, and November, 1602, or nearly a

[1] Adams, *Shakespeare*, 119, notes that Marlowe's father was a shoemaker, Greene's a saddler, Peele's a charity-school clerk, and Lodge's a grocer. By the same token Chettle's father was a dyer, Day's a husbandman, and Munday's a draper. The trade of Dekker's father is not known. Heywood, Drayton, and Chapman appear to have had parents unsullied by trade. Jonson's mother tumbled him from the son of a clergyman to the stepson of a bricklayer.

play a month for four years.[1] Heywood, who was an
actor as well as a writer, was far less active within this
period with less than a dozen plays written mostly with
others; but subsequently and outside of Henslowe's mart,
he became the most productive playwright of the entire
age, declaring, in a well-known passage, that he had had
"either a whole hand or at least a finger" in 220 plays.[2]
However, Heywood's activity was not only incessant, but
of forty years' duration; and a general average of but
little more than five plays a year, often with the help of
others, seems—in view of some of the amazing stories, for
example, of the fecundity of Lope de Vega—not an impossible achievement.

Thomas Dekker was a Londoner by birth and of better
station than has sometimes been reported. He must have
begun his long dramatic career in 1593 or 1594, when just
about of age. Although neither university can claim him,
his writings declare him a man of cultivation, unacquainted
neither with Latin nor with several modern languages.
He appears to have been neither a player nor a tradesman;
he may have trailed a pike in the Flander's wars, perhaps
there to acquire an acquaintance with the Dutch language
of which he makes use in some of his plays. Dekker's
association was at first with the Admiral's men at the Rose
and the Fortune, then with Worcester's at the Rose. He
was employed with Jonson in the devices which welcomed
James to London, and later in other city pageantry. A
writer for various companies thereafter, the Prince's,
Paul's and the Queen's, he spent several years in prison for
debt, but lived to continue his busy career as a pamphleteer
and to collaborate with a new generation of playwrights.
A humane and democratic spirit is characteristic of Dekker, and, despite his talent for somewhat boisterous comedy,
a cleanness and ideality of thought, until the demands of a
declining popular taste partially corrupted him. While

Thomas
Dekker

---

[1] M. E. Hunt, *Thomas Dekker*, 1911, p. 47.
[2] Epistle to the *English Traveler,* 1633.

wanting in constructive ability, Dekker often happily realizes character and, above all, is at need a veritable poet.

Dekker's earliest extant dramatic work is *Old Fortunatus*, the story of the possessor of the inexhaustible purse and the wishing cap, with his consequent adventures and those of his sons. It is recorded as already an old play in 1596. With its Lylyan figure of the serving man, Shadow, first of the series of Dekker's rollicking humorists, and its reminiscences of *Faustus* and *Tamburlaine*, it may well date earlier. It has been assumed, in the absence of an English version, that Dekker had read the story of *Fortunatus*, already extant in German, or perhaps in Dutch, when in the Low Countries; but his fancy has converted the marvels of the old folk-tale into a thing of fresh and almost childlike poetic beauty with a framework of an allegorical contest between Vice and Virtue, the woof of its "trimming for court." It is in this earliest work that we meet the sheer poetry which is Dekker's at his best in song and in the dialogue itself." *The Sun's Darling*, which well displays the poet's delicate love of nature, is perhaps "a bookes of Mr. Dickers" of Henslowe's mention in January, 1598. If so, it has been considerably marred in subsequent revisions by Ford and perhaps others. *The Shoemakers' Holiday* of the next year is the wholesomest example of that other Dekker of genial fidelity to the observed facts of life who will claim further chronicle below. In Dekker's part of *Patient Grissel*, written with Chettle and Haughton for Henslowe, we have once more the exuberant characteristic of Dekker's youth. These earlier comedies are romantic in spirit, and this is more truly the "note" of Dekker, however we shall recognize his power of pathos and his ability to create character in domestic drama, than the stridency of the satire of his *Satiromastix* or the heartless ribaldry of passages of the comedies which he was afterward to write with Middleton.

COMEDY, DOMESTIC AND ROMANTIC

The romantic temper is not so ruling a spirit in earlier Thomas Heywood
plays of Heywood; and yet there is a naïve fantasticality
about his early venture, *The Four Prentices of London*, as
about his efforts to dramatize popularly classical myth.
Not less a Londoner in birth and, at most, but a year or
two Dekker's senior, Thomas Heywood began as a dramatic writer under conditions almost identical. His earliest work must have been staged well before the publication of *The Four Prentices* in 1594; Meres recognized
him in 1598 and he sustained a modest repute through
three reigns in at least as many companies. Up to the
end of Elizabeth's reign Heywood's association was chiefly
with the Admiral's men and the Earl of Worcester's, in
which latter he was a shareholder, following its fortunes
when it became Queen Anne's players in the reign of
James. A more bookish man than Dekker, Heywood fulfilled even more industriously and variedly the hard conditions of a hack-writing pamphleteer. Several of his distinctive contributions to the drama came later with his
work in designing city pageants; but his place chronologically is here with Dekker. There is a modesty, a benignity of spirit, pervading Heywood that endears him
to his readers; and the wholesomeness of his tone, his old-
fashioned piety, and his devotion to the memory of the
great queen, make him one of the most engaging of our
old writers.[1]

Shakespeare's success was established in the final decade Shakespeare's measure in comedy
of Elizabeth's reign; and that success was mainly depend-
ent on his comedies. It has been well said that in comedy
Shakespeare found no such type already in vogue as in
history; wherefore his earliest efforts were experimentally
diverse as we have seen. And now Shakespeare found his
measure. The theme-giver, so to speak, of Shakespearean

[1] Thomas Heywood's probable relation to the family of John Heywood,
the writer of interludes, has been suggested by Miss K. L. Bates, *Journal
of Germanic Philology*, 1913, xii, 1. He appears to have been a Cambridge
man born about 1570. See the Introduction to Miss Bates's ed. of two
plays of Heywood, *Belles Lettres Series*, 1919.

comedy is *The Two Gentlemen of Verona*, in atmosphere romantic, in subject devoted to love and adventure, in attitude sympathetic to the personages involved, in quality refined and poetic. Not that this comedy displays all of these features in perfection, however it contain them potentially. Taking his story from the *Diana* of Montemayor, Shakespeare complicated his plot, as he had complicated the *Errors*, and adapted his personages rather to figure in it than to evolve event out of character. The result has been called "an aggregation of fascinating improbabilities"; but romance is improbability, exploited by the fancy; and its only demands are a continuous whetting of the curiosity in a rising scale and the maintenance of a lively interest, this last being the one tie of the veritably romantic to fact and that unascertainable thing which we call reality.

Wealth of material in *The Merchant of Venice* As we read or witness a modern English play, possessed, let us assume, of some acquaintance with drama in the past, our wonder is at our modern barrenness of idea and poverty in detail. We marvel at a mere episode, expanded to the tenuity of a drawn wire and "simplified" to the protracted pondering of a single theme. A modern drama resembles much the action of a moving picture "slowed down" for comic effect—though the effect is not comic; and we potter over a trivial situation to view it on all sides for a period in which the Elizabethan would have flashed the truth on twenty such. There is no more striking contrast between the old drama and ours than this, nor a more vivid example of it than *The Merchant of Venice:* the quest of an adventurer in matrimony, the trial of a noble friendship, the revenge of a malignant money-lender, a tragedy of racial antipathy, the elopement of an undutiful daughter and the comedy of the ring, all and much more, are but parts of this splendid romance of full-blooded renaissance art, any single episode of which would make two in bulk of "an historical study" by Mr. Drinkwater or a Fabian problem dramatized by the earlier Mr. Shaw. The

Elizabethan neither "studied" nor philosophized his subject. He found no puzzle, either social or racial, in acquisitive and revengeful Shylock, who was simply bloodthirsty and even comic. Bassanio's childlike fortune-hunting, whether we dignify him as the ideal renaissance lover or not, was as acceptable as Portia's delightfully bad law or as Antonio's un-Christian valiancy and insult to the Jew.[1] It is only in oblivion to the nature of romance and in ignorance of Elizabethan conditions that difficulties arise in matters such as these.

Between *The Merchant of Venice* and the three comedies which followed in close succession, in or about 1599, had intervened a return to the chronicle play in the trilogy of *Henry IV* and *V*, its outcome, *The Merry Wives* and the making over of *A Shrew*. Resuming the line of romantic comedy, we have *Much Ado About Nothing, As You Like It,* and *Twelfth Night,* written doubtless in reasonably close succession and marking the height of that sound, joyous and sympathetic note in Shakespeare's art which, more than any of the other phases of his genius, goes to account for his contemporary and lasting popularity. And how popular, how familiar, in these comedies is the dramatist's material. Shakespeare seems to have set little store, if any, on what we call inventive originality of subject, and apparently believed that, with a known story for subject, dramatic success is half won; hence the tale of Hero, repudiated at the altar, a story repeated by Bandello, Ariosto, and Spenser and acted at court nearly twenty years before; the pastoral tale of a popular novel by a some time competitor, Lodge, rewritten not without delicate raillery of the pastoral notions of Tasso and Guarini in *As You Like It;* and the story of Orsino and his page, of a source in Italian drama, repeated, translated, Latinized, at last Englished by Barnabe Riche in prose and by Shakespeare in *Twelfth Night.* They are not for

The joyous comedies of Shakespeare

[1] C. R. Baskerville, *Manly Anniversary Studies,* 1923; and E. S. Stoll, "Shylock," *Journal of English and Germanic Philology,* x, 236.

nothing, these careless, easy titles: *As You Like It, Much Ado About Nothing, What You Will*. But the success of these comedies was not alone in the glorification of old material. It was the verve, the swiftness, the novelty of Beatrice and Benedick—however foreshadowed in Biron and Rosaline—together with admirable Dogberry and his Verges, that made *Much Ado;* and it would be the loss of a bright particular star in either constellation were subtle Touchstone or delectable Feste, choicest of Shakespearean clowns, eclipsed. In Jaques, who is nothing to the plot of *As You Like It*, and Malvolio, who is the pivot of the counterplot of *Twelfth Night*, Shakespeare begins that portraiture of the "malcontent," or saturnine temperament, out of joint with the times, which was to end in *Hamlet*. And in Beatrice, hoyden though she is, and more especially in Rosalind, Viola, and Olivia, the poet continues the series of adorable, capable, dependable women which forms so capital a glory of his plays. Only in *All's Well That Ends Well* do we feel any failing of the standard in comedy set in this incomparable group; and *All's Well* is an older play, rewritten not always with a regard for the clearing away of the chips. And yet, defiant of recent standards as is her story, Helena remains, in her steadfast purpose and splendid self-reliance, one of the finest among the women of Shakespeare. English drama reaches no technique as perfect as that of these comedies, no characters more adequately, more delightfully, more artistically drawn; nor does the poet boast elsewhere, when even at his best, a style more natural, more graceful, or better fitted to the pleasant purpose in hand.

Shake-speare in comedy

The comedies of Shakespeare, after the manner of his time, represent Elizabethan life in its fullness, and elaborately. They offer us a section through that life, so to speak, from Duke Orsino and the Countess Olivia, the lesser gentry Sir Toby and Sir Andrew, to the household in its grades from my lady's steward, Malvolio, her waiting-maid, and her domestic fool to mere servants. In other

plays we go even further outside of the circle of people of
rank to encounter the ignorance, pomposity, and the unconscious humor of Dogberry and his watch, the rusticity
of William and Audrey, and the seductive rascality of the
thieving vagabond, Antolycus. It was reserved for the
artificial next age to limit romance to royalty (or at least
gentility) and its humors, in a separate comedy, to servants
and menials. Indeed, our glib divisions of the kinds of
comedy scarcely apply to Shakespeare, who boldly gives
us, all in the same play, the gross reality of the persecuted
Jew and golden Portia in moonlit Belmont, the dirty
purlieus of Vienna and the pure-hearted steadfastness of
Isabella. Shakespeare is very careless about the trivialities; he does not stop to inquire about the geography of
Bohemia. He does not investigate the fauna of the Forest
of Arden, but admits to it the fabled lioness that will not
touch a sleeping man. It must be confessed that, like
other playwrights, his contemporaries, Shakespeare often
neglects to "motivate," as we call it, or sufficiently to
account for the actions of his personages, imperiling consistency of character for dramatic effect, and perpetrat-
ing inconsistencies which captious prying may discover
and exploit. But in the large Shakespeare is always true
to the passion evoked and sincere and unerring in his
representation of it. With personages, events, emotion,
poetry welded into an artistic whole, we are beguiled into
acceptation whether every detail answer to what we consider the law of probability and consistency, or whether
it square with our own ascertained experience or not.
Shakespeare's dramas declare the futility of the intrusion
of scientific accuracies into the regions of the arts and
emphasize the truth that art must ever run parallel to
nature and that in the confusion of the picture with mere
realities lies its destruction. Wherefore our trouble that
such a lover as Romeo should ever have loved before or
that so jealous a husband as Leontes should ever have had
the chance to love his wife again merely satisfies our own

notions of what we should like to believe. There are conventionalities in this old drama, of course: the happy ending, nearly as great an obsession in Shakespeare's day as in our own, demanded that poor maligned Hero forgive her fickle and credulous lover, Claudio, in *Much Ado,* and that the peerless Isabella, in *Measure for Measure,* give up her devotion to the religious life to marry a duke. The convention that the calumniator is always to be instantly credited makes possible the plight of Posthumus as well as of Othello. Hamlet's fierce reluctance to kill the king at prayer lest his soul be saved may be merely "stage vengeance," not fiendishness. But whether these things are realities or stage semblances, the art is there and none knew better than Shakespeare the unreality of the best of art, especially, when all is said, that it shadows but the unreality of life.

> These, our actors
> . . . . . . were all spirits, and
> Are melted into air, into thin air;
> And, like the baseless fabric of this vision,
> The cloud-capped towers, the gorgeous palaces,
> The solemn temples, the great globe itself,
> Yea, all which it inherit, shall dissolve,
> And, like this insubstantial pageant faded,
> Leave not a rack behind.

Shakespeare in the height of his activity

It would be needless, were it possible, to reconstruct in detail Shakespeare's life during this famous decade. His residence in London is established, up to 1596, as in St. Helen's, Bishopsgate, not far from the Theater; afterward, as in the Liberty of the Clink, Southwark, as convenient to the Globe. His lodging with the tire-maker, Mountjoy, in Silver Street, Cripplegate, was later. Shakespeare's touch with Stratford must have been constant, for he is commonly described in documents as of that town; and the rescue of his father's fallen fortunes, the endeavor to obtain a grant of arms, lawfully to describe himself "gentleman," and his purchase of New Place, all but the largest house

in Stratford, all point to steadily rising fortunes and a
human wish to be esteemed in his world. There is reason
to believe that for the earlier part of his career, Shakespeare's gains may have been less from his dramas than for
his services as an actor.[1] His share in the Globe, and later
in Blackfriars, together with his portion of the substantial
fees for performances at court, brought his income, by the
end of the reign, up to handsome proportions. That the
stamp of industry was upon Shakespeare's life, the amount
and the quality of his work is alone sufficient to attest.
That he was appreciated in his time to his applause and
enrichment, nothing but a stubborn skepticism, intent to
find difficulties, can deny. Acting, planning, writing, deep
in the business of his company, it is not strange that we
hear little of a man so immersed in immediate affairs. His
intimate associates were his fellow sharers, the player folk,
the Burbages, Kempe, Pope, Heminge, Condell, and the
rest. With them he lived in affectionate concord in his
daily vocation. That such a man, according to his station,
should have been more or less intimate, in a larger circle,
with the best minds of his time, needs no proof by document. The meetings of wits and poets at the Mermaid
tavern give us a glimpse into the intellectually free and
socially careless living of the age; and it is good to think of
Shakespeare as a genial participant in them. The early
patronage of the Earl of Southampton is attested by
Shakespeare's dedications of his narrative poems to him
and is strengthened by tradition; and we do not require for
the illumination of these personal relations the corroboration of any strained interpretation of the *Sonnets*, however
ingenious or alluring. Shakespeare's company was often
at court and his plays were as welcome there as at the Globe
or Blackfriars. A certain intimacy with his queen may
be assumed, if we accept the well-known story that we owe

---

[1] In 1596 Shakespeare purchased New Place for £60. Later in the same
year he bought 107 acres of arable land near Stratford for £320, and soon
after, the house next to New Place. See the chapter on his financial
resources in Lee, *Life*, ed. 1916, p. 296.

to Her Majesty's personal request that silhouette of the actual Falstaff, so disgracefully abused by Mistress Ford and Mistress Page. But the highest proof of the degree and stability of Shakespeare's reputation in his own day lies in the many contemporary attestations of the esteem in which he was held alike for his poetry and his plays,[1] in the frequent ascriptions of others' work to his pen, and in the piracies committed on his authorship in efforts to print his plays against his will to the detriment of the rights of his company.[2]

Eliza-bethan publication of plays

Censorship of books, in Shakespeare's time, was directed mainly to the control of utterances political and religious. Copyright meant the protection of printer against printer; the idea of any right in the author, the book once published, was unknown. A new commission to the Stationers' Company had created an office in which registry was demanded of every book to be printed, and, in the theory at least, this was supposed to come only after license by the higher power of church and state. The Elizabethan play was usually published singly, in quarto form and printed, according to the standards of other books, rather carelessly. The size of the edition we do not know; but a popular play like *1 Henry IV* or the two *Richards* often ran into four or five quarto editions within a few years. There were, for example, three quartos each of *Romeo and Juliet*, *Pericles*, and *Hamlet* from the date of the first publication of each to that of the death of Shakespeare. And if publication be the criterion of popularity, we may contrast with these examples the anonymous comedy, *Mucedorus*, printed six times between 1598 and 1616, *Faustus* as many, and Kyd's *Spanish Tragedy*, issued nine times up to the latter date, and thirteen, if we include all the quartos.

[1] *Shakespeare's Century of Praise*, begun by C. M. Ingleby, in 1874, has been expanded to great dimensions by L. Toulmin Smith and F. J. Furnivall, New Shakspere Society, 1879 and 1886.
[2] A. W. Pollard, *Shakespeare's Fight with the Pirates*, 1917, especially 27-54, a book which, with the same author's *Shakespeare Folios and Quartos*, 1909, has modified many opinions.

COMEDY, DOMESTIC AND ROMANTIC

In general it was not to the advantage of the players to have their plays printed, at least while they were holding the stage. They needed protection against performance by another company. Wherefore we hear of the actors' endeavors to "stay" the printing of plays which had come into the printers' hands, and of the gratification of a printer who had succeeded in eluding "the grand possessors' wills," as he says in the case of *Troilus and Cressida*, to get his booty into print.[1] Plays "escaped into print" in various ways, by means of a needy actor, bribed to repeat as much as he could recall, or by means of a shorthand taking down of the play as it was acted. For charactery or stenography, by both of these words, was well known to Elizabethans, the former word at least as far back as the Armada.[2] There were other surreptitious ways of obtaining copy. Heywood declares that there were playwrights who sold their labors twice, once to the stage and again to the press. However, it is not always easy to determine the nature of these transactions. As to Shakespeare, the bibliographical investigations of Pollard have effectively disproved the older idea that any very large proportion of the quartos were actually surreptitious, leaving only five—the first quartos of *Romeo and Juliet, Henry V, The Merry Wives of Windsor, Hamlet*, and *Pericles*— certainly in the category of "bad quartos."[3] It must often have been to the advantage of the players to have their plays printed; and the publication of a "bad quarto" or the printing of a play, which had been the source of one now popular, with the intent to palm it off for the true one, was a sufficient reason for publishing an authoritative quarto. *Love's Labor's Lost* (the quarto of 1598) "newly corrected and augmented by W. Shakespeare," on the basis of a probably earlier quarto, now perished, and *Hamlet*

[1] "To the Reader," quarto of 1609, second issue. *Folios and Quartos,* 56-57 and 77.
[2] Cf. Timothy Bright, *Art of Charactery,* 1588; J. Willis, *The Art of Stenographie,* 1602.
[3] *Folios and Quartos,* 65.

(the second quarto of 1604) "newly imprinted and enlarged to almost as much again as it was," are cases in point.[1] With the less successful companies the appearance of a play in print generally meant that the players had no more use for it; and fertile years in publication are usually those following plague or other misfortune.[2]

The playwright and publication

As to the attitude of dramatic authors towards their works, it is difficult to generalize. There were careless writers then, as now, and careful ones. Plays were generally regarded as ephemeral products, little worthy the care which one might bestow on more serious writing. Shakespeare's poems were carefully proof-read and are practically free from textual difficulties; some of the plays are better "read" than others; and we must keep in mind that Shakespeare could have seen less than half of them in print. It was in Jonson that the sense of editorship as to his own dramatic writings first awoke. To him and to Marston is referable the practice of the publication of plays soon after performance with the apparatus of dedication, epistle, and commendatory verses. And Jonson's col-

Folio and collected editions of plays

lected folio of his own works, up to 1616, is the earliest collection of plays published in England, and the only one until quite modern times, edited by the author. In 1619 there was an attempt to collect Shakespeare's plays;[3] but this was not consummated until the folio of 1623, followed by a second in 1632. Jonson's *Works* were completed with a second volume, varying in date between 1631 and 1642. In 1632 Lyly's *Six Court Comedies* appeared, and, in the following year, the *Tragedies and Comedies* of Marston. Save for these and the great folios of Beaumont and Fletcher, of 1647 and 1679, no dramatist of the older age was collected in his own lifetime or in the generation that followed him.

[1] *Ibid.*, 70, 73-74.
[2] *Ibid.*, 9-64.
[3] On this projected collection of 1619, see *ibid.*, 81-104; and W. J. Niedig, "The Shakespeare Quartos of 1619," *Modern Philology*, 1910-11, viii, 145.

COMEDY, DOMESTIC AND ROMANTIC

Romantic comedy ran in no other channel so purely as in that which Shakespeare made for it; and with every allowance for difference and inferiority, no veritable contemporaneous analogues are to be found for his work. Indeed, save for his comedies, until well past the 'nineties, the examples are rare into which the comic spirit enters otherwise than by way of relief or in support of some other motif, historical, as we have seen, tragic, or realistic. Without here attempting an enumeration of the comedies not already mentioned that fall within this favored decade, a few, at least, may be named. Two anonymous surviving plays of Henslowe's record are *A Knack to Know a Knave* and *A Knack to Know an Honest Man*. The former, which treats, in somewhat belated moral tone, King Edgar and Saint Dunstan, is enlivened, but not very much, with "Kempe's applauded merriments of the men of Gotham." The companion play in title, but not in subject-matter, is a typically naïve comedy of old time involving duels, banishment, tests of love and friendship, and enjoying a deserved popularity. *The Weakest Goeth to the Wall* is derived from one of the stories of Barnabe Rich's *Farewell to the Military Profession*, which also supplied the story of *The Merry Wives*. It begins with dumb show and progresses through a variety of incident to unexpected discovery and reconciliation, differing in these romantic respects not greatly from *The Thracian Wonder*, in which, however, following its source in Greene's popular romance, *Menaphon*, a pastoral atmosphere pervades. Lastly, we have in *Wily Beguiled*, a comedy of everyday life of much naturalness and simplicity, with a romantic turn in the parting and reunion of honest lovers.[1]

A tendency to imitate and repeat certain characters, scenes, and situations is characteristic of the comedies, as

---

[1] *A Knack to Know an Honest Man, The Weakest Goeth* and *Wily Beguiled* have been reprinted by the Malone Society. *A Knack to Know a Knave* is in Dodsley, vol. vi. *The Thracian Wonder,* which has been absurdly attributed to the authorship of Webster, is reprinted in Hazlitt's ed. of that poet, 1857, vol. iv.

of the tragedies, of the last decade of Elizabeth's reign.
It cannot be pure accident that the anonymous *Look About
You* and Chapman's *Blind Beggar of Alexandria* should
both depend on the device of disguise carried out to the
limits of farce and credulity, any more than that the latter
play should not have inspired at least the title of *The
Blind Beggar of Bethnal Green,* in which disguise again
figures, but more romantically and rationally.[1] In *The
Merry Wives of Windsor* there is use of English as broken
in the Welsh speech of Sir Hugh and the French Doctor
Caius; and this device becomes a feature of the three
captains, Fluellen, Macmorris, and Jamy, in *Henry V.*
Haughton's *Englishmen for My Money,* in which three
foreigners court three English girls, each in a jargon of
his own, dates 1598 with these plays of Shakespeare.[2] And
still again, in *The Merry Wives,* we have the "group of
irregular humorists," the Welsh parson, the French doctor,
and mine host of the Garter, the last with the group around
him closely followed in *The Merry Devil of Edmonton.*
These latter two plays also make much of scenes of wandering and cross purposes by night, the one in Windsor
Forest, the other in Enfield Chase. And this motif is
further developed most amusingly in the concluding scenes
of *The Two Angry Women of Abingdon.* Of the several
anonymous plays mentioned in this paragraph, *The Merry
Devil of Edmonton* is by far the best, in its happy combination of a wholesome love tale, a touch of the threatened
supernatural, and the "humors" of low comedy to which
Jonson had just given a new turn.[3] *The Merry Devil* long
held the stage, and scholars have been unusually reticent in
their assignments of an author to it. With *The Two
Angry Women of Abingdon,* one of the most vigorous and
successful of popular comedies, we make a natural transi-

---

[1] On this subject at large, see V. C. Freeburg, *Disguise Plots in Elizabethan Drama,* 1915.
[2] On Haughton, see the ed. of this play by A. C. Baugh, 1917.
[3] On *The Merry Devil,* especially its source in the chap-book of Friar
Bacon, see J. M. Manley in *Representative English Comedies,* ii, 505.

tion to domestic drama. Thoroughly English is this laughable picture of two quarrelsome old women whose difference arrays two families against each other; and admirably is the action sustained through scenes of bustling movement and farcical merriment. The play was so well liked that a second part was called for, and a third entitled *The Two Merry Women of Abingdon*, both of these unhappily known to us only through Henslowe's mention. Of Henry Porter we learn little more than what Henslowe tells us—that he was actively in his employ, in 1598 and 1599, and a borrower of various sums, scaling down at last to twelvepence, that at the height of the success of *The Women of Abingdon*, Henslowe thought so well of him that he engaged him by contract to write only for the Admiral's men. The careful Meres mentions Porter among successful writers of comedy; and, thought to be an Oxford man, on the title of this, his only extant play, he writes himself "gentleman." [1]

Domestic comedy in number becomes legion between 1598 and the end of the reign of James, and falls into certain natural classes according to subject. There is the series devoted to the delineation of the faithful wife, a portrait well drawn, if extravagant according to our standards, in *Patient Grissell*, 1600, by Chettle and Dekker, which treats the Chaucerian theme, long since the subject of a moral-like interlude by John Philip, called *Patient and Meek Grissell* and registered in 1565.[2] And there is the contrasted series devoted to "the shrew," who is nearly as old, if not quite so mediæval, as her patient sister. Here, too, Shakespeare's well-known comedy, *The Taming of the Shrew*, 1594, was preceded by an earlier one, less revised than turned by his adaptable hand into a more perfect focus.[3] Fletcher took up the theme in *The Tamer Tamed*,

Comedies of domestic life

---

[1] The best account of Henry Porter is that of Professor Gayley in the same, i, 515.

[2] Discovered only in 1907. See the reprint of the unique copy by the Malone Society, 1909.

[3] The earlier play is called *The Taming of a Shrew*, and is assigned to about 1589. Many guesses have been made as to authorship.

or the Woman's Prize, 1604, which represents Petruchio's second venture into matrimony with the tables merrily turned; for poor Katherine had died, naturally enough, soon after her taming, having become too good for this world. It is said that the Stuart court delighted in these two plays acted on successive evenings. The plays which deal with the faithful wife often contrast her impeccable submissiveness with her foil, the wanton. Such a play is *How to Choose a Good Wife from a Bad,* by one Joshua Cooke, conspicuous, although he wrote before Elizabeth's death, in the absence of his name from Henslowe's pages. *The Fair Maid of Bristow* is almost parallel in plot and of much the same date, 1604. Another contrast in plays of this type is that between the long-suffering virtues of the wife and the prodigality of her husband, circumstantially and pedestrianly told in the details of a recent actual example in *The Miseries of Enforced Marriage,* 1607, by George Wilkins, known for his reputed part in *Pericles.* It was on the same unhappy theme that the unknown imitator of Shakespeare's manner wrote the short but far abler *Yorkshire Tragedy,* already noted among murder plays. The best drama of the series is Marston's *Dutch Courtesan,* 1604, in which, while both the contrasts just alluded to are well maintained, the emphasis is on the impudence and the fascination of the wanton heroine who gives the play its name. Finally, in Heywood's *Wise Woman of Hogsdon,* also 1604, we have the benign and kindly solution of these relations which we should expect of this humane author, the triumph of the faithful wife, and the regeneration not only of the prodigal, but likewise of the woman who had misled him.

A Woman Killed with Kindness

With a word as to two plays of the domestic class which rise dramatically, as they do emotionally, above the type, we must bring this chapter to a close. Heywood's *A Woman Killed with Kindness* presents frankly and simply two stories of English contemporary life, and in the process suggests rather than delineates a contrast. The minor plot tells of a quarrel over a wager at hawking between two gentlemen and the persistent determination of the loser to ruin his sometime friend by debt, imprisonment, even to the dishonoring of his sister. Here is a situation, however different in motive, shadowing at least that of Angelo and Isabella in *Measure for Measure,* on the stage at much this time. Heywood's Susan is as firm, as constant as Isabella; and her virtue and steadfastness bring about a regeneration—favorite theme of Heywood—in the heart of her brother's persecutor, who substitutes honest love for lust and reconciliation for enmity. The other plot, which gives the play title, is that of the restraint of an honorable man, who, wronged by the friend he had trusted, finds both friend and wife unfaithful, but forbears the customary violence, substituting banishment of the wife from himself and her children; and the play concludes with her consequent death, repentant. In his principal figures Heywood merely outlines the weak woman, sketches Wendoll, the seducer, and gives the strength of his art to Frankford, the wronged husband; but he fails not to record the remorse of Wendoll. His story treads simply and naturally, free alike from the gauds of extraneous ornament as from that parade of cleverness that came soon to corrode honest humor. Nowhere does the humanity of Heywood so shine as in these direct and unaffected scenes. Years after he repeated the theme in a somewhat more romantic situation, in *The English Traveller;* but it is the earlier play which marks the best in the art of him whom the discerning criticism of Charles Lamb christened "our prose Shakespeare." [1]

The atmosphere in *The Honest Whore,* the other play, is more rarefied and the method more elaborate[2]. Moreover, the scene is an imaginary Milan in which, however, London local allusions and customs abound, the two parts

The Honest Whore

[1] *A Woman Killed with Kindness* was first printed in 1607, *The English Traveller* in 1633.
[2] This play was registered in 1604; the second part was printed only in 1630, though doubtless written soon after the first.

147

concluding, the one in Bedlam Madhouse, disguised as "Bethlem Monastery," the other, without disguise, in Bridewell, London's House of Correction. An underplot, in keeping with the taste of the moment, takes for theme "the humors of the patient man," put upon by a petulant tease of a wife and yet maintaining through all a certain dignity. The main plot depicts, at first and without too great coarseness, the life of a harlot, regenerated by a sudden fancy for a man whom she cannot win to evil courses, with her later temptation and triumph over the solicitations of this very man who had saved her. Incidentally, the plays develop two other remarkably well-drawn personages. Matheo, the worthless, unregenerate husband of Bellafront, the heroine, and her brusque but sound-hearted old father, whose parental love returns to sustain her when he finds her truly determined to lead a life free from sin. There is a charm and a winsomeness about Bellafront that impel the reader to accept her notwithstanding her fidelity to her type in a submissiveness to her wretch of a husband, which stops short, however, of wrongdoing and admits no word of disparagement for the father who had repudiated her. The question of Middleton's part in this work has been variously answered by scholars. Its tone, which, barring parts of the minor story, is singularly free from the satirical outlook, should settle the question and ascribe to Dekker the substantial authorship of the whole. Possibly the most remarkable thing about these two great dramas of Heywood and Dekker is the absence of any trace of sentimentalism in either. That blight on the most delicate growths of the emotions was not of the Elizabethan world.

The relations of *Measure for Measure*

It cannot have escaped the reader that in plays such as this we find the drama turning for the first time to scenes of the underworld, to the purlieus of debauchery and vice which flourish for the most part beneath the surface of society. Elizabethan comedy had never been squeamish where "realism," as we miscall such picturing, is concerned:

that was but one feature of the old art's fidelity to the thing seen. But this is something different; for the "realism" of such scenes involved the "humors" of them, in Jonson's sense of that word, as well as that moral attitude of reprobation which, combined with "humor," produces satire. Shakespeare's *Measure for Measure* was doubtless on the stage as early as 1603 and probably preceded Dekker's story of Bellafront; but that Shakespeare was responsible for bringing "repellent characters, situations, and dialogues on the stage" is an affirmation far from proof. It was the satirical bias of Chapman, Jonson, and the slumming in comedy of Middleton that were responsible for this sort of thing. Moreover, the brutal actualism of the scenes of *Measure for Measure* which touch on these forbidding themes is no more the fiber of that wise, sane, and powerful play than are the similar—and far less vividly repulsive—like parts of *The Honest Whore*. *Measure for Measure* contains, in the scenes between Isabella and her unhappy brother and between her and Angelo, heights of emotion, and subtlety and triumph in its delineation beyond which Shakespeare scarcely rose in his tragedies. On the stage, well acted, it is surprising how the essential nobility of the theme, the innate soundness of it morally, shines out above a sordid setting, the very truthfulness of which makes all this possible. The attitude towards life in *Measure for Measure* is at the poles' width from that of Middleton and his school. But it has much in common with the moral soundness of Dekker, however it rises above the unsophisticated honesty of the Heywood of *The Woman Killed with Kindness*.

CHAPTER VIII

Tragedy at its Height

The decade of tragedy

THE first ten years of the sixteen-hundreds have been called for Shakespeare the decade of tragedy. And what was true for him was true for the drama at large; for Shakespeare is always as typically representative of the taste, the spirit, at times even the passing fashions of his age, as he was immeasurably above them in realizing the permanent values to be found even in ephemeral things. The affiliations of *Hamlet*, as we have seen, throw it backward, and there is reason now to place Shakespeare's retouching of the theme earlier than has been hitherto accepted.[1] Between *Hamlet* and *Othello*, the first play of Shakespeare certainly acted before King James, *Julius Cæsar, Troilus and Cressida*, and *Measure for Measure* intervened, and perhaps other plays, especially comedies, usually placed before *Hamlet*. It seems unnecessarily inconsistent to deny to Shakespeare a versatility of mood which is matter of common observation in the natures of lesser men; and inferences of tragedy in the author's life, because the demand of these years was for tragedy on the stage, seem only more ill conceived than the reading of the personal opinion of the author into every rumination of his personages.

Nature of tragedy

Tragedy, whatever its academic definitions, is really less a variety of fiction, poetry, or drama than a way of accepting—or rather of refusing to accept—the vicissitudes, the logic of life.[2] The egotist sets himself against the ·

---

[1] J. D. Wilson, *The Copy for Hamlet, 1603, and the Hamlet Transcript, 1593*, 1918; but see also Chambers, iii, 186.
[2] On the academic question, "What is tragedy?" see the recent paper of Professor Allison Gaw, *Schelling Anniversary Papers*, 1923, p. 151.

150

established order of things as accepted by other men. Macbeth will be king, though murder intervene between his ambition and the crown: Coriolanus, on the horns of a dilemma created by the egotism of his pride is certain of impalement on one or the other. The arrogance of Lear will settle the inheritance of a kingdom by whim, and the petty "selfness" of Richard II—to use an apt word of Greville—tenaciously holds on to kingship when he is in reality no king. Each of these, whether we sympathize with him or not, is but the individual out of step to his overthrow with the inevitable tread of accepted conduct or custom. Even more innocent sufferers— inadequate Ophelia, Desdemona equally a party to her overthrow in her inopportune persistency—represent merely more piteous examples of these dissonances of life which we may explain, if we like, by other figures of speech having to do with Fate or the decrees of a God, more or less theologically conceived; but which lie, dispassionately observed, in a want of articulation, a disjointedness with the adjusted apparatus of the world.

Recognizing tragedy thus, as a mode rather than a kind *Othello* of drama, we may none the less continue to explore our field by such clews as subject, governing motive, and the like may afford. To defer for the moment tragedies on classic subjects with those which measurably followed classic models, the new reign found Shakespeare busy with three great tragic themes: *Othello, Macbeth, King Lear,* a play in each successive year, the first of these and *Measure for Measure* (which immediately followed it) both acted, in 1604, "in the great hall" before King James.[1] *Othello* breathes the conventional romantic air of Italian intrigue only to rise, in passion, vivid characterization, and poetry, the master tragedy of jealousy. The Elizabethan attitude towards this the most venomous of human passions, is prevailingly ironic. When jealousy is

[1] See the now accepted authority of Cunningham's "Extracts from the Revels," *Shakespeare Society,* 1842; E. Law, *Some Supposed Shakespeare Forgeries,* 1911.

not food for the ridicule of comedy, we are left, as in the case of Leontes, with a feeling of contempt for its victim. Such is not the effect of the jealousy of Othello, extorted, as Shakespeare makes us feel that it is, out of the very fervor of the Moor's romantic and honorable love for Desdemona by the machinations of a villain whose wanton malignity is unsurpassed in drama or in life. The noble Moor, Shakespeare found in his source, accept or reject as we will the "thick lips" which Roderigo, Othello's enemy, applies to him, or the "sooty bosom," Brabantio's slur upon the man whom he had introduced intimately into his home. It is doubtful if to Shakespeare, Othello's exotic birth meant anything more than an added touch of the romantic, much as in the case of the Prince of Morocco, Portia's suitor. Shakespeare seldom selects for his major themes the exceptional and the anomalous. Othello's services to the state, his valor and his nobility, are the essential attributes, not his race or his complexion. As to Iago, by depriving him of the vestige of a motive for his practices on his victim, Shakespeare pressed his model, a vulgar, ordinary villain, to the line that divides human wickedness from the depravity of devils. Indeed, this celebrated drama has been severely criticized of late, especially for the want of any sufficient "motivation" for the fatuous credulity of Othello, a want which applies, if we are to judge by the standards which we demand and apply to modern art, not only to Shakespeare elsewhere, but equally to the general range of Elizabethan drama.[1]

Macbeth

In *Macbeth* Shakespeare returned to Holinshed for source, creating, out of a mere hint of the chronicler, that Macbeth had a wife who was possessed of influence over him, that awful figure of unsexed womanhood in which a passionate ambition for the husband with whom she has wholly identified herself, raises her terrible criminality to the sublimity of a complete abnegation of self. The text

[1] E. E. Stoll, "Othello, an Historical and Comparative Study," *Minnesota Studies*, 1915.

of *Macbeth*, as we have it, is incomplete and corrupt, possibly abridged and certainly interpolated with material not Shakespeare's.[1] Moreover, we are compelled to recognize here, in choice of theme and manner of treatment, a glaring example of contemporary considerations limiting artistic freedom, from which even the greatest cannot remain absolutely free. The ministrations of witches interfering in the affairs of men could have been no accident in a play written for performance before the royal author of *Demonology in Form of a Dialogue;* and the promise of regal inheritance to Banquo, a progenitor of King James, is only flattery more finely conceived than the scene lugged in gratuitously concerning the royal touch for king's-evil.[2] But what are these trifles in view of the superb simplicity, effectiveness, and power of this world drama of inordinate ambition and its marvelous dilation of the vulgar figures of witch-lore into mysterious, inevitable ministrants to the flourishing of evil in human hearts? The apparition of Banquo's ghost to Macbeth alone, among his guests, is an excellent example of what some, in these days untaught and careless as to the past, are calling at the moment by a new hard name, "expressionism," and treating as the destined way leading to a new art. The power of such a scene lies in the circumstance that the ghost, which is Macbeth's embodied thought, should appear in the midst of a group of ordinary people who can neither see it nor, even should they see it, understand; and its reality to Macbeth lies in his inability to comprehend why all should not see what is so vivid to him. Another example of this same thing is the daring scene of storm in *King Lear*, where the disturbance of the elements symbolizes not only the tempest in the heart of the discarded king and father, but subtly co-ordinates that passion with

---

[1] Note the borrowing of some of the witches' incantations from *The Witch* of Middleton, a play of uncertain date, a matter not only determinable by the occurrence of these passages in both plays, but by the inapplicability of the interpolations to the story of Macbeth.
[2] *Macbeth*, iv, 1, 112-122 and iv, 3, 140-159.

the whole action of the play: a thing which should be the goal, the very *ne plus ultra* of our new "expressionism."

King Lear *King Lear* was acted in 1606 at court, and here, once more, Shakespeare found the suggestion of his story in Holinshed, but this time with the intervention of an earlier English play, entitled on its publication, when Shakespeare had revived the theme, *The True Chronicle History of King Leir*, and ending, in accordance with its source, in the restoration of the king to his crown and to happiness.[1] Neither drama, nor kindred art, for that matter, knows a more daring *tour de force* than Shakespeare's reinforcement here of the major theme of Lear and the ingratitude of his daughters, not with the usual and obvious underplot of contrast, but with a repetition of that theme in the story of the easy-going Earl of Gloucester and his ingrate son. The parallel is further carried out in the faithfulness of Cordelia and of Edgar and heightened in the despair of Gloucester and the madness of Lear. Moreover, just as the imperious unreasonableness of Lear afforded an original motive for the estrangement of his daughters, so Gloucester's ribald words as to the birth of Edmund lit the spark of undutifulness in the bastard's heart, to blaze into a heartlessness and cruelty the equal of those of the harpy daughters. This tragedy offers another example of this technique of agglomeration, if we may so call it (retaining the idea of massing effect by similar effect and excluding any notion of confusion which the word sometimes connotes). And this is the equally daring juxtaposition, in the scene of storm, of the madness of Lear, with the babble of the sad-eyed Fool and the simulated insanity of Edgar. Dr. Furness, the late eminent Shakespearean, used to declare that the death of Cordelia constituted the one veritable tragedy in Shakespeare; for elsewhere in every case the crime, the folly, or the infatua-

[1] *Leir* was acted by the Queen's and Sussex men in 1594, shortly before it was registered for publication. It did not appear in print until 1605. Lodge is variously mentioned with Peele, Kyd, and Greene as possible authors.

tion of the tragic figure justified, in a measure at least, his fall. Lovely as is the after-devotion of Cordelia, and pitiful her fate, is even Cordelia an exception? Her father's imperious demand for an avowal of filial affection could have been no such extraordinary departure from the habitual conduct of one "the soundest of [whose] time hath been but rash." And Cordelia could have been no stranger to it. Was there just a touch, after all, of the same imperious unyielding spirit in Cordelia that was her father's, that she could not bring herself momentarily to humor a testy old man? Or could she for the nonce have been more intent on being unlike the sisters whose insincerity she so justly despised? In *Lear* we note, if we except *Troilus and Cressida*, the beginning of that difficult, "elliptical and elusive" use of language that came more and more to characterize the later Shakespeare. It is as if the strain of these veritably human emotions in effort to express superlative thought must break the sides of rhetoric and justify in him, who had been as yet a beneficent sovereign of language, the caprices, the violence and the success of a self-willed tyrant.

And now let us consider the tragedies that ransacked for theme the storehouses of antiquity or that exhibited, in their ideals, conduct, or construction, an intelligent return to the examples of the classics. There had never been a time when Elizabethan drama had not before it the example of the ancient world, and never did it cease wholly to draw on ancient story for subject and embellishment. But there was for the poets the constant lure of other themes, newer, more immediate, more startling. The earlier vogue of the classics soon passed at court, though imitation of the ancients theoretically was still practiced by literary courtiers and gentlemen who wrote not for the stage, and the classics remained the standard at the universities. On the public stage in contrast to Kyd's popularization of Senecan ways, Lodge applied somewhat the manner of the chronicle play to his *Wounds of Civil War*, which, treating the struggle of Marius and Sulla, mingles incongruous comic scenes with passages of bombast, disclosing the influence of *Tamburlaine*. Lodge's play is memorable as the earliest to lay under contribution the admirable *Parallel Lives* of Plutarch, so assiduously employed later by Shakespeare. Classical titles, however, are recorded long before, scattered through the 'seventies and 'eighties: a *Cæsar* and a *Catiline* of Stephen Gosson's mention, to name here no others; while the story of Virginia dramatized by R. B. and Preston's popular *Cambyses*, both extant, were even earlier.[1] In the days of "the predecessors" the episode of Panthea (from Xenophon's romance) was dramatized in *The Wars of Cyrus;* and *The Tragedy of Dido*, a subject not long before handled in Latin by Dr. Gager at Oxford, employed the combined activities of Nash and Marlowe.

Classical topics of Henslowe's mention To learn somewhat of the relations of classical to other subjects on the popular stage we may note (remembering the incompleteness of his records) that Henslowe mentions twenty-four titles, undoubtedly referable to ancient story between March, 1592, and January, 1600; but this is in a list of 280 plays. Perhaps none are now extant unless Henslowe's *Phaethon* be Dekker's play, later rewritten as *The Sun's Darling*.[2] Greg calls attention to the popularity of Greek subjects about 1598: *Polyphemus, Orestes, Agamemnon,* and *The Arcadian Virgin* (Atalanta). Chettle, especially with Dekker and Haughton, were chiefly concerned in them. But it is to Heywood, a few years earlier, if we are to accept the identification of these plays with earlier ones of Henslowe's mention, that we must award the most determined endeavor to popularize ancient myth on the London boards.[3] In five plays

---

[1] Fleay's identification of "R. B." as Richard Bower is uncertain. *Malone Society's Publications "Collections,"* iv, 287.

[2] This identification, which is accepted by Greg, *Henslowe,* ii, 190, and questioned by Chambers, iii, 300, would date the play 1600.

[3] These plays of 1595 and 1596 are *Coelo and Olympo,* two parts of *Hercules* and two parts of *Troy;* the identifications, accepted by Greg, *Henslowe,* ii, 175, are Fleay's.

which he subsequently named *The Golden, Silver, Brazen* and *The Iron Age*, we have a series of vital scenes, dramatizing the myths of Jupiter, Hercules, Jason, and the heroes of Troy, the last named culled for the most part from Caxton's *History of the Trojan War* and the rest from Ovid.[1] The series discloses, the difficulties of the panoramic change of subject once acknowledged, a surprising aptitude for dramatic situation and an admirable readiness, inventiveness, and verbal facility.

The relation, if any, of these classical efforts of Heywood to another lost play to which the names of Dekker and Chettle attach, must remain problematic. In 1599, Henslowe records a play by these two authors on Troilus and Cressida, and the fragment of "a plot" of a play on this very topic, doubtless to be identified as the same, has come down to us among the *Henslowe Papers*.[2] Heywood, too, touches on this well-known theme in *The Iron Age*, so that when Shakespeare undertook the story, he worked as usual on a tried and familiar subject. Shakespeare's *Troilus and Cressida* raises many questions. Chronologically it is usually assigned to a position just before *Julius Cæsar*. There are bibliographical difficulties, too, which in detail cannot be set forth here. Licensed, in 1603, by one printer who apparently failed either to obtain copy or was "stayed" in publication, a second published an edition in 1609 of which there exist two issues, the earlier with a title page declaring "as it was acted by the King's Majesty's servants at the Globe," the later substituting for these words a description of contents and printing a curious address by "a never writer to an ever reader: news," in which the statement of the previous title is flatly contradicted, and the play declared a new one "never staled with the stage, never clapperclawed with the palms

Troilus and Cressida

---

[1] E. Koeppel, *Studien*, iv, 15, states that Heywood's main source was the Lefavre-Caxton *History of Troy*.
[2] Ed. Greg, p. 142.

of the vulgar." [1] Various explanations have been offered,
and the inference that the play never reached performance
is perhaps inevitable. Our chief interest, however, in this
advertiser's "news" is for its remarkable appreciation of
Shakespeare, one of the very few contemporary utterances
of a critical nature extant. Here the comedies are described as "so framed to the life that they serve for the
most common commentaries of all the actions of our lives";
and it is prophesied that "when he is gone and his comedies are out of sale, you will scramble for them and set
up a new English inquisition" (which, I take it, means an
indefatigable inquiry for copies of these plays). Again,
there was uncertainty as to the position which *Troilus and
Cressida* should take in the folio of 1623, an uncertainty
referable, perhaps, not only to questions of ownership, but
to the rating of this play as a comedy or a tragedy. In
a sense there is none of Shakespeare's plays so veritably
tragic as this story of disillusion: the very circumstance
that Troilus does not find the death he seeks, or his unfaithful lover the punishment which her levity deserves,
makes it the more so. For the real tragedy is not expia-
tion in death, but the doom to live on in a saddened world.
Shakespeare's sources for this wise, eloquent, mocking, and
forbidding tragedy—for such I will call it—came neither
from Homer nor from Ovid, but from the romantic
mediæval distortions of the Trojan War, and especially
Boccaccio's tale, followed by Chaucer, of the false and
fickle mistress of knightly Troilus.[2] For which reason
nothing could be wider the mark than any notion that
Shakespeare deliberately aimed at a satire on antiquity in

---

[1] See, however, Pollard, *Folios and Quartos*, 66 and 76, who makes
Roberts, who registered this play in 1603, but did not print it, the pro-
tector of the rights of the company, here as elsewhere.

[2] On the Troilus story, see J. S. P. Tatlock, *Modern Language Review*,
1915; H. E. Rollins, *Publications, Modern Language Association*, 1917,
xxxii, 383. The romantic after-story of Cressida, as told by Robert
Henryson in *The Testament of Creseid*, was well known to the age, and
Cressida was as common an Elizabethan word for a light-o'-love as pander
for a go-between. The notion that this play is in any wise autobiographical is hardly worth the expenditure of Adam's honest indignation on so "shallow an hypothesis."—*Shakespeare*, 353.

representing the heroes of Troy as men so essentially un-Homeric. The inequality of the play has been explained as due to a revision by the author of his own earlier work, for *Troilus and Cressida* is unmistakably Shakespeare: in passages equaling the best, the sagest, the most poetic in him.

Before we continue our chronicle of the popular stage, we must record the recrudescence of Senecan tragedy in English in a new impulse, directly traceable to France and mainly to one author, Robert Garnier. Translation from the classics was one of the accomplishments that flowered out of the rigors of renaissance education. The Princess, later Queen Elizabeth, and her unhappy rival, the precocious Lady Jane Grey, both sharpened their Latinity on the translation of bits of Seneca, and another subject of King Henry, Lady Jane Lumley, did the whole of the *Iphigenia in Aulis* into English. Sidney's well-known approval of *Gorboduc* for its adhesion to classical usages marks the attitude on this subject of many cultivated people who, having the progress of English letters deeply at heart, felt that the future lay in a circumspect following of artistic precedent rather than the inspiration of that mysterious thing so little understood, called genius. The Countess of Pembroke followed, in her encouragement of others and in her own practice, however less ably, the ideals of her illustrious brother; and it was from her pen, in 1590, that we have, in her translation of Garnier's *Antoine*, the first example of "French Seneca" in England. A year or two later came Kyd's Englishing of the same author's *Cornelie*, and Samuel Daniel, the well-known tutor to many noble ladies and follower of Sidney in his Italiante lyrical poetry, wrote his *Cleopatra*, an original production, but wholly in the manner of Garnier and his school. The distinguishing traits of French Seneca are dignity, restraint, purity of diction, regularity in verse, a preference for rhyme, and the use of elaborate stanza for the chorus, which is usually of human personages rather than the

French Seneca in England

159

abstractions of earlier Seneca.[1] Daniel's two dramas of
this type—for in 1600 he added *Philotas* to the earlier
Cleopatra—are full of tragic dignity, eloquence and
pathos, exceedingly well written and adequately poetic.
A feature of *Philotas* in particular is the amount of attention given to the abstract discussion of questions moral
and political, the choruses being made up almost wholly of
such comment. We learn from Daniel himself that his
play had fallen under suspicion for an alleged likeness in
the story to the political disturbance known as the Essex
Conspiracy.[2] *Philotas* was acted in 1604 by the Queen's
Revels, and Daniel was called before the Privy Council on
account of it. Another prudent courtier tells us how
he had burned a tragedy of his on Antony and Cleopatra
in fear of incurring a like danger.[3]

Fulke Greville's tragedies This was Fulke Greville, whose long life began in a
boyhood's friendship with Sidney and extended to the be-
friending of the young William Davenant in the reign of
King Charles I. A favorite of Queen Elizabeth, Greville
rose to the dignity of a royal councillor in the reign of
King James and, as Lord Brooke, was sometime owner of
Warwick Castle. To such a man poetry and drama, in
both of which he was proficient, were no more than a means
to the expression of abstract moral and political ideas;
and he avows it as his purpose "to trace out the high
ways of ambitious governors" (we should say rulers) "and
to show" that the greater their worldy success, "the more
they hasten to their own dissolution and ruin." [4] The two
extant tragedies of Greville are *Alaham*, which dates about
1600, and *Mustapha*, some six years later. Both conform
to the variety here under discussion, but rise in a species
of intellectual radiance, in an unexpected and searching

[1] "France makes Seneca more academic than he was. . . . Action is
almost dispensed with, stirring incident is banned, dialogue becomes monologue . . . language acquires the perpetual gloss of rhetoric—in short a
French Senecan drama is drama in little but name."—Kastner and Charlton, *Works of Sir William Alexander*, cxxxviii.
[2] "Apology," prefixed to the quarto of 1607.
[3] Fulke Greville, *Life of Sidney*, ed. 1652, p. 178.
[4] *Ibid.*, 242.

power, at moments, of insight into feeling, not only above their class, but into comparison with the triumphs of the contemporary popular stage. The employment of Eastern subjects, in the drama, in which Greville was not alone, calls for a momentary comment in passing. In Elizabeth's day the Turk was still a menace to Europe and the world was interested in his doings. Wherefore, a number of "Turkish histories" and other stories of the East held the popular stage. *Tamburlaine* is such, and *Soliman and Perseda* even more strictly. And there was *Selimus*, variously attributed to Greene or to Marlowe, besides a lost *Turkish Mahomet* by Peele. To Chapman, somewhat later, has been assigned a fine tragedy, *Revenge for Honor*, treating much the same events as those of Greville's *Mustapha*. And there were grosser melodramas such as Mason's *Mulleasses the Turk* and the rant and bombast of several plays on Ottoman history by Thomas Goffe.[1] Aside from the atrocities that form so repellent a feature in some of these plays, but which must have attracted in their day, such topics lent themselves to elaborate staging and led on, we may well believe, to the triumphs in this kind of Dryden and Southern. Excepting a name or two such as Samuel Brandon, author of a dignified and well-written tragedy, *The Virtuous Octavia*, strictly in the mould, French Seneca comes to an end in the *Four Monarchic Tragedies* of Sir William Alexander, later Earl of Stirling, complete in 1607.[2] Stirling was one of the Scottish gentlemen who followed his sovereign to his new and opulent throne in England. He was tutor to Prince Henry and rose to important place in the state. It was natural that he should fall in with aristocratic Sidnean literary ideals. Stirling's plays are tedious and prolix,

Later Senecan plays

[1] Mason's play was called merely *The Turk* in the ed. of 1610. John Mason was a Cambridge man and a member of the King's Revels in 1608. This, his one play, has been edited by J. Q. Adams in *Materialien*, 1913. See also G. C. Moore Smith in *Mod. Lang. Rev.*, viii, 371. Goffe lived between 1591 and 1629. His chief plays are *The Raging Turk, or Bajazet II*, and *The Courageous Turk, or Amurath I*. Both belong to Goffe's student's days at Oxford.

[2] Brandon is known only by this play.

and least of any of the group could they have been thought of for acting.[1]

Julius Cæsar as a subject for drama

It is clear, then, that in turning to classical history Shakespeare was broaching no new topic for drama.[2] The mention of some five or six plays touching Julius Cæsar find place between 1562 and 1600, the date of Shakespeare's tragedy. Chronologically the *Richards* and *Hamlet* intervene between *Romeo* and *Cæsar*. The method of chronicle history is still apparent in the last. Following Lodge, it was in Plutarch's *Lives* that Shakespeare found his source of first resort for ancient history, and, save for an intervening play, it is unlikely that he often went further afield. And here the poet met with a higher order of material than annals of events or recounted intrigues and adventure. For Plutarch is essentially biographical and occupied with character and personality. It has been observed that "*Richard II* marks the beginning of Shakespeare's interest in men who fail," and that while *Richard III* recounts the rise and fall of a hero and *Richard II* only the hero's fall, *Julius Cæsar* marks—after the manner of several two-part plays contemporaneously on the stage—Cæsar's fall and, in the overthrow of Brutus, Cæsar's revenge.[3] In a sense it is true, as often remarked, that this tragedy is more truly that of Brutus, whose idealist's rejection of realities brings about his overthrow, than of Cæsar, whose imperialism was not quite accurately timed to his age. But from another point of view, it is the spirit of Cæsar, as contrasted with the man who was mortal, that dominates the play. With a subject already so hackneyed on the stage and in literature, Shakespeare may well have chosen deliberately this larger spiritual theme in preference to the usual picture of a conqueror

[1] Stirling's dramatic works have been recently edited by L. E. Kastner and H. B. Charlton, 1921, with an informing introduction which overhauls the entire subject of Seneca in his influence on the literature of western Europe.

[2] M. W. MacCallum, *Shakespearean Roman Plays and their Background*, 1910.

[3] R. M. Alden, *Shakespeare*, 1922, p. 249.

triumphing in politics and war. Least of all can we accept the notion that the poet was obsessed with any prejudice against the greatest man of antiquity or failed to understand him in thus presenting him only in the period of his decline. When all is said there is a dignity and an emotional temperance about this famous tragedy that comport well with the subject, and a brevity and effectiveness alike in the conduct of the scenes and in the superb diction which rank it high among the works of Shakespear's maturity.

Several other plays on Julius Cæsar followed Shakespeare's, among them one of the *Four Monarchic Tragedies* of Stirling already mentioned, and the *Cæsar and Pompey*, published years after by Chapman with an apparent pride in the fact that it had never been acted.[1] Confusion of incident and intrusion of irrelevant detail mark this as a work which adds little to the fame of the translator of Homer. An academic play, described on the title page as "privately acted by the students of Trinity College in Oxford" and dated 1607, usurps the titles of at least two other plays as *The Tragedy of Cæsar and Pompey, or Cæsar's Revenge*, but bears no relation to either Chapman or Shakespeare. A Latin *Julius Cæsar* by Thomas May, the historian of Parliament, of much later date remains extant and, I believe, is yet unprinted. His English tragedies on Cleopatra and Julia Agrippina, 1626 and 1628, are effective dramas with the ideals of the ancients clearly in view.

Later plays on Cæsar

The next tragedy of note to follow Shakespeare's *Cæsar* was Ben Jonson's *Sejanus, His Fall*, acted at the Globe by the new King's men in 1603, with Shakespeare, according to the list of actors in the Jonson folio of 1616, taking a part; what part it is impossible for us to tell, as the actors' names are not listed to parallel the *dramatis personæ*. That popular Shakespeare should have preceded scholarly Jonson in achieving for a tragedy on Roman history suc-

Jonson's Sejanus

[1] Dedication to the Earl of Middlesex, ed. Parrott, *Tragedies*, p. 341.

cess on the public stage, is interesting in itself; and the contact of the two great names in *Sejanus* is arresting. It has been thought, too, by some that a closer relation in authorship as to *Sejanus* may possibly be hinted, as in Jonson's preface "to the readers," in which he speaks of "a second pen" as having "good share," which in printing he has honestly expunged rather than "defraud so happy a genius of his right by my loathed usurpation."[1] Perhaps, however, when all is said, it was Chapman rather than Shakespeare who was here Jonson's earlier collaborator. The story of Sejanus, favorite of the Emperor Tiberius, is that of a political adventurer with his overthrow. "The tragedy of political adventure," as it has been well called, was flourishing at the moment. These were plays, like Chapman's "French histories," of plot, conspiracy, and usurpation; and it is not unlikely that they may have owed much of their popularity to the excitement attendant on the actual conspiracy and trial of the Earl of Essex.[2] However, that a very conscious scholarship was Jonson's in the writing of his Roman plays, and the joy of superiority in showing it, is not to be denied. His had been a stern apprenticeship, both to the classics and to the drama; and his claims for his *Sejanus* are not excessive as he formulated them: "truth of argument, dignity of persons, gravity and height of elocution, fulness and frequency (which here means sufficiency, not recurrence) of sentence."[3] Recent opinion has interpreted this effort of Jonson's as "a deliberate reshaping of an ancient tradition for the right use of the modern stage," an attempt to reform "the people's Seneca without destroying its popularity."[4] The response, as usual to deliberate efforts at reform, was failure.

[1] *Jonson*, Gifford-Cunningham ed., iii, 6.
[2] Introduction, "Jonson," *Mermaid Series*, by the late Brinsley Nicholson, n. d. i, p. xxxv.
[3] "To the Readers," as above.
[4] *Works of Alexander*, as above, i, clxxiii, as to Jonson in Senecan tragedy.

TRAGEDY AT ITS HEIGHT

Marked is the contrast between Jonson's scholarly integrity in the use of his authorities, honestly cited, and the pedantic and verbose *Tragedy of Claudius Tiberius Nero, Rome's Greatest Tyrant* (1607), which, with much the same material, is the work of "a young scholler," we are told, "especially inward with Cornelius Tacitus." A better play is *The Tragedy of Nero*, "newly written," as the quarto of 1624 declares, but equally unknown as to date of writing or authorship. Even greater is the disparity between these more or less scholarly efforts in the reproduction of the spirit of antiquity and the trend of the age that gave to every story a bias romantic and adventurous. Thus Marston turned to Painter's *Palace of Pleasure* for the immediate source of his *Sophonisba*, adding much by way of curious invention and making the most of the romantic and heroic element in this world story; and Heywood popularized the pathetic story of *The Rape of Lucrece* in a manner alike perfunctory and below the level of his usual dramatic ease and excellence.[1] Both belong close to the period of the acting of Jonson's *Sejanus*, as does the ambitious Latin play on Nero of much celebrity in its day by Dr. Matthew Gwinn, dedicated to the queen. Lastly, at what time the dignified and restrained *Appius and Virginia*, published with Webster's *Works*, was really written is uncertain. It fits so ill with the unquestioned work of that great romantic tragedian and differs, with all its merits, so wholly from his manner and style, that we may agree that it is not his, unless in very superficial revision. *Appius and Virginia* is much in the manner of Heywood and may tentatively, at least, be accepted as his.[2]

It was not until 1611 that Jonson returned to tragedy on Roman history. *Sejanus* had not proved successful

[1] A. M. Clark in *Modern Language Review,* xvi (1921), gives this play to Webster.
[2] On the subject, see Rupert Brooke, *John Webster and the Elizabethan Drama,* 1916, pp. 165-210; and A. M. Clark, in *Modern Language Review,* January, 1921, who makes out a good case for Heywood while retaining Webster as a collaborator.

Jonson's
Catiline's
Conspiracy

and the author's careful citation of his authorities, when the play was published, had been ridiculed. But Jonson was never tractable under criticism. Dedicating his new play "to the reader extraordinary," he chose the conspiracy of Catiline for his subject and, following the story of Sallust, produced a tragedy more classical in certain features than *Sejanus*, yet lightened by the flash of comedy and consciously decorated with passages of poetry. It has been well said of *Catiline* that it was not written for laymen, but for such as could bring to the reading of it a knowledge of the setting and atmosphere of the Roman world. It is not that Jonson overcrowds his pages with learning, but that he assumes too much on the part of his reader, elaborating niceties in his art where essential features have not been made altogether clear. Jonson is said to have prized *Catiline* above all his other work. With its conscious ornament, elaborated eloquence, scholarly completeness in detail, and high demands made almost wholly on the intellect, *Catiline* makes clear how completely antithetical were the serious elements in Jonson's art to the spirit of the age in which he lived. *Catiline*, too, failed on the stage; and Jonson wrote no more tragedy.[1]

Timon of
Athens

Our consideration of Jonson in Roman tragedy has carried us forward. It was between his two plays that Shakespeare turned once more to drama, on ancient story. *Timon* and *Pericles* were on the stage by 1607. The latter we may leave to find place among the "romances." *Timon of Athens*, with a theme of childish, if natural, misanthropy, can scarcely be considered more than the work of some inferior playwright touched here and there with the hand of the master. The tale was a popular one, accessible in Painter as well as in Plutarch, and it had been employed, a few years before, in an academic

---

[1] The fragment of a play on Mortimer in the folio of 1642 indicates an intent on Jonson's part to write a play on even stricter Senecan lines. Whether this could be one with the *Mortimer* of Henslowe's mention in 1599 and 1602 is questionable.

drama, the relations of which to the Shakespearean tragedy remain food for surmise.[1]

With *Antony and Cleopatra* and *Coriolanus*, both in *Coriolanus* 1608, Shakespeare returned to Roman history, though obviously it is the mad, romantic passion that dares and loses all of the first, as it is the splendid, overmastering, and ruining pride of Coriolanus that must have attracted the author. The story of the haughty patrician, unable to bend to the arts of popularity, has been thought to offer an analogue to Shakespeare himself, especially as to the artifices of the plotting tribunes, and the fickle instability of the crowd against him are effectively emphasized. But aside from the patent danger of reading an autobiographical significance into anything assigned to a dramatic character or situation, the universal benignity and charity of Shakespeare's attitude towards life must flatly contradict any such supposition. Here, once more, success in the realization of the chief personage must not lure us from a recognition of Shakespeare's inventive power in the creation of subsidiary characters, Menenius Agrippa, the old friend and adviser, testy, human, pathetic in his devotion, the splendid Roman matron, Volumnia, and the gentle, silent wife, perfectly presented in a rôle in which scarcely two hundred words are uttered, these are creations of the artist's own and as vital as they are convincing.[2]

In *Antony and Cleopatra* Shakespeare once more hit *Antony and* upon a subject perennially the theme of poetry and drama. *Cleopatra* English treatment of the story theretofore had been purely academic. It was characteristic of Shakespeare that, telling the ancient tale with circumstantial frankness, he should have raised it out of the category of mere lust and faithlessness, in which the bald facts leave it, into the realm of an ideal and imaginative passion. We approve

[1] J. Q. Adams, *The Timon Plays*, 1910.
[2] Virgilia appears in only three scenes and utters actually 183 words. See "Virgilia, a Neglected Heroine of Shakespeare," L. Strachey, *Shakespeare's Final Period*, 67.

neither Cleopatra nor her vacillating Antony. There is
no concealment of his treachery to Rome, his heartless
neglect of Fulvia and Octavia, or his pitiable weakness
where we expect in manhood strength; and there is no
pathos in his lamentations for the lost honor which he
has deliberately cast into the fire of his passions. And
yet unaccountably, like Enobarbus, we love him and find
ourselves disposed to extenuate his conduct against our
better judgment. As for Cleopatra, willful, wanton, capricious, and unutterably mendacious though she is, we are
fascinated, as was Antony, by her inexpressible charm and
her infinite variety; and we find ourselves seduced into
forgetting her as the meretrix that she is and into imagin-
ing that the ruin which she has brought upon herself and
all that she loved is somehow atoned in the high heroic
resolve of her death. In comparison with other Cleopatras,
the scheming harlot of Fletcher's *False One*, even the dignified tragedy queen of Daniel and other classicists, we
recognize the immeasurable superiority of Shakespeare's
imaginative truth and ethical soundness. Nowhere is his
art more supreme than in this extraordinary play which,
like *Hamlet*, treats with all but complete disdain the petty
restraints of the stage.[1]

Jonson and Shakespeare in Roman drama   In neither of these latter Roman plays does Shakespeare
allow himself to be tied to those small consistencies of
setting and environment which have often made the repute
of inferior productions. If we must contrast the methods
of the scholar, as practiced, perhaps to the height of
success in its kind, by Jonson, with this artist's realization
in his work of the deeper mainsprings of passion, which
stir all mankind and not merely Romans, we must award
to the latter the higher praise. In that capricious distribution of gifts which Fate, blind and inscrutable, makes
to men, all but the greatest learning of the age, the best

[1] Two suggestive essays on this immortal topic are that of the late
C. T. Winchester in *An Old Castle and Other Essays*, 1922, p. 64; and
the earlier one of Arthur Symons, reprinted in *Studies in the Elizabethan
Drama*, 1920.

of skill in the devising of plot and superlative powers of eloquence and verbal felicity are as nothing before the divining sympathy of unlettered genius and the uplifting wings of unparalleled poetry.

In a former chapter we considered a series of plays known specifically as the "revenge plays," which, taking their rise in Kyd's masterpiece, degenerated, especially in *The Revenger's Tragedy*, attributed to Tourneur, into a production which, despite a gross effectiveness, presents the most hideous picture in Elizabethan drama of the wanton, cynical, and godless living prevalent in certain circles of the life of contemporary and earlier Italy. Other plays followed, such as *The Second Maiden's Tragedy*, the author unknown, which Sir George Buck, Master of the Revels, licensed in 1611 under that title, "for it hath no name inscribed." [1] But the older type, however perverted by strong men or diluted in weaker hands, was still vital and produced one author of eminence who stands out, not only superlative in his class, but raises the type to a place beside the greatest. Of John Webster we must repeat the dispiriting formula that we know next to nothing.[2] "Born free of the Merchant Taylors' Company," he appears first in *Henslowe's Diary* in 1602 as the author, with four others, of a play called *Cæsar's Fall*, written for the Admiral's men, and, a year later, as writing for Worcester's company, again with as many more collaborators, a "history" of *Lady Jane Grey* and a comedy, now lost. Webster's apprenticeship reveals collaboration with seven authors in three varieties of plays, and his extant works add Middletonian comedy of manners and romantic tragedy to his versatility in his craft and one more name to the list of his coworkers. Dekker was the chief among them; the others need not concern us. Webster's author-

Marginal note: John Webster and later contributions to the tragedy of revenge

---

[1] In the Mss. of this play Greg, 3 *Library*, ii, 232, distinguishes four hands. Though registered in 1653, it was not printed until 1825. Authorship is pure guesswork.

[2] Chambers, iii, 509, suggests that Webster may be one with the actor of that name abroad in 1596 as a member of Brown's troupe, and that authorship may have come to him late in life.

ship falls into three periods: that in which with other men he wrote whatever fell to the lot and took on the color of his collaborators; that in which he came into his own; and that in which he relapsed into mere imitation. Passing the second period for the moment, in the third Webster fell, like so many of his lesser fellows, under the curiously pervasive spell of Fletcher. It is in the intervening time alone that Webster is himself and it is as amazing that a man with such an apprenticeship should thus suddenly have burst into something so distinctive as it is all but unprecedented that he should have deserted his strong tragic bent to write, with Rowley, Fletcherian comedy such as *A Cure for a Cuckold*.

The master tragedies of Webster The distinctive repute of Webster rests on two tragedies of Italian intrigue and crime: *The White Devil*, which is the story of the Duke of Brachiano, and the crime by which a notorious courtesan, Vittoria Corombona, supplanted his duchess and with his connivance murdered her; and secondly, *The Duchess of Malfi*, telling the unequal vengeance of two princely brothers on their sister for the misstep of a misalliance. This latter play comes, as to source, from the time-honored quarries of Bandello and Painter, not without an assiduous reading, we are informed, of Sidney's *Arcadia* and the *Essais* of Montaigne—strange as it may seem—for dramatic effects.[1] *The White Devil* was based on occurrences almost contemporary, as the actual Vittoria Corombona was murdered in 1585. But whether Webster's source was a novel or a previous play, or whether the story may possibly have come to him by word of mouth, as some have thought, remains undetermined. The writing of this play has been assigned to 1610; *The Duchess of Malfi* was on the stage, at most, within three years thereafter.[2]

It is to the arrogant, scholarly, and satirical school of Jonson and Marston that Webster essentially belongs,

[1] C. Crawford, "John Webster and Philip Sidney," *Collectanea*, 1906, i, 20.
[2] Brooke, *Webster*, 1916.

and with them he hated the crowd and loved books. Although one of "the rearguard of a great age" and a close
student and borrower of it, Webster's "reaction to life,"
to put it contemporaneously, was an emotional one, for
all that his method of work was slow, pottering, and that
of a master of mosaic who worked with bright bits of
other men's color and metal, twisted and fashioned by his
genius into new and startling combinations. Webster is
distinguishable among his fellows for certain old-fashioned
mannerisms, such as occasionally all but irrelevant couplets
of comment and lugged-in anecdotes told at length; and
his liberties with his measures at times amount to license.
But his speech is always vernacular and often racy, and
his imagery concrete and original. Full of that commentary on his story which must be accepted as of the essence
of drama, whether shut off in choruses, devised in solilo-
quies and asides, or paraded in prefaces, Webster, with
much originality, makes all this a part of the personality
of his characters, especially in such, for example, as malev-
olent and foul-mouthed Flamineo in *The White Devil* and
that strange but, it is to be feared, not wholly unhuman
personage, the clear-seeing, hopelessly abandoned villain,
Bosola, of the other play. Equally individual to Webster
is his uncanny ranting, a characteristic of both of these
personages; and his probing for the hollow places in life,
so to put it. To the simplest of observations he gives a
sinister twist: "Pleasure of life!" he exclaims, "what is it?
Only the good hours of an ague." He cannot think of the
day of judgment without the sinister foreboding:

> Yet remember
> Millions are now in graves, which at the last day,
> Like mandrakes, shall rise shrieking.

Even more distinctive is Webster's terrible "trick of playing on the nerves"; witness especially the overpowering
scenes of the torture of the unhappy Duchess of Malfi
and the effective use which the poet makes of the old and

worn stage device of the echo, here employed ominously
to presage the impending fate of a doomed man in the
same tragedy. Brooding persistently on death, the violent moment of dissolution seems to have a fascination for
Webster; and in the same breath he is contemptuous and
pitiful as to wretched humanity. But Webster's, too, is
the poet's revealing power of phrase joined to the dramatist's instinct to place it. The words of the unnatural
brother looking upon the dead sister whom his machinations have brought to ruin:

> Cover her face; mine eyes dazzle: she died young,

are constantly quoted. Scarcely less effective are Vittoria's
dying words:

> My soul, like to a ship in a black storm
> Is driven, I know not whither;

or Bosola's dying comment on mankind:

> We are only like dead walls or vaulted graves
> That ruined yield no echo.

At the poles from what Rupert Brooke aptly called "the
ready rhetoric of Fletcher" and unsustained by any such
"perpetual inspiration" as was Shakespeare's, Webster's
is a grasp of passion in the moments of its impetuosity, a
power to inspire horror, terror, and compassion that stands
alone.

Middleton in tragedy Into the romantic tragedies of Fletcher and his school
we shall not here enter. They present a new departure.
Nor shall we pursue the older types or romantic tragedy
in their recurrences later. Middleton's master tragedy,
Women Beware Women, lies in point of date between
Webster's two great plays and appears to have been written to emulate them in its terrible picture of human depravity. Even more certainly here than in the case of

Vittoria Corombona, it would seem, have we an effort to stage a *cause célèbre*, that of the historical Bianca Capello, mistress of Francesco de Medici, and her degeneracy from wantonness to crime. With no such mastery of phrase as Webster and no such poetic power to create the surrounding atmosphere of horror and gloom by touches really extraneous to his story, Middleton tells his tale, when once under way, with a swift directness and certainty of touch, with a clear realization of personage and discrimination of incident that proclaim him veritably of the great Elizabethan brotherhood. Another great tragedy of the type is *The Changeling* (1623), in which Middleton had to assist him the more virile, if coarser, genius of William Rowley. Here once more the theme is the degeneracy of moral nature in contact with crime, but a wholesomer general tone prevails. It is always a relief to turn from the overwrought passions of these tragedies of Italian crime to Shakespeare's purer atmosphere, however we find in *Othello* a subject altogether cognate to the type. In intrigue and heartless villainy "honest Iago" may well compare with ugly, insinuating De Flores, who, in *The Changeling*, drags to perdition the merciless if delicate lady who imagines that she can disavow the instrument of a crime which she shudders to put into words, or with Bosola, necessitous creature and instrument of the cruel brothers in their torture of the suffering Duchess of Malfi. We do little justice to Elizabethan dramatists if we disregard the versatility which is so amazingly theirs. And yet, however Shakespeare, Middleton, and some others succeed in comedy and tragedy alike, Webster fails outside of his limited field, as Ford failed after him; and Dekker and Heywood seem happier in lighter, or at least less tragic, moods than when they attempt the satirical banter of Jonson or the taunting, ironic horrors of Marston and Webster.

CHAPTER IX

THE BIAS OF SATIRE

The ironic view of life IT cannot have escaped the reader that, save for a few examples in which the subject-matter has carried us forward into the reign of King James, the plays of Elizabeth's time are characterized by a certain simplicity and sincerity, in tragedy maintaining, even in exaggeration, a seriousness, at times involving almost a purpose, in comedy, a species of naïveté, or naturalness, even among the irrationalities of romance. In a word, the Elizabethans—using the term strictly—saw the world with open eyes; they viewed things candidly and took delight in what they saw. And they looked upon the world, too, at times, with dilated pupils which, dazzled with light, beheld everything transfigured with the radiance of a rare poetic beauty. As we approach the reign of King James there came about a new way of looking at the actions of men. Eyes were often now half closed and narrowed into scrutiny. Things were not so much seen as examined, peered into, to seek out their peculiarities and imperfections, to distinguish, comment on, moralize, unmask. In a word, the time of James infused into the drama, as into other literature, a new ingredient, that of satire, and a prevailingly ironic view of the world came into vogue.

It seems less likely that literature should have led in this than that the writings of the new reign should have chronicled an actual change in attitude and feeling. There was weariness and disillusion as the long reign of the old queen approached an end. There was greater wealth and greater luxury, and the competitions of life had become keener. Prosperity had enriched especially the merchant, and a pleasure-loving class of idlers was developing between the gentry and the tradespeople who claimed their own amusements and found before long their own dramatic laureate. From the side of literature, it is not accidental that three clever young men, Donne, Marston, and Hall, should almost simultaneously have turned their attention to writing satire on their own times, cloaked in an imitation of Horace and Juvenal; or that Jonson, greater satirist than any of these, should, under the same impulse, have turned English comedy deliberately to satirical purposes.

Ben Jonson was London born, and some ten years after Shakespeare. His father was a north-country clergyman from the region of Scotland, which far later begot Thomas Carlyle; but he died just before Jonson's birth, and his mother, remarrying beneath her, her son was "poorly brought up." To the famous antiquary, William Camden, Jonson's tutor at Westminster School, the poet owed his induction into the classics and perhaps much of the bias of his subsequent studies. His poverty prevented his going to either university, yet he became by his own diligence one of the best read of English scholars. After brief service abroad as a soldier, Jonson began his converse with the theater as an actor and playwright in the employ of Henslowe. But a duel, in which he slew a fellow actor and for which he suffered imprisonment, narrowly escaping the gallows, severed his relations with Henslowe for a time and thrust him into a wider field. Tradition relates that Shakespeare encouraged young Jonson. Certain it is that *Every Man in His Humor* was staged in 1598 by Shakespeare's company, Shakespeare himself acting a part in it: which, unhappily, we do not know, but the elder Knowell has been suggested.[1] *Every Man out of His Humor, Cynthia's Revels,* and *Poetaster* followed in the three succeeding years with varying popular success. These plays are known especially as Jonson's dramatic

Ben Jonson

---

[1] The order of the actors is that of their precedence in the company and does not correspond with the order of the *dramatis personœ*.

satires and mark not only the poet's further practice of
the comedy of humors, but likewise his capital contributions to the *poetomachia,* or war of the theatrical poets,
of which more below.

Jonson and
the classics

Jonson began really in the manner of Chapman, writing
in *The Case Is Altered,* which preceded *Every Man in His
Humor* and was never acknowledged, a better comedy of
its kind than most of Chapman's. But he soon developed
his strong satirical bent and an originality of plot and
characterization beyond classical or other models. There
is a duality, so to speak, about Jonson which we must
recognize if we are to understand him; and thus far we
have met him only as a scholar, applying his scholarship
to the writing of tragedy on Roman historical subjects.
But Jonson lived in the midst of Elizabethan life and knew
it intimately from the tavern to the court. Moreover,
he was a part of that life and observantly critical of it.
In his art as a dramatist Jonson was from the first a man
with a theory, which he frankly avowed and aired in practice on every occasion. He was intimately acquainted
with the classics not only of Rome, but likewise of Greece;
and, like most men who intelligently know them, he found
in them guidance, example, and inspiration. But it is a
mistake that no one really knowing Jonson will make, to
suppose that he was a reactionary theorist, deriding his
own time and hypercritical as to it. Jonson was impatient
of anything but the best; although he believed in adapting
the old to changed conditions, while he knew that there was
much to learn from the past.[1] It was out of his deep
knowledge of ancient theory and practice plus a keen
satiric observation of life about him, then, that Jonson
evolved his famous comedy of humors which through the
comedy of manners, practiced in many varieties and modi-

[1] See, as to this especially, the Introduction, *Every Man Out of His
Humor.* A sane and scholarly discussion is that of P. Simpson, "The
Portraiture of Humours," in his ed. of *Every Man in his Humor,* 1919,
xxxvi-lxiv.

fications after him, profoundly affected English drama for
generations to come.[1]

In Jonson's comedies, character develops incident, not
incident character. In contrast to Shakespeare but wholly
in accord with ancient theory, the author's attitude and
that of the spectator is not sympathetic with the characters, but critical of them and judicial. For which reason
a certain detachment is demanded of Jonson's readers that
many find it difficult to give. But to proceed more specifically to his theories, a "humor," according to Jonson, is a
bias of disposition, a ruling trait, such as governs the
nature of a man and shapes his conduct and his story.
This ruling trait Jonson used alike to emphasize and to
simplify complexity of character and reduce it, so to speak,
to its most striking feature, if not always its lowest denomi-
nator. Brainworm in *Every Man in His Humor* sets out
to fool and manage everybody. Bobadil is ruled by a
ridiculous habit of exorbitant boasting; Epicure Mammon
by a magnificent greed to be a grandee. Jonson confirmed
a practice at least as old as the moral play of naming his
personages to suggest each his salient "humor": Fastidious
Brisk, Morose, Asotus (the prodigal) Fungoso (the upstart). But he is careful to disclaim the making of some
triviality of speech or dress a "humor," although his imitators readily fell into this perversion of his idea. Jonson,
too, succeeded measurably in keeping his "humorous"
personages individual and from falling into mere types, in
which again his imitators were not always so successful.
But Jonson did not escape from the logic of his adaptation
of the comedy of the ancients to English conditions which,
with the simplification of character to a trait and a worship of wit and cleverness, divides the world into a clever
folk and their dupes, the knaves who exploit things and
the fools who are exploited. With a sturdy sense of right
worthy of admiration, and a penchant for moralizing al-

The
theory of
"humors"

---

[1] Despite the learned opinion of Professor C. R. Baskerville, *English
Elements in Jonson's Comedy,* I cannot but agree with Mr. Simpson that
Jonson "had no English theories to guide him." *Ibid.,* xxxix.

most as strong as his irresistible itch to satirize all things, it is somewhat remarkable that Jonson should have fallen into this worship of mere intellectual cleverness, however this worship continues in a cult, far less honestly avowed, in the several generations that have followed him.

The "War of the Theaters" The novelty of *Every Man in His Humor* took the town. In a plot of his own invention Jonson showed himself a master of the art of comedy, of ready witty dialogue, and of this new kind of satirical characterization. But his success encouraged him arrogantly to point his succeeding play, *Every Man out of His Humor*, with personal satire; and, whether he was actually the aggressor or not, the poet was soon involved with his fellow playwrights, especially Marston and Dekker, in a merry theatrical war, conducted by means of play retaliating on play. For the details of this episode the reader must be referred elsewhere.[1] Suffice it here to say that Marston, the reviver of the revenge play and an aggressive satirist after the manner of Juvenal, appears to have been Jonson's chief opponent, supposedly alluding to Jonson and more or less lampooning him in *Histriomastix*, an unacknowledged drama of 1599, *Antonio and Mellida* and other plays. Jonson retaliated in *The Case Is Altered*, in *Every Man in His Humor*, and more especially in the three dramatic satires just named, mixing literary criticism with personal lampoon, by no means confined to Marston, from the first; and Dekker was called in later in his *Satiromastix*, the hurried adaptation of a chronicle play on William Rufus, to reply to Jonson's *Poetaster*.[2]

Shakespeare and the "war" A list of the several other plays which have been variously thought to reflect this ebullition of personal satire in the playhouses is not for a picture on this scale. Of more interest is the question whether Shakespeare could have had anything to do with the "war." Or perhaps,

[1] See especially *Poetaster* and *Satiromastix* edited together, 1913, by J. H. Penniman, with an excellent introduction in which the "War of the theaters" is admirably treated.
[2] Marston's hand has been found by some in *Satiromastix*.

to put it more aptly, how could Shakespeare in active practice of his profession have escaped being involved in an affair so notorious and so much discussed? Shakespeare's Chamberlain's company acted Jonson's *Every Man out of His Humor* and *Poetaster*. *Poetaster* was also acted by the Chapel children at Blackfriars, and they acted *Cynthia's Revels* there as well. Marston's plays were staged by Paul's boys, and so was Dekker's *Satiromastix* privately, but publicly by the Chamberlain's men also. At Christmas time of this same year, 1601, a play called the second part of *The Return from Parnassus* was acted by students of St. John's College, Cambridge, in which the "war" is clearly alluded to and Burbage and his fellow actor Kempe (as notable for his comedy parts as was Burbage for tragedy) are mimicked on the stage. "Few of the university pen plays well," declares Kempe to Burbage:

> They smell too much of that writer, Ovid, and that writer, Metamorphosis, and talk too much of Proserpina and Jupiter. Why here's our fellow Shakespeare, puts them all down: aye, and Ben Jonson, too. O that Ben Jonson is a pestilent fellow: he brought up Horace giving the poets a pill: but our fellow Shakespeare hath given him a purge that made him beray his credit.

The "pill" forms the climax of the action of Jonson's *Poetaster*. The "purge" has been variously interpreted to mean Dekker's *Satiromastix*, which, though on the other side of the quarrel, was acted by Shakespeare's company, or to refer to a play of Shakespeare's, possibly *Troilus and Cressida*.[1] Finally we have the famous reference to the "war" in Hamlet's conversation with the players from which it appears that "a certain company of boy actors, who are likened for their forwardness to a nest full of fledgling hawks, are in great popularity for their high-pitched eloquence and for the satirical intent of their plays.

[1] On the whole topic see Penniman, as above, and the many authorities there cited. Professor Tucker Brooke is conspicuous in rejecting most of the opinions as to the "war," and surmizing last parts of *Hamlet* as containing Shakespeare's contribution.—*The Tudor Drama*, 1911, pp. 372 onward.

There was controversy between them and other companies, and the town did not hesitate to set them ('tarre them') like dogs upon each other, and to grant that the boys, who apparently looked down upon their opponents' theaters as 'common stages,' had the better of the argument." And Hamlet's (which is Shakespeare's) kindly comment on it all is:

> Will they not say afterwards, if they should grow themselves to common players . . . that their writers do them wrong to make them exclaim against their own succession?

Personal satire in the drama

Personal satire was no new thing on the Elizabethan stage. Nash had fallen into difficulty about his now lost play, *The Isle of Dogs,* acted, it would seem, at the Swan by Pembroke's men in the summer of 1597.[1] It has been surmised that Jonson had a hand in the writing of this comedy as well as in the acting of it. He was in prison with others for it. Jonson's quarrel with Marston has been thought, too, to link backward to earlier representations and satirical allusions of the former to Gabriel Harvey, Spenser's friend, and to Samuel Daniel, the court poet who appears to have aroused the enmity of Jonson from the first.[2] However, when all has been said which ingenious scholarship can devise in the way of identifications of person and incident, the "war" really resolves itself into one of several efforts at novel and startling attractions, staged by those who revived the boy companies in their efforts to take over to themselves the cream of the theatrical business from their adult competitors. It adds to our wonder to think of these difficult satirical plays as acted by children. How far the whole thing was personal is also difficult to say. Jonson told Drummond that he had quarrels with Marston, beat him, and took his pistol away from him. He also designated Dekker a rogue. But

---

[1] Chambers, iii, 453-455. As to the probable subject-matter of this play, see Nash's *Summer's Last Will,* line 779, "The ship of fools would have staid to take in fresh water at the Isle of Dogs."

[2] Penniman, as above, xxxii.

this was in the free talk of intimates long after.[1] The "war" was practically over by the end of 1602. And strange as it may appear to us in reading the plays involved, the town awarded the victory, not to Jonson, but to his opponents. In an incredibly arrogant and self-complaisant *Apologetical Dialogue* (only published, however, in 1616 when *Poetaster* was collected into his folio), Jonson withdrew haughtily from the fray and turned his dramatic talents, as we have seen, to tragedy. That the "war" could have been no very serious matter even to the principals involved is clear, as we find Jonson joining his friend Chapman and his "enemy" Marston in the writing of *Eastward Ho* only three years after.

Leaving Jonson for the moment, let us turn to the work in comedy of his friend, George Chapman, which in some respects more nearly resembles his own than that of any of his contemporaries. The chronology of Chapman's earlier work is a matter of some difficulty, owing to the current practice of changing the name of a play between acting and publication, as well as to Henslowe's exasperating habit of identifying for himself any play by any catch phrase or character that might recall it to his mind. Thus Henslowe's *Comedy of Humors*, of 1597, is doubtless the play that we have under title of *A Humorous Day's Mirth*, and *All Fools* was known by at least two earlier titles. The use of the word "humor" in a title two years before Jonson's employment of it is allaying; but the play that we have is "pure comedy of intrigue." Chapman's earliest extant dramatic work, *The Blind Beggar of Alexandria*, a trivial comedy of great popularity in its day, was on the stage early in 1596. It corresponds in date with other

Chapman in comedy

---

[1] See *Drummond's Conversations with Ben Jonson* for this and other like examples of free talk. It is of interest to note that two recent writers view the war of the theaters very differently, Adams, *Shakespeare, 223,* making it a very real affair, with Jonson challenging Marston to duel and "the Chamberlain's men bent on revenge"; while Chambers, following Small, whose cue it was to differ with Penniman, minimizes identification with actual personages as far as possible. If Jonson dealt not in personalities in these plays, they must have been pointless in their own day. Jonson is not elsewhere chary of personalities.

comedies in which disguise is employed to an extravagant degree: *Look About You*, for example, and *John à Kent and John a Cumber*. Chapman's comedy is disfigured by a preposterous disregard for probability or the most rudimentary conception of ordinary human conduct. In addition to the comedies already mentioned, Chapman wrote *May Day, Sir Giles Gooscap*, and two comedies into which a fine romantic spirit enters, *The Gentleman Usher* and *Monsieur D'Olive*, concluding with *The Widow's Tears* about 1606. *All Fools* has been highly praised, and there is inventiveness of plot and cleverness of dialogue in it above Chapman's other comedies. With Roman comedy for his chief inspiration and frequently his immediate quarry, Chapman borrowed likewise from Italian comedy and was deeply influenced, of course, by the new comedy of humors as it developed in the hands of his friend, Jonson. Chapman's comedies are unequal, and, though uniformly well written, an atmosphere of unreality pervades certain of them, as if the poet regarded this pulling of the wires of intrigue and this dancing of the puppets of his clever devising as matters largely extraneous and bearing little relation to actual life. In comedy Chapman's greatest success is in his "humorous" figures, among them none more whimsical and delightful than Monsieur D'Olive, conceited, good-tempered, witty light-weight that he is, fooled into an embassy which never comes off and yet always master of himself and unnettled. In his romantic plays, too, the poet succeeds at times in giving to his personages a certain noble aloofness, such as that of Vendome in this same comedy, or the development of character under suffering, as in Strozza in *The Gentleman Usher*. A conspicuous position as a forerunner of tragicomedy and a high quality of excellence have been claimed for this last play.[1] As I reread it, I find it extraordinarily unequal, descending in tedious foolery below Chapman's wont; however, it contains passages of unusual beauty. The grace

[1] See T. M. Parrott, *The Plays of Chapman, the Comedies*, 758.

and fluidity of Chapman's blank-verse must be acknowledged, and the frequent happiness of his style. Chapman
is never easy reading, but seldom does he disappoint the
effort bestowed upon him.

Let us turn back once more to the notable period of the
appearance on the stage of Jonson's *Every Man in His
Humor*. Recent comedies were *The Two Angry Women
of Abingdon* of Porter and Haughton's *Englishmen for
My Money*. *The Merry Wives of Windsor*, too, is almost
precisely contemporary with Jonson's new departure in
comedy, and Dekker's *Shoemakers' Holiday* could not have
long preceded it. In these plays we may note several things:
English scene, localized to Windsor, Abingdon, London;
an effort to represent English contemporary manners
among tradesmen and the lesser gentry; and an endeavor
to make less of mere situation and intrigue and more of
character than had been common in comedy heretofore.
We may recognize in these earlier examples of the comedy
of manners several types: the good-humored and merely
realistic picture of English life, chiefly rural in *The Two
Angry Women*, localized to town or city by Haughton
and Dekker in the plays named above. Thirdly, there is
Chapman's contribution in which we feel the satire none
too serious and the personages none too real. Then comes
Jonson with the significant irony of the comedy of humors,
which, once launched, became a model more or less affecting
the graver comedy of his contemporaries. Ancient Pistol,
Falstaff himself, Malvolio, these are some of Shakespeare's
personages conceived in the method of "humors." Marston
fell into the mood at once, but gave a darker, more saturnine significance to "humor" in his original and gloomy
drama, *The Malcontent*, than was ever Jonson's even in
his dramatic satires. Marston, however, was quite capable
of employing comedy more lightly, as in *The Fawn* and in
The Dutch Courtesan, both of which fall somewhat later.
A quasi-romantic atmosphere hangs over these two comedies, which, like Chapman's *Monsieur D'Olive* and *The*

Jonson's "humors" and earlier comedy of manners

John Day

Gentleman Usher, lay the scene in foreign lands. Here, too, should be mentioned John Day, who began in Henslowe's mart with Chettle and Dekker, but lived to do choicer things. Day was a Cambridge scholar, but expelled for stealing a book, goes the report. His independent work ranges from the popular "historical" adventures of *The Blind Beggar of Bethnal Green* and imaginative travels dramatized, such as those of the three Shirley brothers, to light, humorous comedy, delightfully freed from the slightest contact with anything like the realities of life. There is a curious impersonality and aloofness about Day's writings, a feeling that he was either indifferent to popular praise or not quite in touch with his time. *Humor Out of Breath*, in its sprightly prose dialogue and bandying of wit, is reminiscent of the repartee of Lyly and *Love's Labor's Lost*. *The Isle of Gulls* indulges in satire of the king's favoritism for the Scotch, so patent that "sundry were committed to Bridewell in consequence." Day was of about Jonson's years and his work for the stage lies between 1600 and 1608. He is best remembered for his dialogue or characters, *The Parliament of Bees*, a delicate, original, and poetic piece of writing, but assuredly not within the widest category of drama. Bits of the dialogue of *The Bees* which occur in certain plays have been variously explained.[1] Widely differing as were all these writers of comedy, among them is not to be forgotten the name of Middleton, dramatic laureate, as I have called him, of the London citizen.

Middleton and the comedy of citizen life

Thomas Middleton was born in London about 1570, the son of a gentleman, and his education was a legal one, pursued chiefly at Gray's Inn. He became a pamphleteer, a writer of plays and especially of city pageants, holding later the post of chronologer to the city of London in 1620, vacated by Jonson. In 1602 Middleton was writing in the usual collaboration for the Admiral's men; and the assistance that he rendered Dekker in a welcoming

[1] Chambers, iii, 287.

entertainment for King James apparently led to the continuance of this collaboration. *The Honest Whore* concerns, in the minor plot, it will be remembered, a patient tradesman, one Claudio, sorely afflicted with a shrewish wife. Here Middleton appears, already following the lead of Dekker's comedy of London tradesfolk; however, both the Italian scene and a new spirit, scarcely to be described as other than heartless, contrast with that earlier and wholesomer mode. Dekker, in this departure, worked with another collaborator at least as early as any of Middleton's independent ventures. The three comedies, *Westward Ho*, *Eastward Ho*, and *Northward Ho*, are unmistakably of the citizen type and date successively 1603 and the two years following, the first and third by Dekker and Webster, *Eastward Ho* by Jonson, Chapman, and Marston in reconciliation after the theatrical "war" of which we have heard. The titles of the first two come from the well-known cries of the Thames watermen, calling for custom to Westminster or the city. *Northward Ho* extends the idea to a journey to a disreputable haunt in that direction. *Westward Ho* details the intrigue of three idle citizens' wives, their unmasking and the counter-unmasking of their precious husbands who are no better than they. *Northward Ho*, which is of similar material, supposedly satirizes Chapman under the ridiculous scholar Bellamont, and doubtless raised less indignation among his genial fellow dramatists than among modern critics, in whom the proprieties hold greater sway. Both plays are devoid of any moral standard, and to criticize them for the want of it is as wide of the mark as to object to their copious flow of bawdy talk, one of the things that the Jacobean theater-goer wanted and got, alike from learned Jonson, reverend Chapman, crabbed Marston, and even from the gentle Shakespeare himself. The late Mr. Archer in an able, if somewhat exasperating, book remarks with much justice: "I suggest that it was not a merit, but an unpleasing defect in the Elizabethans, that they loved to hale into the foreground of their pictures all the unsavory incidents of life which modern sanitation tries to hold aloof, not only from our eyes, but from our nostrils." [1] But it is scarcely the business of the historian to lecture the Elizabethans on their sins, or to assume that because they yielded to the demands of their groundlings, we must assume airs of artistic superiority on the score of our comparative restraint and reticence. Without the slightest disposition to justify the coarseness and uncleanness of men like Marston, Middleton, and Webster, there are few things so superficially temporary as slang and vulgar colloquialism; and fastidiousness of speech, it is ever to be remembered, is not always identical with purity in thought.

The repertory of Middleton in comedy When Middleton, then, about 1604, threw himself fully into the production of this kind of comedy, it is impossible to say whether it was he who, after the type of the underplot of his own *Blurt Master Constable*, had perverted Dekker's wholesome picture of city life by a descent into the slums, or whether he was only following a practice already established in the collaboration of Dekker with Webster. At any rate, from this time onward, for some years, Middleton put out unaided a series of comedies, depicting the seamy side of London life, its usurers, sharpers, gamesters, prodigals, and women of bad life, unequaled in their easy fidelity to things as they are, and void alike of any redemption in beauty, generosity or magnanimity as of any serious moral reprobation. In *Michaelmas Term* and *A Trick to Catch the Old One*, *A Mad World, My Masters*, *The Roaring Girl*, and *A Chaste Maid in Cheapside*, we may wander as among the crooked, dirty byways of Elizabethan London, meeting a diversity of rascals, each amusing in his kind, tricking and tricked, shameless, cheerful, unregenerate, and human, ever sure of bustle, confusion, humor, filth, laughter, and diversion. If there is anything in the oft-repeated cry of the critics, "Write of the things about you, nearest to you. See, don't read; and,

[1] W. Archer, *The Old Drama and the New*, 1922, p. 79.

above all, invent your own stories," then this easy, competent, realistic and unbookish art of Middleton should find
a higher niche than criticism has yet accorded it; for his
personages are often repulsively true to an experience
that comes not to the modest man.   Middleton's plots run
easily, encumbered neither by the fine phrases of Chapman's moralizing nor by the wealth of satirical comment
with which Jonson embroiders even ordinary converse.
There was another Middleton who showed the aspiration
and the sense of the romantic and the passionate that was
the birthright of his age; but the Middleton of the citizen
drama, which particular thing he did better than anyone
else of his time, with all his readiness, lightness of plot,
and realization of personage, should be enough to put
merely realistic theme forever out of court.   Realism in art
carries not to the next generation unless preserved with
the salt of satire.   It is not a discredit to human nature
that we recoil from mere reality to seek the atmospheric
beauty of romance or the stimulating condiments of the
ironic.

Middleton's own work in citizen comedy continued **Followers**
throughout the reign of King James, *No Wit, No Help* **of**
Like a Woman's, take it all in all, quite the best of the series, **Middleton**
dating 1613, *Anything for a Quiet Life* and *A Match at
Midnight*, in which Rowley may have assisted, falling after
the twenties.[1]   But far earlier, the imitation of his comedy,
more or less tinged with the "humorous" vein of Jonson,
had become the ruling quality of the comedy of manners,
however tempered with a somewhat greater superficial refinement before long in the hands of Fletcher and those
who imitated him.   Passing *The Fair Maid of the Exchange*, about 1602, in its humor and pathos more of
the type of the earlier Dekker and possibly of Heywood's
authorship, we find the manner of Middleton imitated in
several comedies by minor writers, Edward Sharpham,

---

[1] *Anything for a Quiet Life* has recently been assigned largely to the
authorship of Webster. See H. D. Sykes, in *Notes and Queries,* September, 1921.

Robert Armin, and others.[1] Two of these Middletonian
comedies enjoyed a contemporary popularity above Middleton's own. These were David Barry's vulgar bustling
Ram Alley, 1607-08, and a few years later, *The City Gallant,* by John Cooke, rechristened *Green's Tu Quoque* from
a catch phrase in the clever impersonation of a humorous
Nathan servant, Bubble, by the comedian Thomas Greene. The
Field two breezy comedies of Nathan Field, *Woman Is a Weath-
ercock* and *Amends for Ladies,* also belong here.[2] Field,
as a fatherless schoolboy, had been kidnaped by the notorious Giles and forced to become a player. He made his
repute in Jonson's dramatic satires and is said to have
been noted for women's parts. Jonson, the story goes,
befriended him and taught him play-making. His comedies amply declare his master. Field gave up the stage
to become a stationer. The date of his death is unknown.

In 1605 Jonson returned to comedy. In the interval
he had gained for himself a recognized leadership at court
Jonson's in the devising of masques, a subject to claim us below.
Volpone This time Jonson wrote in collaboration, as we have seen,
with Chapman and Marston in the excellent comedy of
London life, *Eastward Ho,* which remains conspicuous in
its class for its honest acceptance of a sound moral standard in its telling contrast of the careers of the good and
the bad apprentice. In conduct of plot as well as in the
success of its personages this play rises so well above the
best work of the other collaborators that it is difficult not
to assign to Jonson a major share in the planning, if not
in the writing, of it.[3] The following year witnessed the
performance of *Volpone,* in some respects the most powerful and surprising production of Jonson's pen. The

[1] Sharpham, who was of the Middle Temple, wrote two comedies, *The
Fleir,* 1606, and *Cupid's Whirligig,* 1607; he died of the plague in the next
year. Armin was an actor and satirical writer. His only certain play is
Two Maids of Moreclack, 1609. As to Sharpham, see M. W. Sampson in
J. M. Hart Studies, 1910.

[2] Field's two comedies date 1609 and 1611. The dramatist's name appears to have been Nathan and not Nathaniel, who may have been a
brother and the bookseller.—Chambers, ii, 316.

[3] See, however, T. M. Parrott, *Chapman,* Comedies, 841-848.

story is that of the Fox, a Venetian schemer and grandee who pretends the approach of death, in order to receive the gifts (really bids for heirship to him), of several scoundrels, appropriately designated by the Italian words for the crow, the raven, and the vulture. Volpone is attended by a clever, conscienceless rogue, named Mosca the Fly, who in the end betrays his master; and the latter overreaches himself in the very triumph of his villainy. The play ends with the moral discomfiture and punishment of practically the entire *dramatis personæ*. In *Volpone* Jonson put personal satire behind him, but maintained the method of "humors," while restraining its exuberance. At a recent revival in London of this famous comedy, well acted by professional actors, the effect was overpowering and the success complete.[1] The brilliancy of dialogue, the swiftness and sureness of movement and effective characterization, however it be that of caricature, literally carried away the audience. The atmosphere of depravity seemed not to hang so heavy as when the play is read, and the moral expectancy is not hopelessly outraged. It was interesting to note the surprise, the pleasure and immediate acceptance of this play by a cultivated and well-read woman, who had fallen into a prevalent error (on the part of those who do not read him) of confusing Jonson's physical weight with an alleged heaviness of style and dreariness of content.

In his subsequent comedies Jonson reverted to English scene, even transplanting the setting of *Every Man in His Humor*, on the reprinting of it in the folio of 1616, from Italy to England. *The Silent Woman* was written in 1608. It is a huge farce the dénouement of which contradicts both words of the title; a splendid fabric of improbabilities so logically built one upon the other that the question of reality enters not into criticism. Two years later came *The Alchemist*, most popular of Jonson's comedies, satirizing alike the charlatan and his dupes in

Comedies of Jonson's maturity

[1] That of the Phœnix Society, in May, 1923.

their contributory rascality, in a series of scenes woven together into a whole constructively all but perfect. Lastly in genial, vulgar, robust *Bartholomew Fair*, 1614, we cannot doubt that Jonson came closest to an actual picture of London low life as it disported itself at that notorious, recurrent and disreputable festivity. In this Rabelaisian comedy Jonson laughs more broadly and moralizes less than in any of his plays. And yet none of his satire is keener or more to the point than that in which the hypocritical Puritan Zeal-of-the-Land Busy is held up to ridicule, that Puritan who, with the realities to back him, was only too soon to prove no laughing stock to the playwrights and their fabrics of facile imagination.

Jonson's art in comedy Several things call for comment in these famous comedies of Jonson. First, their essential originality in the face of a constant and openly avowed employment of "the substance or riches of others" to his own use. Plautus, Aristophanes, Ovid, Tacitus, and orations of Cicero, a satire of Horace, an episode from Lucian, a phrase from Martial, even a situation from a modern Italian comedy of Bruno, all are rifled, woven into the fabric of his plays, only to be bettered in the process.[1] From his immediate contemporaries alone, especially in drama, did Jonson disdain to borrow. And he held their amateurishness and empirical practice in undisguised contempt. Vastly in contrast is this alchemical transmutation of the immediate small riches of others to Shakespeare's faithful rendering of some old story, transfigured by the radiance of his genius into something wholly new. Again we note in Jonson's original plots a constructive excellence quite beyond that of any of his contemporaries. Huge and elaborate as are some of these dramatic contrivances of his, once under way, they move with an amazing ease and smoothness. Commonly the Jonsonian comedy, after ancient example, is pivoted on some one dynamic personage

---

[1] On the subject see "Jonson and the Classics" in the present writer's *Foreign Influences in Elizabethan Drama*, 1923.

who starts all the scheming and devising, the rest of the *dramatis personæ* falling into two groups, his passive or his protesting victims. It is thus that Face runs *The Alchemist*, Brainworm *Every Man in His Humor*, and the Fox, with his Fly, *Volpone*. And at times Jonson so admires these active creatures of his imagination that he condones their moral delinquencies in consideration of their wit; for in his heart, like many another moralist, Jonson hated stupidity beyond any rascality if only it contrived to involve cleverness. The characterization of Jonson's best comedies escapes mere type, despite the theory on which it is based; and this is due to the observant realist in the poet who studied the men about him assidu-ously with an eye for absurdity, pretense, and other raw material of satire unequaled in literature outside a very few names. The bias of Jonson's power, as of all veritable satire, lies in a moral robustness that we cannot but feel, despite the fascination which successful chicanery exer-cises upon him. Jonson once reported to Drummond that, "of all styles, he loved best to be called honest," and an essential honesty is the basis of Jonson's work. Lastly, the brilliancy, wit, and complete adaptability of Jonson's diction is not to be forgotten. Rarely is he difficult in verse or in prose because of any obscurity or intricacy of thought or expression, although his reader is often on the stretch because of his learning, agility, and the copiousness of his allusion and illustration. Jonson's success was, save for Shakespeare's alone, the greatest of his time. None was held in greater repute or exercised a stronger influence on his own or following generations. All the gifts of talent were his, even poetry, though we find little intrusion of it, where it does not belong, into these comedies of "humors." But there are greater gifts even than those of the highest talent and learning, and only one of Jonson's contemporaries was fully possessed of them.

191

CHAPTER X

THE STAGE AND ITS CRAFT

King James
and the
companies
of players

WITH the accession of King James, the London theatrical companies came under the royal patronage:
the Lord Chamberlain's as the King's, the Admiral's as
Prince Henry's, the Earl of Worcester's as Queen Anne's
men. In the royal patent to the King's players Shakespeare's name stands second in the list of nine actors,
that of Burbage following, Laurence Fletcher's leading.
Fletcher, who had not been previously connected with the
Chamberlain's men, was already in favor with the new king
before his coming to England and was perhaps accountable
for the early patent which this company procured in
advance of its rivals. The other members of the company
at this time were Phillips, Heminge, Condell, Sly, Armin,
and Cowley. From time to time new names appear in the
list of the King's men—Lowin, Cooke, Osteler, Field, and
Taylor—some of them destined to become leaders in the
"quality." Shakespeare seems not to have acted after
1603;[1] but Burbage continued the leading tragedian to
his death in 1619, and Heminge and Condell lived to sign
the introductory matter prefixed to their friend's collected
plays, in 1623, and to appear in a new patent, granted to
the company by King Charles, two years later. Under
King James's patent each player received an annual wage
of £3. 6s. 8d., besides such rewards as were customary
when the company played at court. A picturesque detail
of their office as servants to His Majesty was their livery
of a scarlet doublet, cloak, and hose, with the royal arms

---

[1] That is the year of his acting in *Sejanus*. There is no later list with
his name as an actor.

and cognizance embroidered on the sleeve, for which an allowance was provided, as we learn from the entry in the books of the Lord Chamberlain.[1] Moreover, leading members of the company, in accordance with the custom of Elizabeth's reign, were appointed Grooms of the Royal Chamber; and on extraordinary occasions, such as the entertainment, at Somerset House, of the ambassadors of Spain and Austria, in 1604, acted as attendants on these important guests. The profession of the player had advanced from the days of "rogues and vagabonds" to recognition such as this. But where could King James have found better-mannered men to wait on princes, or more adaptable?[2]

Up to 1608 the King's players acted only at the Globe on the Bankside. In that year, Burbage resumed the lease of the theater in Blackfriars which he had given to Evans and his children of the Chapel; and thenceforward the King's men acted at both houses, at Blackfriars especially in winter. In 1613, the Globe was burned, only to be rebuilt on a larger scale. But towards the end of the reign, Blackfriars supplanted the Globe in popularity and became the chief playing place of the company. While Jonson, Webster, and lesser authors wrote at times for the King's men within the lifetime of Shakespeare, it was John Fletcher who succeeded to Shakespeare's place as the leading dramatist of the company and the age; and in the reign of Charles, Massinger briefly assumed that position and Shirley upheld it to the end. Besides these, and Jonson at times, Ford, Davenant, and Brome all wrote for the King's men, whose repertory had become a valuable one and was carefully protected from the inroads of other

The King's players [marginal note]

[1] Adams, *Shakespeare*, 358, quoting *The Officers of England Collected in Anno 1608*, a manuscript recently sold in New York.

[2] An interesting picture of the Somerset House Conference, often reproduced, hangs in the National Portrait Gallery; E. Law, *Shakespeare as a Groom of the Chamber*, 1910, p. 21, prints in facsimile the entry in the accounts of the "Treasurer of the Chamber" as to the payment made to the King's players for waiting and attending on the Constable of Castile, in August, 1604.

companies and piratical publishers. The leadership of the King's company during both reigns was safe and beyond assail, a primacy due, we may well believe, to practical business sagacity as well as to the excellence of the plays which the King's players habitually offered.

Successors to the Admiral's men

Among rival adult companies a chief continued the sometime Admiral's men who acted at the Fortune under the patronage of Prince Henry and afterward of the Palsgrave who married the Princess Elizabeth. The Fortune was owned by Alleyn, who had now ceased to act, and was let to his tenants under various conditions, at length in 1618, at an annual rental of £200. In 1621 the Fortune, like the Globe, was destroyed by fire, but was soon re-erected as "a large round brick building." Samuel Rowley was an actor-playwright of this company, and Dekker, Middleton, and Field wrote for it. In 1630 it took for patron the infant Prince Charles and thereafter occupied at times other theaters, the Red Bull and Salisbury Court playhouse among them. The Red Bull was a large open-air house erected in 1605 at the upper end of St. John's Street in the parish of Clerkenwell. The Salisbury Court playhouse was only built in 1630, a private house in St. Bridges, Farringdon without.

The Queen's players

The Earl of Worcester's men, towards the close of the reign, had variously occupied the old Boar's Head Inn and the Curtain. On becoming Queen Anne's players, they leased the Red Bull; and, later, in 1617, occupied the new Phœnix, or Cockpit, in Drury Lane, a playhouse of private type, perhaps continuing the Red Bull as their public playing place. The leader of the Queen's men was Thomas Greene, a popular comedian; their most famous author, the prolific Thomas Heywood. On the death of Queen Anne in 1619, the company fell into difficulties. Some were licensed as the King's Revels, and others went over to other companies. There was much litigation, the details of which are difficult to interpret, but which furnish us almost our only information.

An important later company of the time of King James Other companies was the Lady Elizabeth's, which, uniting with "Rossiter's second Queen's Revels," made a gallant effort at the new Hope theater with Jonson's *Bartholomew Fair* to attain a position of leadership. This was in 1614 and the Hope was the latest of the circular public theaters on the Bankside. Field was an actor and playwright for this company; but vicissitudes carried it at length away to the provinces. In its brief day of success the second Queen's Revels staged other important plays, of Beaumont and Fletcher, of Middleton, Rowley, and Ford, and acted, next to the King's men, most frequently at court. Henslowe died in 1616, Alleyn ten years later, and the stage now ceased to know a financial dictator. In the reign of Charles I, Christopher Beeston most nearly succeeded to this place of manager's control. It was he who ruled the new Queen Henrietta's company which acted usually at the Cockpit.[1] His repertory was the best, next to that of the King's men, and included most of the writers represented in the rival list.

It remains to recount in brief the activities of the boy The Chapel children and Blackfriars companies. On the accession of James, the successful Children of the Chapel, acting as Blackfriars, became the Queen's Revels. The poet, Samuel Daniel, then newly in favor at court, was appointed to license the company's plays; and Marston, now a sharer, became one of its poets. But it was not long before his *Dutch Courtesan* and Daniel's own *Philotas*, 1604, brought the company into suspicion; and *Eastward Ho*, 1605, for ridicule of the Scots, if not of the royal brogue, sent Chapman and Jonson to prison. Marston, who was the real culprit, escaped by flight, but in 1606 sold his share, and the company was officially deprived of its royal title. However, the children continued to act under a new manager, but only to fall into new difficulties on account of Day's satiri-

---

[1] Beeston was owner of the Cockpit from 1617 to 1637, when he was succeeded by his son. There he housed several companies successively.— Chambers, ii, 302.

cal comedy, *The Isle of Gulls*, which gave offense at court. In the next year this series of indiscretions was crowned in Chapman's *Charles, Duke of Byron* by the representation of the King of France on the stage in unseemly domestic altercation. The French ambassador complained and the suppression of the company followed. It was at this juncture that Burbage resumed his lease of Blackfriars, and this playhouse remained thereafter, as we have seen, the winter theater of the King's men.[1]

Paul's boys and their successors As to Paul's boys, they had ceased playing for some reason about 1591, but are heard of again in 1600 and onward up to 1606. Jonson, Marston, Middleton, Chapman, Dekker, Webster, and Beaumont all wrote for them on the little stage of their "singing school" "behind the Convocation house"; and they produced there some of the most important plays of their time, appearing, too, occasionally at court. Disbanded in the next year and their master bribed that the company should no longer act, a new troupe was formed, known as the King's Revels, with a playing place "somewhere in Whitefriars." This has been identified with that projected by the poet, Michael Drayton, for which a theater was constructed out of certain rooms of the old Whitefriars' Monastery, much as Farrant had converted parts of Blackfriars.[2] In his venture Drayton associated a moneyed man named Woodford, who, retiring, sold his shares to David Lord Barry, a son of Viscount Buttevant, and an aspirant to dramatic authorship; and the two authors engaged Martin Slater, a well-known actor, to manage the new company.[3] Their repertory included Day's lively comedy, *Humor Out of Breath,*

[1] Ibid., ii, 50-54; T. S. Graves, "Political Use of the Stage," *Anglia,* xxxviii. The former notes that the boy companies were much more closely under the influence of their poets than the adults and that their plays came more readily into print.

[2] Adams, *Playhouses,* 312; also Chambers, ii, 66, and *New Shakspere Society's Transactions,* 1887-90, p. 269.

[3] A mistake of generations' standing describes Barry as Lodowick. This was set straight by Adams in *Modern Philology,* ix, 1912, and the identification of Barry with the heir of Viscount Buttevant was made by W. J. Lawrence in *Studies in Philology,* 1917. Barry was but twenty-four when he died in 1610.

Middleton's satiric attack on an extreme sect of the Puritans, *The Family of Love*, Barry's own vulgar, vivacious *Ram Alley*, and Mason's *Mulleasses the Turk*, a blood-curdling melodrama. It is likely that Drayton, an old hand at play-making from his earlier converse with Henslowe, was ready to contribute as well. But the venture was short-lived; and the closing of all the theaters in 1606, because of the complaints as to Chapman's *Byron*, together with the plague which broke out immediately after, combined to wreck the new company and leave to posterity a couple of lawsuits disclosing the circumstances. In less than a year Drayton's company was no more, and the children who had been acting at Blackfriars, dispossessed by Burbage's resumption of his lease, took up the Whitefriars house, Robert Keysar and Philip Rossiter at their head. This company by 1610 had become a new Queen's Revels and Rossiter alone was in control. It is somewhat disconcerting to our sensibilities to learn that the King's men entered into an agreement with Rossiter to keep the Paul's playhouse silent at a "dead rent" of £20, that they might have no rival among the private theaters.[1]

By 1610 Rossiter with a new and second Queen's Revels had gained a practical monopoly of the children's activities. But the line between children's and adult companies had become by this time much obscured; and we find Rossiter's players joined, before long, with the Princess Elizabeth's men under Henslowe. In 1615, the indefatigable Rossiter organized a third Queen's Revels, for which, even, a new theater, Porter's Hall, near Puddlewarf in Blackfriars, was, it would appear, actually built; but an order of the Privy Council demolished it within the year, and the activities of the third Queen's Revels are to be traced thereafter only in the provinces. Finally in the late 'thirties Beeston organized a "King and Queen's Company" of boys and acted at the Cockpit. The fitful suc-

Later companies

---

[1] See the case of Keysar *vs.* Burbage, discovered by C. W. Wallace, *Nebraska University Studies*, 1910.

cesses of these various children's companies in their efforts to rival alike the combinations of Burbage and of Henslowe, constitute an interesting feature in the history of the stage. Their plays appear to have been addressed to more cultivated auditors, and they commanded the best dramatic talent among their writers. Indeed, save for Shakespeare alone, there is scarcely a name of note that does not appear among the writers for the children of Paul's or of Blackfriars.

"Representations" of the playhouse

Let us turn now to that vexed question, the probable construction of the stage of the Elizabethan public playhouse. Unhappily for anything approaching exactitude of detail, no authoritative picture of a pre-Restoration stage is extant, and the only contemporary description involving any degree of fullness is imaginatively embellished to the detriment of mere information. As to pictures, there are the two little cuts on the title pages, respectively, of *Roxana*, 1632, and *Messalina*, 1640; but they come very late for generalizations as to the whole period, and exhibit scarcely any detail; while the frontispiece of *Kirkman's Wits*, originally printed in 1662 and long miscalled "the interior of the Red Bull," has been shown to be an improvisation of Commonwealth times, exhibiting contradictory features of both public and private playhouses.[1] There is left for us, then, only the well-known sketch of the Swan theater, about 1596, from the drawing of John De Witt; and even this has been discredited, if somewhat hastily, as second hand and wanting in certain features of which we may feel sure, at least as to other playhouses, from other evidence.[2] As to description, there is the passage in the English *Wagner Book* of

[1] *Messalina* in this connection was first mentioned by Reynolds, *Some Principles of Elizabethan Staging*, 1905.
[2] Lawrence in *Englische Studien*, xxxii, 36, 1903; but see H. Child in *Cambridge History of English Literature*, vi, 292; also Chambers, ii, 527, and 519 for fuller details as to these cuts. W. Creizenach, *The English Drama in the Age of Shakespeare*, 1916, pp. 374 and 379 reproduces two interesting Dutch analogues of the structure of the Elizabethan stage, dating 1561 and 1539.

1594, headed "the tragedy of Faustus seen in the air and acted in the presence of 1,000 people of Wittenberg, Anno 1540." Shorn of its imaginative ornament and fantasy, this passage reads:

They might distinctly perceive a goodly stage to be reared . . . upon many a fair pillar. . . . Therein was the high throne wherein the king should sit and that proudly placed, . . . and round above curious wrought chairs for diverse potentates. There might you see the groundwork at one end of the stage whereout the personated devils should enter in their fiery ornaments, made like the mouth of an huge dragon. . . . At the other end in opposition was seen the place wherein the bloodless skirmishes are so often performed on the stage, the walls . . . environed with high and stately turrets; . . . and hereat many in-gates and out-gates, . . . many large banners and streamers were pendant. Briefly nothing was there wanting that might make it a fair castle. There might you see, to be short, the gibbet, the posts, the ladders, the tiring house, there everything which in the like houses either use or necessity makes common. Now above all was there the gay clouds *usque quaque* adorned with the heavenly firmament and often spotted with . . . stars. . . . This excellent fair theater erected, immediately after the third sound of the trumpets, there entereth in the Prologue attired in a black vesture and making his three obeisances, began to show the argument of that scenical tragedy.[1]

During the last few years consideration of the several descriptions of English theaters by foreign visitors and other matter, together especially with a careful examination of the stage directions and the action of plays of the whole period, have done much to further our knowledge of the Elizabethan stage. And the correlation of that stage with mediæval staging and the after-developments of the Restoration picture stage, as well as the relations of all this to the theories and practices of early staging abroad and the development of the masque in England—

Investigation as to the Elizabethan stage

[1] This passage is apparently not in the original German, but is an addition of the English translator who is otherwise conversant with the English stage. See A. E. Richards, "Studies in English Faust Literature," *Literarhistorische Forschungen*, 1907, xxxv, 67-69.

all have been helpful in a difficult subject.[1] Most recently we have Dr. Chambers's diligent and exhaustive inquiry into the problem anew, the distinguishing merit of which lies in his grouping of the evidences of the plays in a manner more historically methodic and complete than that of his predecessors.

Construction of the theater

The Elizabethan popular stage was a platform thrust into the middle of a yard: in Alleyn's Fortune the thrust was forty-three feet in a building along fifty-five feet square within, so that the spectators stood around the stage instead of sitting before a picture, set, as with us, in a frame. Auditors even sat, at times, on the stage itself and in balconies above it, as well as before it.[2] All this lent a nearness and an intimacy unknown to our separation by curtain and footlights of the actor from his auditors. A second feature of the Elizabethan stage was the tiring house which backed the stage and, constructed primarily for the utilitarian purposes of a dressing room and a place in which to keep properties, served as a permanent background, whatever temporary modifications by way of hangings or properties might be made before it. The tiring house was provided with two doors, one on either side of a central structure which, supported by pillars and roofed for protection from the weather, covered, if we are to trust the De Witt drawing, only the middle part of the stage.[3] This structure was equipped with a contrivance somewhat like a false ceiling, stretching across in front and beneath the roof and known as the "heavens," which simulated apparently a strip of sky by means of painted stars; and underneath it, across the stage and over the doors, ran a balcony or gallery divided into rooms known as the "lord's room," "twelvepenny

[1] See especially the excellent summary and critique of the subject up to its date by G. T. Reynolds, himself an important contributor, "What We Know of the Elizabethan Stage," Modern Philology, ix, 1911; and Chambers, iii, 1-154, with the incidental bibliographical references.
[2] See Reynolds, as above, 81; and C. R. Baskerville, "The Custom of Sitting on the Elizabethan Stage," Modern Philology, 1911.
[3] This structure was later suppressed. See the specifications for the building of the Hope theater, Henslowe Papers, 19.

room," and perhaps the "music room," as at St. Paul's. Somewhere beneath the general superstructure and below the level of the gallery, a curtain was arranged (though not represented in the Swan picture) ; and this curtain, when drawn, cloaked a third and middle entrance and divided the stage into a fore and after part.[1] (The drop curtain concealing the entire stage was totally unknown.) We have thus an outer and an inner stage, the two doors mentioned above disclosed and leading out on to the former even when the curtain obscuring the third and middle entrance at the back of the stage was closed. And we have, above, a balcony, often curtained, and practicable for use as an upper stage. To this we may add that the whole was surmounted by a turret from which the play was announced by a trumpet; and that certain contrivances must have been placed there as well as beneath the stage for the lowering and raising of properties.

As to all this most scholars agree; but here difficulties arise. Why should not the superstructure have covered the whole stage, as Chambers thinks?[2] Why may not the music room have been in another story above the balcony stage where Adams recently puts it?[3] Were the doors in a line, as they are represented in the picture of the Swan? Or were those on either side obliquely set as represented in Mr. Godfrey's reconstruction?[4] This would be a position almost inevitable, if such a stage were arranged in a circular or octagonal building. And what was their position forward? Was it these, or possibly other entrances still nearer the audience, as Chambers

Difficulties as to construction

[1] Reynolds's *What We Know*, 58, modestly states his contributions to the subject to consist in, (1) that "the curtain, at least in some theaters, did not conceal the whole end of the stage, but instead of hiding the doors, hung between them; that (2) instead of the usually accepted two doors . . . there were . . . three such entrances; and (3) that the curtain did not hide the balcony, which had a curtain of its own."
[2] Chambers, iii, 90.
[3] Adams, *Shakespeare*, 286.
[4] W. Archer, "The Fortune Theater," reprinted in *New Shakespeareana*, 1908, vii, 96.

queries in his diagrams, which developed later into the proscenium doors, as Lawrence thinks? [1]   Moreover, what was the nature, and especially the size, of the inner stage— that is, what proportion of the whole stage did the curtain mark off?   Did the inner stage fill the greater part of the floor space between the back and the supporting stage pillars, as the present writer once argued.[2]   Or was it a narrow corridor between the doors, a species of alcove, running back and taking in perhaps the depth of the tiring room itself at need, as Chambers suggests? [3]   Leaving the answers to these questions to develop with the subject, let us avail ourselves of the valuable results of this latter scholar's approach to the whole topic from a new angle, recognizing that we can only outline his conclusions, for the detailed evidences of which the reader must be referred to his book.

Settings of the public stage   Carefully distinguished chronologically and with the differences between private and public theaters in mind, the evidence as to the staging of plays in the latter declares for a system in which different localities were represented, not simultaneously as prevalently at court and in the plays of Lyly, but successively, each in its turn occupying the stage.   The method of representation was simple and suggestive, involving, besides a curtain run on a rod and hanging from beneath the balcony, the use of frames hung with arras and on occasion painted cloths, properties at times of considerable dimensions, to designate houses with practicable doors and windows, walls that could be leaped over, trees that could be climbed, besides lesser objects, thrones, arbors, gibbets, wells, and furniture.   Deliberate pause in the continuity of the action (within the act, at least) was avoided, undoubtedly in some cases, by the employment, during the action before it,

---

[1] Chambers, iii, 84, 85; Lawrence, "Proscenium Doors, an Elizabethan Heritage," ii, 157.

[2] "The Elizabethan Playhouse, *"Numismatic and Antiquarian Society of Philadelphia,* 1908, p. 155.

[3] Chambers, iii, 82-86.

of the part of the stage, back of the curtain, in which,
in close proximity to the tiring room, the tire-man might
prepare changes in the setting of the alcove, to be "discovered," as the word went, by the drawing of the curtain. That this was the only means by which scene succeeded scene, or even the more frequent method, is not supported by the evidence. Quite as often, if not more usually, continuity of action was sustained by a rapid change
of properties effected by lowering from above, raising from
under the stage, or thrusting forth from the tiring room
through a middle aperture of considerable dimensions.[1]
The actors themselves were doubtless employed, besides
more formal assistants, in a manner, more or less incidental to the action, in this shifting of pieces of property,
effecting such changes much as Hamlet is used to drag
off the dead Polonius, or Falstaff made to groan under
the heavy load of Hotspur's full-armored body.[2] While
it is not to be denied that there are scenes in these popular
plays which are not localized and might be acted practically without any setting, the number of such scenes is
perhaps much smaller than has sometimes been argued.
On the other hand, it may be accepted that there are scenes
of small interiors, studies, prisons, chapels, bedchamber
scenes especially, which from their nature are fittingly
set in a small space and often appropriately "discovered,"
as we have seen. But it is easy to exaggerate, too, their
number and to forget that many scenes suggesting an interior appear, when carefully studied, to have been managed on a full stage.

It would appear that neither before 1600 nor after,
was the action restricted to one "house" only at a given
time on the stage; though often, of course, one would

Change of scene

[1] "Enter a spruce courtier a horse-back," *Woodstock (1 Richard II)*,
iii, 2; and see *Soliman and Perseda*, i, iv, 47; "Enter Basilisco riding of
a mule." Chambers queries the bringing in of large pieces and notes the
occurence in the inventories of the Admiral's men of "i wheel and frame
in the siege of London," iii, 97. Adams, *Shakespeare*, 376 n, notes several
other cases of horses on the stage.

[2] Archer, *Quarterly Review*, ccviii, 454, finds over a hundred plays in
which dead bodies are removed by stage direction.

suffice. Such structures, where more than one, were usually contiguous or grouped, although they might stand
apart, like the two opposing inns of *The Merry Devil of
Edmonton,* or be conceived of as at a distance, one from
the other to be measured—Chambers calls it "foreshort-
ened"—as in *Bonduca* when the Roman army enters at
one side of the stage, out of sight of a rock "half a fur-
long off," visibly held by Caratach, before us in the center of the stage. Among the several kinds of scenes,
more or less carefully distinguished, it would seem that
out-of-doors scenes are by far the most numerous, including those of the open country, war scenes, garden
and park scenes, and such as are conceived as taking place
in some public spot within a city. These last are frequently the *locus* of threshold scenes which serve often
to evade the necessity of an interior setting (especially in
earlier plays) and offer an analogue to neo-classical Italian
staging. A tendency, in later plays, to make more use
of set interiors points, not to any increased employment
of the alcove for such purposes, but to a recognition that
its limitations as to size, distance from the body of the
house, and dinginess—even if lighted by back windows [1]—
marked it out as fit only to visualize the obscurity of a
cave or prison, " 'an unsunned lodge' or a chamber of
horrors." In a word, scholarship has now definitely disposed of the theory that the dramatic art of Shakespeare
and his fellows was seriously disturbed by any mechanical
necessity of alternating a scene behind the curtain with a
scene in progress before it, that the stage settings (imagined confined to the inner stage) might be leisurely arranged behind it.

Still there are queries that remain difficult to answer.
To what extent was there any attempt to harmonize the
various properties on the stage into a scenic whole? Where
was the wall placed which Romeo overleaps into Capulet's

---

[1] Lawrence, "Light and Darkness on the Elizabethan Stage," *Elizabethan
Playhouse,* ii, 1-22, and the following essay on windows in particular,
45-50.

over, the question of ordering it was commonly quite important, witness the chronicle histories, panoramic successions of scenes often with little cohesion save that of sequence in time, or the disjointed classical dramas of Heywood in which the *dramatis personœ* changes three or four times in process of the play. Of course there came to be far better things, and men like Jonson theorized as well as practiced an art of dramatic construction. But a great deal of time has been wasted in the application to our old drama of principles of an imaginary dramaturgy of which Elizabethan writers for the stage were far more innocent than our own children. Loosely told as loosely conceived, none the less the Elizabethan playwright demanded more help of his auditor in the exercise of the imagination as to atmosphere, place, and situation than we demand. Whether read or seen acted, the Elizabethan solicited the assistance of his auditors' understanding to the total effect to be produced, however well interpreted by the actor; and much was suggested, or left to be fitted in, where, in that lazy man's literature, the modern novel, all is told circumstantially and to repletion.

Again, the Elizabethan play was not only "a story told rather than realized," but there was an allowed and accepted manner—not to say mannerism—in the telling. Contempo- rary de- mands of the actor In a comparatively small auditory, with the audience packed close and none too tractable if not continually interested, the acting had to be direct, vigorous, and incessant; and individual effects, with a close succession of them, were far more important than consistency of parts or any sense of design, to be appreciated only by the lettered and the critical. The acting even of men like Burbage and Alleyn must have been far more declamatory and facially active than ours, and far more circumstantially realistic, for much more depended on it. An actor might be hissed off the stage for a want of skill in fence or for clumsiness in dancing the lavolta. For although the author's hearers might be as blind as he as to the

geography of Bohemia or the fitness of a striking clock
in the Rome of Brutus, they watched with critical acuteness the accuracy of the use of terms applicable to hawking or current gentlemen's games of chance, and judged
the writer less by his lore in antiquity than by his cleverness in topical allusion and passing slang. It is this quality of an absolute contemporaneousness that makes the
·best of these old plays so valuable a mirror of their age,
as it is the childlike oblivion on the part of their authors
(always excepting the conscious scholars) that leaves them
so fresh and unspoiled by literary affectations.

Idealism
and oppor-
tunism

And, indeed, it was just this experimental and un-
professional spirit of the better part of these old writers
that prolonged the old feud as to literature between classical idealists, like Sidney, dreaming of a past which had
really never existed, and the romantic opportunists, like
Shakespeare, who took everything for his own and made it
such by the daring of his genius. As the age advanced,
much was learned by practice and experience, and the
powerful influence of Jonson came to mean more and
more. Jonson was far more rationally for restraint and
the sense of design in the application of ancient practice
to English conditions than were ever the theorists, who
could see for English letters at large no future except
that which might be hoped decorously to come in the leading strings of classical imitation.

Eliza-
bethan
dramatic
construc-
tion

Constructively the drama improves in the reign of
James. Instead of a string of episodes more or less
loosely connected or the tossing together of two stories,
little related, there is a more frequent articulation of parts
and an effort at a completer unity. Aside from prologue
and epilogue, which are really parts extraneous, the older
drama was fond of certain other devices that fall without
the action. The induction is one such, as that in which
Sly the Tinker figures in *The Taming of the Shrew*. It
is significant that Shakespeare dropped off the conclusion of the older play, his source, in which Sly is returned

to finish his drunken sleep on the steps of the alehouse: it interfered with the completeness of the effect of the intervening story of Katharine. Jonson, from his almost Shavian itch to comment on everything that he wrote, is a prime offender in respect to this framing of his drama, and in some of his plays he even interpolates "inter-means," as he calls them, which, as in *Henry V* or *Pericles*, carry forward the action by way of narrative between the acts.[1] The Elizabethans were never sensitive as to continuousness in the action; and it is not often that the poet is as careful as is Shakespeare in *The Winter's Tale*, to indicate that Perdita from a babe has grown up to marriageable womanhood. In Stuart times, the masque, which had often been employed as a device of plot, came to be used as an embellishment often impairing the dramatic effect, or at least delaying the action, as in *Cymbeline*, for example.[2] There is nothing so dead as the unities, Aristotelian or Italian; and the wiser Elizabethans knew it and found in the success of their plays, often in open violation of all three, on an eager stage, a sufficient answer.

But if the drama improved constructively with the influence of Shakespeare, Jonson, and Fletcher fully upon it, the same cannot be said of characterization. The concluding chapters of this book will set this more fully forth; but without question there is a difference between the spontaneity that lays everything under levy for material, and the conscious art that comes with a realization of how much has gone before. The greatness of the dramatic structures reared by those who wrote in the reign of the great queen obscured to their successors the wideness of view which had been theirs; and these successors became imitative in their representations of character and repe-

Decline in characterization

[1] See especially *The Staple of News. Intermedii* of spectacle and dance were well known to the Italian stage. Cunliffe finds them an influence producing the English dumb show. *Modern Philology*, iv, 597.

[2] Dr. Furness used to remark, on reaching the scene (iv, 4), in his readings, in which the apparitions begin to appear to Posthumus, "At this point Shakespeare lost all interest in the story."

titious in episode and story, and less eager to find out
ways of their own.

Eliza-
bethan
insight into
human
nature Looking back once more at the age as a whole, it is
folly to expect of an art so spontaneous and unlabored
that deeply considered consistency, that pondered "philosophy of life," which we are accustomed to demand of
every second-rate novelist today. Not only did the old
playwrights mingle homely every-day ideas and, to us,
irrelevant mirth with the lofty diction of thrilling tragic
moments, but they admitted almost every conceivable in-
consistency, instability, and uncertainty into the make-up
of human nature, to the distress of the modern psycholo-
gist, as they awarded a frequently unequal distribution of
rewards and punishments, to the scandal of the moralist.
It is not to be denied that certain recent strictures as to
insufficient "motivation," rudimentary psychology, and
the lack of unity and continuity in Elizabethan conceptions of character are points well taken. And the efforts
of enthusiasts to justify every Shakespearean imperfec-
tion and follow up with admiration what Lowell once
called every "Elizabethan goose-print," have not improved
matters. Aside from the fact that no product of the romantic imagination can stand the acid test of what we
call scientific inquiry, it would seem wise to grant that
every art has its conventions—conventions of thought as
well as conventions of manner and style—and that equally
has every age, therefore, its own standard of judgment.
No Elizabethan, in all likelihood, was troubled in the least
by the easy credulity of Othello or Posthumus, by Olivia's
ready forgetfulness of the dead brother for whom she was
sorrowing, or by Oliver's sudden transformation from an
unbrotherly monster into a fit romantic lover for Celia.
The Elizabethan accepted all these things as belonging to
the sanctioned no-man's land of romance and the stage,
and as of substantially the same conventional fabric as
the aside, the soliloquy, deception by means of disguise,
eavesdropping for information, and the property machin-

ery of a lost letter, a charmed handkerchief, or a ring. And we fall into serious error about all these things, whether we seek to justify them as what we call "true to life," which they are not, or complain of them as serious blemishes on an art the essential verity and force of which carry such trifles lightly on its flood. The art of any age is justly to be appraised only on the basis of the accepted conventions of the life of that age; and the intro- spection and subtilized "motivations" of our contemporary fiction and drama are open to precisely the criticism that this is (perhaps a passing) convention, like the brash and unaccountable moods, passions, and changes so frequently deplored in the personages of the old drama. Are we altogether sure that in the abstract our incessant ques- tionings are any the less a convention than the Eliza- bethan criminal or other personage of quite unaccount- able conduct according to the canon of our latest psy- chiatrics? When all is said, the Elizabethan playwrights seem to know by an intuition which is far above the trial balances of experimental science where art is concerned, that the heart of man, enigmatic and unexplainable by generalizations in the abstract, is to be surprised and way- laid, at times in the individual, by the insight and sym- pathy of the poet. Making every allowance for an age, somewhat, but not so very, different from our own, and looking at this great literature of the past with all its faults and shortcomings, but looking at it as a whole, the present writer feels that he can place a more implicit reli- ance on the perception and comprehension of human nature, possessed by Shakespeare and his fellows at large, than he dare trust to a wilderness of psycho-analysts. But in this, perhaps, he proclaims his own limitations; for, if he dare claim some acquaintance with these old worthies of the stage, he must confess that his ear has been only too willingly deaf to the chatter of the wilderness.

CHAPTER XI

"Romance" and Tragicomedy

Tragi-comedy

THE word "romance" has become one of those counters in current language which by long and inexact usage has ceased almost to convey a meaning. And among several misapplications and inaccurate uses is that which applies the term "romances" to the latest three or four plays of Shakespeare, largely, it would seem, because they come under set definitions neither of comedy nor of tragedy. "Tragicomedy," declares Fletcher, in doubtless the earliest English effort to define it, "is not so called in respect of mirth and killing, but in respect it wants death, which is enough to make it no tragedy, yet brings some near it, which is enough to make it no comedy," [1] It is with no purpose either to defend or to enlarge the significance of either term that both are used in the heading of this chapter; but rather in a recognition of the fact that the distinctive feature of the plays of Beaumont and Fletcher and of those who came under their powerful influence is a certain heightening of sentiment, a mitigation of the realities, a greater dependence on chance and adventure, a more persistent search after the striking, the unexpected, the picturesque and theatrical, all of which we habitually associate with the word "romance." All this tends to obscure the old line of demarcation between the serious ethical ground of tragedy and the light-heartedness, or the irony, at least, which we associate with the comic spirit. Tragicomedy intensifies the emotions of comedy, but alleviates the moral rigors of the tragic. Tragicomedy is

[1] *The Faithful Shepherdess*, "To the Reader." For a discussion of the subject see F. H. Ristine, *English Tragicomedy*, 1910.

a bid to stir as with tragedy and please simultaneously after the manner of the comic. The demands of tragicomedy are less on the intellect, the taste and judgment, than on the emotions, a thoughtless glut of the eye and sedative of the feelings. Variety, activity, ingenuity, and excitement, rarely anything of that reminiscent pleasure that is the measure of veritable art. All this may be blanketed as of the motion, the unreality, the charm and the success of dramatic romance.

In Beaumont and Fletcher professional dramatic author- *Social status among the playwrights* ship reaches a new class, for both were gentlemen born, in an age in which a genuine importance attached to station. Sackville, Hughes, and their like were gentlemen entertaining their sovereign; to Gascoigne and Lyly the drama was only a means to court employment. Heywood, Marston, Chapman, Jonson, too, were of decent stock, but not socially recognizable. It was different with Beaumont, younger son of a justice of Her Majesty's Court of Common Pleas, descended of a line of distinguished lawyers and nobly connected; and with Fletcher, too, the son of the Bishop of London, a sometime favorite of his queen, although fallen from favor by an unwise second marriage and impoverished by munificence and unthrift. Indeed, it may be suspected that not a little of the eloquent tribute to the worth, however deserved, of Beaumont in particular, which graces the occasional poetry of the time, may be referable to a sense of the importance of his station, his condescension, as well as his art.

John Fletcher was born in 1579 and admitted to *John Fletcher and Francis Beaumont* Bene't College, Cambridge, in 1591. There is no record of his degree; but his was a literary family, as witnessed in the well-known contemporary work of his uncle, Dr. Giles Fletcher, and the latter's sons, Phineas and Giles the Younger, both of them eminent poetical followers of Spenser. The disfavor and death of his father in 1596 must have thrust John into the world and may well account for his leaving the university. At any rate, we have no word of him until his emergence as a dramatic writer, about 1606 or 1607. Beaumont was five years Fletcher's junior and matriculated at Broadgate's Hall, Oxford, after the manner of the time, when but twelve years of age. He, too, lost his father while yet a youth. But the justice was a man of substance, and young Beaumont's brother, coming into the estate, made ample provision for him, if not in the beautiful homestead of Grace-Dieu in Charnwood Forest, in some other way. The Beaumonts, too, were a literary family. Sir John became a poet of recognized repute and long survived the dramatist, his brother. The education of the sons was that of their ancestry. For after the university both were entered at the Inner Temple, where their father and grandfather had been benchers, Francis in 1600. The atmosphere of the Inns of Court was charged with drama and the young playwright could have had no better school. Beaumont began authorship in imitation of Shakespeare's erotic *Venus and Adonis,* and both brothers appear to have been intimate with Drayton. Unlike his friend Fletcher, Beaumont must have drifted into theatrical Bohemia out of choice and not necessity. There he met that potent spirit, Jonson, ever fond of young men and encouraging them. Tradition gives us the glimpse of a Bohemian *ménage* on the Bankside in which Beaumont and Fletcher shared like brethren, and only fortune bore them subsequently apart.[1]

Independent efforts of Beaumont and of Fletcher
The two were doubtless friends in the earliest years of King James; for we find both commending, in prefatory verses, Jonson's *Volpone,* in print in 1607. Both poets appear to have begun, independently and experimentally, Fletcher perhaps with *The Tamer Tamed* in an earlier version than that now extant, dating 1604, and Beaumont in *The Woman Hater,* in 1606. This latter play is frankly of the Jonsonian school of humors, but a promising pre-

[1] See G. M. Gayley, *Beaumont, the Dramatist,* 1914; and O. L. Hatcher, *John Fletcher, a Study in Dramatic Method,* 1905.

cursor, in its mirth and diction, of what was to come. It is suggestive, too, of the later inventiveness of Fletcher, that he should have chosen for so early an endeavor the topic of Shakespeare's *Taming of the Shrew*, with the tables, as we have seen, completely turned. And now each young author, still working independently, it would seem, was diverted to a more original venture, Beaumont in *The Knight of the Burning Pestle*, ridiculing, in rollicking parody and satire, the contemporary penchant for impossible romantic adventure and citizen love of it, and Fletcher in a poetic effort to place on the English stage that Italian potted flowering plant, pastoral drama. These plays were acted, respectively, in 1607 and 1608, and both by children's companies. And although both proved their worth on revival and have remained, for their respective and very diverse excellences, in high repute ever since, both failed in their day. The citizen playgoer could not endure to have his favorite absurdities ridiculed by a superior young playwright, however cleverly; while Fletcher, in his effort to be true to the poetic ideals of Guarini as he interpreted them for the English stage, defeated expectation, as he says, in an audience that looked for "a play of country-hired shepherds with curtailed dogs in strings." [1]

In these two plays the contrasted characteristics of "the twin dramatists" already appear, although not wholly to advantage, because the more serious and significant Beaumont is here given over to burlesque, and the lighter, more buoyant comedy spirit of Fletcher expresses itself only in the artifices of the pastoral. *The Faithful Shepherdess* is an exquisitely poetical play, and if we accept its delicate artificiality—which is much that of *Comus*—delightful.[2] Whether actually before their collaboration or not,

Characteristics of Fletcher

---

[1] *The Faithful Shepherdess*, "To the Reader"; see also Jonson's comment in *Conversations with Drummond*, ed. 1846, p. 4.
[2] The beauty and poetry of this play were a surprise to many who saw it acted by the Phœnix Society in London, in June, 1923.

Fletcher's *Monsieur Thomas* may be taken as the theme-giver of strictly Fletcherian comedy. Here at once we meet the incessant action, the struggle of wits, coincidence, and improbability overworked, but cleverly made to appear likely, the gayety, inventiveness, and bubbling optimism which characterize this resourceful playwright. And here, too, we have Fletcher's easy repetitious and mannered diction, his long loose line, his license of speech, and also his suggestive salaciousness. This last most disagreeable and persistent feature is recognizable as a blot on the beauty of *The Faithful Shepherdess*, in which the plan of the poem demands a representation of love in its gamut from sexual passion to a deification of chastity which is scarcely less distasteful to our modern spirit. Fletcher's method is that of heightened contrast, and this has been pleaded in extenuation in this particular case. But on the other hand, it may be surmised that Fletcher's license of speech, which is as reprehensible as Marston's nastiness and far more so than the mere healthy animalism of earlier times, is only one of his several concessions to the vulgar taste. The ultimate standard of Fletcher's art seems to have been solely the applause of his audience. This he gained as none, not even Shakespeare, had gained it before him; and, with Beaumont his coadjutor, he kept it for three generations.

The collaboration of Beaumont and Fletcher

It was about 1609 or 1610 that the famous collaboration of Beaumont with Fletcher began; and, as Beaumont married about 1613 and, retiring to the country, died in 1616, a month before Shakespeare, obviously the actual partnership could not have been of long duration. Face to face with this, we have the two folio editions of *The Comedies and Tragedies written by Beaumont and Fletcher*, 1647, and *Fifty Comedies and Tragedies*, 1679, and the total has been subsequently enlarged to some fifty-four or fifty-five dramas. The problem of this joint authorship has occupied critical attention now for years, with general results that may be accepted.[1] In just a dozen of these plays, considered chronologically, have we any reason to look for the hand of Beaumont, and three of these (*The Woman Hater*, *The Knight of the Burning Pestle*, and a masque) are his alone. About a dozen more are solely Fletcher's, and the rest are Fletcher, variously in collaboration with Massinger or in revision by him, with Field and others.[2] It is likely that one or two plays, of the second folio especially, are not Fletcher's at all, but Massinger's, and even (in one case) Shirley's. To no one conversant with the practices of Elizabethan printers need this confusion present anything startling. Already in the generation following them, there were claims and counter-claims as to the authorship and the proportion of authorship in these plays; and the problem has only yielded at last to the application of tests of style and verse, as to the efficacy of which it is as easy to set too great a store as it is to minimize them. *The Coxcomb*, an inferior production, is believed to be the first play in which Beaumont and Fletcher collaborated. For our purposes, but three more are memorable: *Philaster*, *The Maid's Tragedy*, and *King and No King;* and these are the indubitable master-dramas of the entire group.[3] Roughly stated, to Beaumont is now allowed the deeper nature, a more genuine originality, a greater power of satire, the choicer diction, and a stronger, more truly musical flow of verse. Fletcher is more facile, nimbler of wit, more cleverly inventive; in diction careless, even repetitious and mannered at times,

---

[1] See especially the works, mentioned above, of Professor Gayley and Miss Hatcher, in the latter of which will be found an excellent summary of opinion and the accompanying bibliography involved, from Fleay's important paper in *Englische Studien*, ix, 1886, to E. H. Oliphant's several papers in the same, xiv, xv, xvi, 1890-92. Later bibliography will be found in Gayley.

[2] As to Field, see H. D. Sykes, *Notes and Queries*, February and March, 1921, viii, 141.

[3] The usually accepted dates for the earliest acting of these plays are 1609-11, and in the order named. See, however, W. J. Lawrence, "The Riddle of Philaster," *Times Supplement*, November, 1921, who thinks the play originally Fletcher's, written for a boy company about 1608 and revised only in 1613 by Beaumont for the King's men.

in verse more lithe and supple, displaying a fondness for redundant syllables and an overuse of them, yet wonderfully effective withal. Both men were at need admirable poets. And if Beaumont's is the truer insight into the human heart, Fletcher has rarely been equaled as a sprightly chronicler of human conduct. In the three great dramas named above, Beaumont has been given an overwhelming share, and I doubt not with justice.

Elizabethan dramatic collaboration In an excellent monograph on Elizabethan dramatic collaboration, the author has noted certain differences in the nature of this universal practice.[1] Henslowe, desiring the ready dramatization of some matter of passing interest, for example, would assign the writing of a play at times to as many as three, four, or even five writers, who, working all but independently, produced a patchwork of little coherence. Such a play as *The Travails of Three English Brothers*, a brother assigned each to Day, Wilkins, and William Rowley, is left at the end on a trisected stage, each observing the other with perspective glasses or telescopes.[2] A better method than this, and a frequent one, is the assignment of the more serious plot of a play to one author, the relieving comedy to another. It is the opinion of this critic that Fletcher worked, whether with Beaumont or Massinger, "on a fairly stable agreement based on a structural division of the plays." According to observation, Fletcher, in collaboration with Beaumont, seldom begins the play, but comes into it late; and he is likely to leave the opening and the final act to Massinger, when working with him, writing usually mostly the intervening three. "Under neither arrangement was it usual for one author to have exclusive charge of a separate plot or character." Our authority even suggests that Fletcher received "his first lessons in playwriting" from Beaumont;

---

[1] E. N. S. Thompson, "Elizabethan Dramatic Collaboration," *Englische Studien*, 1909, xl, 30.

[2] It is fair, however, to add that this is rather "an appeal to the imagination," as Chambers puts it, iii, 118, than an argument for the simultaneous existence of three localities on the stage.

and he accounts for the want of unity, which we must agree with him is characteristic of many of these clever Fletcherian plays, in the obvious risks attendant on such a method.[1] Leaving these sagacious inferences with a cordial recognition of their worth, I do not combat designations of scene and line by the critics to this poet or to that; though one can, at times, take refuge in the critics' disagreements. I waver with the praises of Beaumont or the preferences for Fletcher, though I cannot follow the former extolled in the utterances of Bellario alone, and Fletcher damned in the words of his own scapegraces. Moreover, did these old dramatic collaborators never work up a scene jointly? Was there at no moment an informing spirit, a momentary amanuensis? Have we never the voice of Jacob and the hands of Esau?

The story of *Philaster* is that of an impetuous young *Philaster* prince in the court of a usurper whose daughter he loves, with the pathetic devotion to the prince of a lovelorn lady, paging it in disguise, and the contrast of the "pure" and devoted love of Philaster for his peerless princess contrasted with the gross amours of a poltroon rival. The play is packed with sentiment, incident, surprise, idyllic situations, and threatened danger, suspicion aroused, and death averted; it is alike romantic, unhistorical, improbable, and delightful. *Philaster* was an immediate success and as epoch-making in its way as was Jonson's *Every Man in His Humor*. In *Philaster* is embodied to the full the idea of tragicomedy. *Philaster* marks, too, the transfer of the talents of its two authors from the children's companies to the King's men. This success was followed up by *The Maid's Tragedy*, which is precisely the same species of play as *Philaster*, save for a certain weightening of the emotions and for its sensationally tragic situations and ending. *The Maid's Trag-* *The Maid's* *edy* is the story of the unhappy Amintor, who, at the de- *Tragedy* mand of his king, forsakes Aspatia, his plighted bride, to

[1] Thompson, as above, 37, 38.

be married to Evadne, the royal mistress; of Evadne's awakening to her crime, of her vengeance on the king, and of the pathetic death of Aspatia. The power and pathos of this great play and its several scenes which lend themselves to the virtuoso in acting kept it a favorite on the stage for generations. *King and No King* is the story of a struggle against unlawful passion in the hearts of one, supposed a king, and a princess, believed to be his sister, with the averting of their impending doom in the discovery that they are not really allied in blood. The plot is developed from hints and situations variously to be found in Xenophon and Herodotus,[1] but otherwise the story is as completely the invention of the authors as either of the other plays and almost, save for the feeling that it should have been tragedy, their equal. *King and No King*, too, enjoyed a long popularity on the stage.

"Decadent" features of the *Philaster* group   Previous criticism has made much of certain alleged decadent features, thought to be discoverable in this group of plays, such as of their unreality of atmosphere, improbability in action, and their running to type in personage. That all these things came to characterize later productions of the Fletcherian school, none will deny; but the model is not answerable necessarily for distortions of it. However, to take the matter of types first, much is to be said for the idea that these clever young dramatists were following Jonson in simplifying complex humanity for their romantic tragicomedy, much as their master had simplified it for satirical comedy with his "humors" personified. The unreasoning precipitate young hero, Philaster, Amintor, too; the lovelorn lady disguised as a page, Bellario, Aspatia; the outspoken, honest soldier, Melantius; the boastful poltroon, a coward and lecherous, Pharamond—not to pursue the enumeration here into comedy—all are of the "humorous" stuff, in the simplicity of the qualities constituting them, of which Jonson's comedy

[1] *Cyropædeia*, bks. iii, vi; Herodotus, bk. vii.

220

personages are made, although none of them, of course, is humorous in the modern sense of the word. As to unreality and improbability, the truth of both charges must be acknowledged at once; though we have here merely that universal atmosphere of romance which time out of mind has been accepted and admired. Moreover, the degree of this exaggeration, this departure from what we call "life," is only a part and parcel of that more emphatic emphasis, that higher spicing, which is a dominant quality in the new art. To be fair, do any of these Beaumontesque and Fletcherian extravagances really outdo those of either *Pericles* or *Cymbeline?* With respect to decadent features, as to these master-dramas of Beaumont and Fletcher, we may offer, if not a denial *in toto*, at least a qualified defense. *The Maid's Tragedy* is often cited as an example of the poet's devotion to the doctrine, "the King can do no wrong"; and indeed the wretched Amintor's will to avenge the unspeakable tyranny exercised upon him at the hands of his king drops dead at the thought. But why not quote from the same play the straightforward, successful vengeance of Melantius who has no qualms on the subject and receives no punishment for regicide.[1] There is in these great plays a dallying with the emotions not common before them, an intensity of feeling, and this led on in time to sentimentalism, to an overwrought heroic ideal, and to a distorted ethical code. But in *Philaster* and *The Maid's Tragedy*, as yet, right is right and wrong is wrong; and even in *King and No King*, however, the story turns on a theme later to be dangerously abused by Ford, the real issue is evaded, somewhat to the destruction of the play as a play, but with no evasion of the moral question involved. A rereading of these great dramas after years of familiarity with them leaves me,

---

[1] That the following age recognized more truly than we the true motive of *The Maid's Tragedy* is shown in Waller's attempt to mitigate the realities of regicide, by writing a new fifth act in which the story ends happily. See J. Genest, *Some Account of the English Stage*, 1832, i, 337.

when I remember Webster, Tourneur, and Marston before them, with no impression of an ethical outlook on life materially impaired. Their lapses of this nature seem rather such as displease us with the outrageous wager of Posthumus or with the questionable ruse by means of which Helena fulfills the hard conditions put upon her by her husband, Bertram.[1]

Shakespeare's relations to Beaumont and Fletcher

The relations of Shakespeare to the two young dramatists who thus were bringing fresh laurels to his company remain food for conjecture. That both, in the new romantic drama, were his avowed disciples rather than that he, the older man, the greater artist, should have been lured by their sudden success into following in their wake, seems to the present writer, now as heretofore, the better opinion.[2] It is less important to determine the priority on the stage of *Cymbeline* or *Philaster* than it is to note that the idea of tragicomedy is as old at least as Greene's *James IV* or *The Merchant of Venice*, that the pathetic, lovelorn page occurs at least as far back as *The Two Gentlemen of Verona*[3] and that, however it differ in its alliance to the romance of travel and adventure in strange lands, rather than in an atmosphere of intrigue, *Pericles* has features, too, in common with the new tragicomedy. In his latest work for the stage, Shakespeare is no decadent, bolstering his art on the inventiveness of other men, although it is not to be denied that he went over wholly to romantic tragicomedies in the end to which his own art in comedy had long been tending. As to *Pericles*, this unequal production appears to have followed close upon *Timon of Athens* in 1608, and it would seem that here Shakespeare did little more than

Pericles

[1] *Cymbeline*, i, 4; *All's Well That Ends Well*, iii, 7.
[2] On this topic see the well-known essay of Thorndike, *The Influence of Beaumont and Fletcher on Shakespeare*, 1901; Gayley, as above, pp. 386-395; and the present author's *Elizabethan Drama*, ii, 197-204.
[3] Shakespeare uses the girl disguised as a page five times. On the general topic see V. O. Freeburg, *Disguise Plots in Elizabethan Drama*, 1915, pp. 61-99.

touch up the work of George Wilkins,[1] a mediocre pamphleteer and author for the company of a circumstantial drama of contemporary happenings called *The Miseries of Enforced Marriage*. The story of *Apollonius*, which the authors amended to read *Pericles of Tyre*, is a straggling romance of adventure, and ill adapted for reduction to theatrical representation; but it enjoyed an unusual popularity on the stage and was read subsequently in no less than five quarto editions during the lifetime of Shakespeare. None can doubt the hand of the master in all that pertains to Marina and the recovery of her mother, Thaisa. These scenes were enough to make the play.

Cymbeline, The Winter's Tale, The Tempest are com- **Cymbeline** monly dated from 1609 to 1611. In them, while we rise to no such heights of passion as animated the great tragedies, we have, none the less, serious emotion, deep and penetrating insight into human feeling, and the presentation of personages on the stage in which only the most captious criticism can find any falling off in art. *Cymbeline* paints, on the background of a revolt of the ancient Britons against Rome, derived from Holinshed, the story of Belarius and his surreptitious nurture of the king's sons, and the tale of Posthumus, his mad wager of his wife's honor with her devotion and the reconciliation of all, this last from a well-known story of Boccaccio. The result exhibits all the action, multiplicity, variety, and scenic possibilities of *Philaster*, although, in his battle scenes at least, Shakespeare reverts to an older technique. It is in the personality of his characters and their reality despite the improbability of their adventures, that Shakespeare holds his lead. We are so accustomed to think of Shakespeare as the great exponent of elaboration, rich and full of utterance, even occasionally, it is to be con-

---

[1] As to Wilkins, see H. D. Sykes, *Sidelights on Shakespeare.* The activity of Wilkins lies between 1604 and 1608. A "George Wilkins the poet" was buried in August, 1603; a George Wilkins was fellow witness with Shakespeare in the case of Belott *vs.* Mountjoy in June, 1612. Are there two or three?

fessed, to an interference with the supremacy of his art, that we forget that he may be cited elsewhere as the supreme example of that artistic brevity, that economy of stroke which is recognized as one of the chief glories of Greek art. The tragedies afford us of this our best illustrations: the sleep-walking scene of Lady Macbeth, the death scene of Cleopatra, the last utterance of Lear. But even in the elaborate tragicomedy of *Cymbeline* there is such a moment gradually led up to in the scene in which Iachimo maligns the husband of Imogen to her face and she, at length through the armor of her innocency, understanding the lewdness of his advances, exclaims:

> Away! I do condemn mine ears that have
> So long attended thee. If thou wert honorable
> Thou wouldst have told this tale for virtue, not
> For such an end thou seek'st, as base as strange.
> Thou wrong'st a gentleman who is as far
> From thy report as thou from honor, and
> Solicit'st here a lady that disdains
> Thee and the devil alike. What ho, Pisanio!

The Winter's Tale

In *The Winter's Tale*, the poet returns to a greater simplicity of plot and a greater unity of emotion. The story is taken over bodily from a prose tale of Shakespeare's old rival, Robert Greene, entitled *Pandosto*, and treated in the process much as he had previously treated Lodge's *Rosalind*, his model for *As You Like It*. In the face of all the unities, as to time Shakespeare boldly cuts his play into two pieces with the lapse of sixteen years between, but deprecates our criticism with a graceful word. Defiant of geography as well as of unity of place, he follows his source in making Delphos an island and giving Bohemia—like all Shakespearean countries—a port and a seacoast. But in recompense he inverted admirable Paulina, her sequestration of her beloved mistress Hermione, the device of the statue, the reunion of mother and daughter, and the reconciliation of husband and wife; while, not least, he gives us Autolycus, most delightful of rogues.

"ROMANCE" AND TRAGICOMEDY

It was in these years of *Cymbeline*, *Philaster*, and *The Winter's Tale* that these authors came together. Save for his *Masque of the Inner Temple*, no play of Beaumont's was published in his lifetime. It is not unlikely that a feeling as to the impropriety of avowed authorship for the stage on the part of a gentleman may have actuated this reticence. With Fletcher necessity was pressing, and tradition, as well as the nature of the texts, agrees that there was, at some such date, a collaboration of Shakespeare with Fletcher in several plays. One, *The History of Cardenio*, from a story of Cervantes, though recorded as acted at court in 1613, is now lost. *The Two Noble Kinsmen* was printed in 1634 as "by Fletcher and Shakespeare." This is a dramatic version of Chaucer's *Knight's Tale of Palamon and Arcite*, long since dramatized in a play by Edwards, now lost. Opinion is still at variance as to whether Shakespeare really shared in this play. It is absolutely of the type of the new tragicomedy, and there are passages in it not unworthy of him.[1] Lastly, we have work in our present version of *Henry VIII* in a style and versification unmistakably Fletcher's.[2] What were the actual terms of this combined authorship? Did Shakespeare, after an earlier practice, contribute a touch here, a scene there, an improvement, an embellishment, to work, already in form by Fletcher? Or did Shakespeare, now returning to Stratford more frequently, leave certain plays, sketched and projected, which Fletcher finished? Or did the older dramatist, seeking retirement to the town of his birth and the fine house that his wealth had bought him there, take the younger, promising spirit into a species of apprenticeship, suggesting, helping, encouraging? This would have been assuredly in the manner of "the gentle Shakespeare."

Shakespeare's alleged collaboration with Fletcher

[1] Sykes, *ibid.*, 1-17, denies Shakespeare's hand in *The Kinsmen* and assigns it to Fletcher and Massinger. A. H. Cruickshank, *Philip Massinger*, 1920, denies Massinger's hand in this play or in *Henry VIII*.
[2] Sykes, *ibid.*, 18-47, gives *Henry VIII* wholly to Fletcher and Massinger, regarding it as "early work." The question was raised as long ago as 1850 by James Spedding in *The Gentleman's Magazine* of that year.

The Tempest

The Tempest is generally reputed the latest of Shakespeare's plays. Its place of honor as the first of the comedies at the beginning in the folios bears out this repute. More than most of his plots a combination of suggestions rather than the borrowing of a story, his delicate handling of the supernatural, the scene a desert island haunted with strange sounds and enchantments, places this beautiful play poetically and imaginatively apart. In this story of a magician and his power over the elements, designated in the spirit Ariel, his innocent and lovely daughter, Miranda, her girlish love at sight, the machinations of evil foiled by enchantment and, below, the ground tones of the drunken revelry of menials and the uncouth semi-monster Caliban, we have exemplified almost the whole range of Shakespeare's magic art. Let us not ask what Ariel and Caliban may signify, ranging as each does beyond our human world; nor be too curious to know if Shakespeare meant himself by Prospero and an allegory of his farewell to the stage when the magician sinks his book forever "deeper than a plummet's sounding."

Last days of Shakespeare

Tradition assigns to Shakespeare a life of comparative seclusion after the performance of *The Tempest* in 1611; but there is reason to believe that he was still more or less in touch with the activities of the Globe and Blackfriars, where his dramas, as at court, continued constantly to please.[1] Adams finds a reason for Shakespeare's return to London in 1612-13 in Beaumont's withdrawal from writing for the stage. The coincidence of these two events with the date of the supposed collaboration of Shakespeare with Fletcher is striking. Somewhat earlier than this Shakespeare had lodged with a Huguenot refugee and tiremaker, Christopher Mountjoy, at Silver and Monkwell streets in Cripplegate, and lived on friendly terms with his family. It was in consequence of this intimacy that the poet was called, in 1612, as a witness in a lawsuit which

---

[1] C. W. Wallace, "Shakespeare, the Globe and Blackfriars," *Nebraska Studies*, x, 261; Adams, *Shakespeare*, 432.

had unhappily arisen within this family, thereby adding
in a deposition signed by his own hand, a sixth signature
to the five previously known.[1] The poet's intimacies, we
may well believe, lay chiefly among those of his own profession. Among his fellow sharers, Phillips left him a bequest of remembrance, and Heming and Condell affection-
ately signed the "Address to the Reader" and the dedication of the famous first collection in folio of his plays,
1623. Burbage, who must have been nearer to him than
any of these, had died four years before, and more than
one anecdote is related of their intimacy and friendship.
A glimpse into the avocations of Shakespeare and Burbage
is offered us in an item of the accounts of the young Earl
of Rutland, who took a prominent part in the tournament
of 1613 commemorating the king's accession to his crown.
The word *impresa* signifies a symbolic and heraldic device
painted on the shield of a contestant in a tournament,
with an inscription appropriate to the knight and the occasion. The "item" reads: "31 Marti 1613, to Mr. Shakespeare in gold about my Lord's *impresa*, xliv s. To Mr.
Richard Burbage for painting and making it, in gold,
xliv s.[2] Burbage is elsewhere elebrated as "an excellent
both player and painter"; and an apocryphal story assigns to him the original of the Droeshout portrait of
Shakespeare. In the year previous to his death, Shakespeare was involved with others as plaintiffs in a suit to
recover certain deeds and other writings curiously enough
brought against one Bacon—not Francis, but Matthew—
who detained them.[3] Into the many family affairs and
relations of Stratford it is impossible to enter, even for its
greatest figure, in a book of this size. Shakespeare married both his daughters well; his only son, Hamnet, had
died in 1596. Among his neighbors at Beauchamp Court

---

[1] C. W. Wallace, in *Harper's Magazine*, 1910, cxx, 489.
[2] *Historical MSS. Commission's Report on MSS. in Belvoir Castle*, iv,
494; and Sir S. Lee, in the *London Times*, December 27, 1905.
[3] Also discovered by Professor Wallace. *The Standard* newspaper,
October, 1905, and *Shakespeare Jahrbuch*, 1906.

was Sir Fulke Greville, a dramatist, we have seen, of very different mood; among Shakespeare's friends was the poet, Michael Drayton, not without his experiences, too, with the stage. Shakespeare died April 23, 1616, on the day reputed his birthday.

Fletcher in tragedy

To return to Fletcher, we have had occasion thus far to name a scant dozen of the plays with which his name is associated; more than forty more remain, an enumeration of which would be idle. The public taste, long since surfeited on horrors, demanded fewer tragedies; they muster less than ten in the whole group. Among the more memorable is *Bonduca*, a "history" of ancient British times, combining cleverly the story of Caractacus with that of Boadicea and involving a pathetic child prince, to be accepted and enjoyed or captiously criticized as the reader's nature is possessed of a touch of sentiment or is rigorously devoid of it. *Bonduca* was on the stage in the year of Shakespeare's death, and *Thierry and Theodoret* and *Valentinian* must soon have followed it. The former lays tribute on early annals of France, not without surmise of cloaked allusion to more recent French history.[1] All but repulsive although the subject is, repeating the favorite situation of the lustful tyrant and the steadfast wife, *Valentinian* is a tragedy of much power and represents the author at his best. Later plays on Roman theme are *The False One*, which concerns Cleopatra's amour with Cæsar, and *The Prophetess or the Tragedy of Dioclesian*. In both of these Massinger had a hand in collaboration or revision. In all this work the spirit is purely that of romance. Tragicomedy has spread its spell, and the accident of a violent ending scarcely distinguishes the plays which so conclude from the score of dramas which may logically claim the more cumbersome title.[2]

Later tragi-comedies of Fletcher

Among tragicomedies, *The Loyal Subject, The Humorous Lieutenant*, and *The Knight of Malta*—the latter

[1] Fleay, *Chronicle*, i, 205, and Ward, ii, 190 n. Oliphant places *Valentinian* as early as 1611 or 1612, *Englische Studien*, xv, 358.
[2] *A Wife for a Month* is an example of this variety of near-tragedy.

shared in by Massinger and Field, as were several others—
may be named as typical. They belong to the years immediately preceding 1620, when Fletcher was ruling, the
undisputed dramatic successor to Shakespeare. *The
Humorous Lieutenant* is of the usual fabric of a romantic love tale, set in an imaginary court; but the droll, if
Rabelaisian, personage whose humors give rise to the title,
is one of those happy Fletcherian variations of an old
figure in the preposterousness and ribaldry of which generations continued to delight. In *The Knight of Malta*
and *The Loyal Subject,* both of them plays of extraordinary variety and inventive fertility, we breathe a new
exotic atmosphere, more strained even and ultra-romantic
than was ever that of *Philaster.* Derived partly from the
French prose romances of the day and partly from Spanish
ideals, we are presented to a world which is governed by
a strange and overwrought sense of honor, by a conventional code of chivalric conduct and a Quixotic obligation
to the word once plighted, although it defeat the spirit,
which came in time so to rule the drama that a definite
new species, the heroic play, emerged out of it all. The
present writer has been recently criticized as one who
has "exaggerated" the influence of Beaumont and Fletcher
on the heroic drama; and the point has been made that
"Beaumont and Fletcher hardly seem to make any attempt at epic dignity; [that] their exaggerations of virtues and vices appear to be due to a desire for contrast;
[and that] they aim at startling sensation rather than
grandeur" . . . while Dryden's extravagance is referred
"to a deliberate endeavor to raise the pitch of the drama
above that of ordinary life." [1] We may grant this as a
valuable distinction and accept the author's "notes" of
the heroic as "epic construction [whatever that may mean
in a play], unity of tone and predominance of the hero."
But assuredly we must submit the essentially epic nature

The
"heroic"
ideal

[1] See especially *Elizabethan Drama,* ii, 348-352, and B. J. Pendlebury,
Dryden's Heroic Plays, a Study in Origins, 1923, p. 6.

of these two plays of Fletcher with their multitude of episode and fertile invention and their unity of tone, however they have for theme rather the test of loyalty and a struggle for honor than the glorification of a single hero. The heroic idea, with its artificial code of an ideal of conduct, was taken up at once for its dramatic possibilities. To mention no others here, Heywood paralleled rivalry in courtesy in *The Royal King and Loyal Subject* and returned later to a theme of honor in *A Challenge for Beauty*. *The Lover's Progress*, 1623, was Fletcher's latest contribution to the species. The diffusion of the heroic idea in the drama in the reign of King Charles with the cult of Platonic love belongs below.[1]

Fletcher in romantic comedy

Yet with all this lead and prominence in other things, it is the Fletcher of comedy who chiefly endures. Between the time of his collaboration with Beaumont and his untimely death, by the plague, in 1625, Fletcher's hand appears in some twenty comedies, variously assisted, in some of them by Massinger, Field, William Rowley, Daborne, perhaps Middleton, and possibly even Jonson. That Fletcher was the ruling spirit in all is not to be questioned, however they range from comedies of manners, that vie with Middleton in the representation of contemporary life, to serious romantic dramas, shading off in gravity of plot into the regions of tragicomedy. To these latter more especially belong Fletcher's many borrowings of story from Spanish sources, chiefly Cervantes. These are from fiction and through French or other intermediaries. It

Romantic plays of Spanish sources

was Massinger, and not Fletcher, who first opened the rich stores of Spanish drama to English imitation.[2] There are no more pleasing plays than *The Chances*, 1615, from one of the novels of Cervantes, or *The Pilgrim*, 1621, from a story of Lope de Vega. In the former we may study the method of this master-playwright in dealing with nar-

---

[1] Below, pp 270, 271.
[2] On Spanish influences see Miss Hatcher, 48; *Elizabethan Drama*, 206-218, and the present writer's contribution to this subject in *The Cambridge History of English Literature*, vii, 124.

rative material. The story involves a clandestine marriage, a lost child, a veiled lady seeking protection, disguise, mistake, a duel, generosity, discovery, and reconcilement. The original is full of recital and episode. Fletcher throws everything into action, develops the possibilities of the entanglements, and creates new and original personages on the basis of a hint. Take up these semi-romantic, semi-humorous comedies where we will—*The Spanish Curate, The Little French Lawyer* (the absurd little fire-eater of the title, alone enough to make any play), *The Maid in the Mill* or *The Fair Maid of the Inn*— and we find charm, incessant movement, lively personages, witty, sprightly dialogue, and diverting adventure.

There remain the comedies of manners in which Fletcher had been to school alike to Middleton and to Jonson, and had learned how to avoid the too veritable low life of the one and the too rigid "humors" of the other. In comedies, such as *Wit at Several Weapons, The Scornful Lady, Monsieur Thomas, Rule a Wife and Have a Wife* and *The Wild Goose Chase* we have the very soul of this born master of comedy, his verve and "go," his ready adequacy, his inventiveness within the strict limits of the game, and his success in meeting precisely the expectations of his age in the way of an amusing and none too exacting entertainment. *Fletcher's comedies of manners*

Postponing for the nonce our consideration of Massinger, whose work continued much into the reign of King Charles, the name of the Fletcherians, even in the time of James, is legion. Old authors departed from their former ways to try to write like him; new ones used him alone as the sufficient example. Dekker's *Match Me in London* repeats the all too hackneyed theme of the tyrant king and the chaste wife tempted, to make, however, a fine drama in the process. Heywood essays, as we have seen, the Fletcherian theme of a contest for honors; and Middleton and Rowley, of whom more below, followed, too, with Massinger, the enticing lead of Fletcher into roman- *The influence of Fletcher* tic Spain. Younger Fletcherians will claim a later mention as well as the greater men, who carried forward into the next reign the comedy of manners, persistent in a repetition of Jonson's "humors," or accepting the lighter, sprightlier mode which marks here, too, the ubiquitous influence of Fletcher.

CHAPTER XII

THE ROYAL DIVERSION

LYLY'S ideal of a drama, at once artistic and fitted to the tastes, the prejudices, and the limitations of the court, failed less because of any inadequacy on his part than because it could not abide the vigorous rivalry of the popular stage which, in the essential democracy of the age, addressed itself to a constituency that included every class in the nation. There are recurrent records of popular plays acted, as we have seen, at court, and references in Henslowe and elsewhere to the "trimming" of such plays, by way usually of some extraneous addition for performance before the queen. It is significant that the popular playwrights wrote few plays primarily for court performance, however we may recognize the special fitness of some over others. In the regular drama it was the court that came to the taste of the town, not the town to the taste of the court. However, there was at no time a cessation in the customary embellishments of the court's amusements, many of which partook of a nature dramatic; while conservative influences prevalent at the universities and the Inns of Court conspired to give a preference, in theory at least, to plays which conformed more or less to classic theory and Italian example. With the advent of Shakespeare and Fletcher to the leadership of the professional stage such preferences little availed. We are here less interested in popular successes, repeated at court, than in the development of that quasi-dramatic by-product, the masque, and in the kinds of plays which diligent courtiers selected on occasion at the universities and elsewhere as fit to entertain royalty. For this undercurrent, often a

The court and the drama

233

current counter to the earlier popular taste, came by the time of Charles seriously to affect the nature of popular performances in subject-matter as well as staging.[1]

Masque in the *Gesta Grayorum*

Mention of court festivities involving dramatic elements has already found place in a former chapter, with incidental reference to some of the probable means and ways of presentation. Little save their elaboration distinguished such undertakings as the *Gesta Grayorum* of 1594, a painstaking parody of an actual royal court, prolonged intermittently from St. Thomas's Eve (December 20) to Shrovetide. One peculiarity of this solemn feigning was the important place within it of several devices by way of allegory, in one at least of which we recognize several features later characteristic of the Jacobean masque. This *Masque of Proteus* is the work of Francis Davison and Thomas Campion (as to a song or two), well-known lyrical poets, the latter likewise an eminent musician; and Queen Elizabeth was present on this occasion to receive in person that obvious flattery of the prince which remained to the end a salient characteristic of the masque.

The Jacobean masque

The dramatic and scenic developments of the masque belong to the reign of King James. They were inspired almost wholly by the poetic genius of Ben Jonson and carried out by the inventive talents of Inigo Jones, the king's architect.[2] While the word *masque*[3] was employed with much latitude both before Jonson's time and after, in the heyday of its vogue, a masque meant definitely an entertainment of royalty, usually given at court, in which the nucleus is a dance; a lyric, scenic, dramatic frame, so to speak, or setting for what we should now call a ball. An invariable feature is the group of dancers, from eight to sixteen in number, called the "masquers," and usually

---

[1] The most recent important work devoted to the masque is that of P. Reyher, *Les Masques anglais,* 1909. On the definition, see Appendix 1.

[2] On the importance of Jones, see Chambers, i, 179, and the authorities there cited.

[3] Jonson, with Lyly before him, seems responsible for the spelling *masque, ibid.,* i, 176.

noble and titled people. These take no part in the dialogue nor in the music, but by means of their grouping and graceful pose, their handsome costumes and stately presence in the midst of gorgeous and appropriate setting, mark and hold the center of interest. Such dialogue and action as the masque involves was, from the first, in the hands of professional actors, as was the arrangement of scene and decoration, the music and prearranged dancing. In form the masque was made up of three essential parts, the "entry" which included the first appearance of the masquers, their march from their "sieges" or seats of state in the scene, followed by the first dance; secondly, the "main" or principal dance, and lastly the "going out." All these were carefully prearranged and rehearsed. But between the latter two fell the "dance with the ladies" and the "revels," this last made up of galliards, corantos, and lavoltas; and these were extempore. Two forms analogous to the masque were distinguished with equal precision by Jonson; these are the "entertainment," in which the nucleus for the allegory and dialogue is a speech of welcome; and the "barriers," in which a sham fight or tournament is similarly set and introduced.[1]

The new king's journey from Scotland to London was marked with acclaim and panegyric. In this last, which took the form of "entertainment," several of the dramatists figured, particularly Jonson and Daniel. Between these two there was a rivalry of long standing; for Daniel, with his ideals of French Seneca, his Petrarchan sonneteering, and his Italianate over-refinement, was anathema to the sturdy Anglo-classical spirit of Jonson. Both poets celebrated the king before he arrived in London; but Daniel won the commission for the first royal masque, his *Vision of the Twelve Goddesses* being presented by the queen (Anne of Denmark) and her ladies at Hampton

First masque of James's reign

[1] For examples, see *The Entertainment of the Two Kings at Theobalds,* and *Speeches at Prince Henry's Barriers,* Gifford's *Jonson,* vii, 103 and 147.

235

Court in January, 1604. Daniel, of whom we have heard before, had found a congenial place as tutor in the Pembroke family and, gaining through them the favor of Queen Anne, later became one of her gentlemen in waiting and Master of the players known as the Queen's Revels. Daniel's masque, *The Vision of the Twelve Godesses*, is graceful, courtly, poetical, and totally undramatic. It was distributed in several pageants about the hall, and the allegory was expounded by a Sybil as presenter.[1] A year later, the masque was Jonson's, celebrated in the old banqueting house at Whitehall. The scenic setting, now concentrated at the end of the room, was that of Inigo Jones; and these fortunate coadjutors at once became the accepted entertainers at court. *The Masque of Blackness*, for such this was called, turns somewhat unhappily on the disguise of the queen and the masquing ladies as "the daughters of Niger"; in which, says a contemporary letter-writer, "instead of vizards (or masks) their faces, and arms to the elbows, were painted black." But the costumes of azure and silver were splendid and the setting novel, the masquers appearing in a concave shell, the torch-bearers borne "by sea-horses with other terrible fishes which were ridden by Moors."

The scenic devices of Inigo Jones

In later masques Jones achieved many novelties: a haven and castle with ships moving on the sea; a cliff over which a cloud breaks for the chariot of Venus; a perspective of porticos leading to Sybilla's trophy, an obelisk of Fame (obviously a Serlian motif); circles of moving lights and glasses, and changes, as in *The Masque of Queens*, where "the whole face of the scene altered" from the representation of "an ugly hell" to the House of Fame, "a *machina versatilis* which showed first Perseus and the masquers and then Fame.[2] All this new craft of the stage was the result of much study in similar devices

---

[1] L. B. Campbell, *Scenes and Machines*, 165, and Chambers, iii, 176, who finds in this dispersed setting the influence of the French ballet comique.
[2] This device was first employed in England by Jones at Oxford, in 1605.

employed in contemporary Italy, whither Jones had traveled, acted on by an ingenious and inventive spirit well provided with the means to achieve these ends.

Jonson wrote, within some thirty years, twenty-three masques, two antimasques, nine entertainments, and three barriers. Of a total of thirty-seven masques presented in the reign of King James, twenty were Jonson's. And this predominance was founded on quality as well as the mass of his work. In place of enumeration, let us take a typical masque of Jonson as illustrative of his work. *Hymenœi* was written to celebrate a noble marriage at court, and was followed the next night by a barriers. Let the story be told in the words of an eye-witness: *The masques of Ben Jonson*

> The conceit or soul of the masque was Hymen bringing in a bride and Juno's pronuba's priest a bridegroom, proclaiming those two should be sacrificed to nuptial union, and here the poet made an apostrophe to the union of the kingdoms. But before the sacrifice could be performed, Ben Jonson turned the globe of the earth standing behind the altar, and within the concave sat the eight men masquers representing the four humors and the four affections which leaped forth to disturb the sacrifice to union. But amidst their fury Reason that sate above them all, crowned with burning tapers, came down and silenced them. These eight together with Reason, their moderatress, mounted above their heads, sate somewhat like the ladies in the scallop shell last year. Above the globe of earth hovered a middle region of clouds in the center whereof stood a grand consort of musicians, and upon the cantons or horns sate the ladies, four at one corner and four at another, who descended upon the stage, not after the stale downright perpendicular fashion, like a bucket in a well; but came gently sloping down. . . . The men were clad in crimson; the women in white. They had every one a white plume of the richest heron's feathers, and were so rich in jewels upon their heads as was most glorious.[1]

Gigantic golden figures of Atlas and Hercules were employed in this instance as supporters of the scene, the framing of the picture—this being apparently a new

[1] John Pory to Sir Robert Cotton, January 7, 1606, reprinted by Miss M. Sullivan, *Court Masques of James I*, 1913, p. 199.

thing in England; and the dances and the music were alike elaborate and novel.[1] In *Hymenæi* Jonson's poetry rises to its highest level, especially in the beautiful *Epithalamion* with which the whole concludes.

Character-
istics of
the masque
We have here obvious allegory and familiar classical personages, both of which fall readily into the comprehension of the gentle and cultivated folk who went to constitute such a court as that of Elizabeth or James. We have, too, except for a speaker or two and those responsible for the music and the mechanism, only the select group of court people, the masquers, taking part. Later masques developed a more difficult and recondite allusiveness on which Jonson piqued himself not a little. In this same *Masque of Queens* he incidentally compliments "the capacity" of his spectators to comprehend what he elsewhere calls these "high and hearty inventions . . . grounded on antiquity and solid learning" . . . "where men, beside inquiring eyes, are understood to bring quick ears and not the sluggish ones of porters and mechanics."[2] But it is in the development of dramatic possibilities that Jonson's services to the masque chiefly lie. Beginning with the masque just mentioned, Jonson devised what he called the antimasque as a foil to emphasize in its contrasted grotesqueness and drollery the dignified beauty of the masque

The anti-
masque
proper. *The Masque of Queens* contains an antimasque of witches, *Love Freed from Ignorance*, one of She-Fools and Follies; *Love Restored* opens with a lively piece of farce satirizing the difficulties of plain people in their efforts to see one of these exclusive court entertainments. Jonson is as fertile in the variety of his antimasques as he is poetically resourceful in the masque itself. King James greatly rejoiced in Jonson's antimasques; so much so that the poet wrote two or three, especially *The [Anti] Masque*

[1] Miss Campbell notes, as above, 166, that in *The Hue and Cry after Cupid*, as Gifford called Jonson's *Lord Haddington's Masque*, 1608, we have the earliest reference to the framing arch of the stage. In *The Fortunate Isles*, 1624, the full stage is shut off by drawing together two halves of a curtain.
[2] Gifford-Cunningham, *Jonson*, vii, 113.

of Gipsies, nicely calculated to the coarse and salacious temper of the British Solomon; and was liberally rewarded for it. Elsewhere Jonson's appeal to his royal master was more creditable to his love of erudition.

Beaten out of the masque, Daniel tried a diversion, and presented before His Majesty, on his visit to Oxford in 1605, a pastoral drama modeled on Guarini, whom he had met in Italy, and whose *Pastor Fido* he admired. This Daniel called *The Queen's Arcadia* and, preceding Fletcher's *Faithful Shepherdess,* as it did by several years, Daniel's play marks the earliest effort of its exotic kind in English.[1] However, the pastoral mode was by no means a new one; Spenser had long since popularized it in *The Shepherds' Calendar* and Drayton and lesser poets reveled in it. From Sidney's little interlude, *The Lady of May,* 1578, to Peele's *Arraignment of Paris,* as in two or three of Lyly's plays, the court had known the pastoral spirit in its entertainments, in greater or less admixture with other elements; and John Day, more especially than any other one writer for the popular stage, preserves "a sort of Arcadian fancy" in his sprightly and frequently poetic comedies.[2] However, *The Queen's Arcadia* was something more exotic alike and more ambitious. It is, indeed, a charming, inventive, and gracefully written production, with all its preservation of the conventional shepherds and shepherdesses in an entanglement of happenings at eternal cross purposes in love. An original feature is a satirical underplot in which a bid is made for the approval of King James in an attack on tobacco, which His Majesty detested almost as much as he detested witches, and had written against as well.[3] But although applauded and successful, the pastoral drama, as yet, could make little headway in the royal esteem against the masque.

Daniel's pastoral, The Queen's Arcadia

[1] In general, see W. W. Greg, *Pastoral Poetry and Pastoral Drama,* 1906.
[2] *The Isle of Gulls* and *Humor Out of Breath,* especially, 1605 and 1608.
[3] *The Counterblast to Tobacco,* 1604.

Other pastoral dramas

It was not until the successes of Beaumont and Fletcher in tragicomedy had recalled attention to their other work that other attempts were made at the pastoral drama. Robert Daborne, a hack writer for Henslowe, wrote, much about this time, a pleasing pastoral comedy, too little known, *The Poor Man's Comfort;* and the mode was revived at the entertainment of Prince Charles at Cambridge in 1613 by Samuel Brooke in his *Scyros* and again by Phineas Fletcher in an elaborate variant of the species, *Sicelides, a Piscatory,* or fishers' pastoral. Daniel, too, repeated his experiment in *Hymen's Triumph,* employing a pastoral play for the usual masque at a noble wedding celebrated before the king in 1614. This is a work of much elegance and refinement; but it bears no comparison with the richer coloring of *The Faithful Shepherdess* or with the exquisite fragment which Jonson left in *The Sad Shepherd.* This was found among his papers at his death in 1637, and opinion differs as to whether it may have coincided with the later effort of Daniel in an endeavor, characteristic enough of Jonson, to outdo his rival in his own field, or may have been an experimental recurrence in old age, on the part of the poet, to a form still holding esteem in court circles.[1] *The Sad Shepherd* is no limb of Tasso and Guarini, but a happy and poetical effort to work into a plot of English country life the familiar figures of Robin Hood and his Maid Marian in an atmosphere charged with the homely folk-lore of the countryside.

Masque of Jonson's rivals

But it is not to be supposed that Jonson was without rivals. *The Masque at Lord Hayes' Marriage,* January, 1607, was Campion's; it is notable alike for its poetry and the elaborate incidental music. Forty-odd instruments— a bandora, a double sackbote, a harpsichord, with treble violins, even six cornets—sound oddly insufficient in these our days of monster orchestras. In June, 1610, Daniel

---

[1] The question is discussed by W. W. Greg in his ed. of "The Sad Shepherd," *Materialien,* i, 1905, especially pp. v-xx, with the conclusion that "the date cannot be fixed with certainty" and a leaning towards "a few years before Jonson's death."

achieved his greatest effort in the masque in *Tethys' Festival, or the Queen's Wake,* celebrated at Whitehall. The masquers were thirteen nymphs representing as many English rivers, led by the queen, who was Tethys herself. Besides the scene, there was a "Tree of Victory" to the right of the stall which figured in the dancing. The stage was cloaked with a traverse representing a cloud, and the scene was changed under cover of moving lights. A feature was the appearance of the little Duke of York in a sort of antimasque "between two great Sea Slaves . . . attended upon by twelve little ladies, all of them daughters of earls or barons," writes the obsequious author; and he adds, not without a fling at Jonson: "In all these shows, this is to be noted, that there were none of the inferior sort mixed among these great personages of state and honor (as usually there have been), but all was performed by themselves with a due reservation of their dignity." [1] On the death of Prince Henry, Jonson had gone abroad as tutor to Raleigh's son, so that he was absent in the next year, 1613, when the Princess Elizabeth was married to the Palsgrave. Three great masques signalized the event. *The great masques of 1613* These were Campion's *Lords' Masque,* "the prospective with porticoes" prepared by Inigo Jones; Chapman's *Masque,* "presented by the gentlemen of the Middle Temple and Lincoln's Inn," which was preceded by a grand procession to Whitehall; and Beaumont's *Masque of the Inner Temple and Gray's Inn,* which offered the novelty of a preliminary flotilla by night on the Thames. Much was made in all of the antimasques which vied each with the other in variety and novelty. It was Campion, too, who wrote the masque to celebrate the ill-omened marriage of Robert Carr, Earl of Somerset, the king's favorite, with the divorced wife of the Earl of Essex, in December of

---

[1] The elaborate ingenuity of some of the dances must have taxed the apprehension of the court, some typifying the girdle of Venus or the winding of the river Thames. One of the dances of Jonson's *Masque of Queens* "graphically disposed into letters" the names of royalty. On such devices Bacon comments, "Turning dances into figure is childish curiosity." See Reyher, as above, chap. viii, especially 444.

this year. A bit of realism in this case was the representation of a scene along the Thames with a grotesque dance of "skippers"; who apparently came and departed on "barges" which moved off the scene. An Italian rival of Jones was responsible for this novelty. But Jonson returned to take his part in the Somerset marriage festivities and to maintain his lead in inventiveness and fancy.[1] The anonymous *Masque of Flowers* which the gentlemen of Gray's Inn contributed to these festivities, with Beaumont's masque mentioned above, are memorable as having been financed by no less a personage than Francis Bacon at an expenditure, it is said, for the former, of some £2,000, a wedding gift or a provident investment to insure the royal favor, as one looks at it.[2] Indeed, this matter of expense for court entertainments had become a public scandal, and, after 1615, there were efforts at less exaggerated display. In this year Jonson quarreled with his old coadjutor, Jones, and thereafter lampooned him in later masques. But the poet succeeded in retaining the patronage of the king to the end of the reign. Only one other Jacobean masque need be mentioned here; this is that of William Browne of Tavistock, the pastoralist, entitled *Ulysses and the Sirens*, distinguished alike for the beauty of its poetry and a coherency unknown in general to the species. This appears to have been a private masque of the Inner Temple and not acted at court or elsewhere.

Plays at Cambridge However, the royal Stuart taste was not satisfied alone with masking and pastorals. Aside from the recurrent performances of popular plays at court, the colleges adhered to Latin models, if not always to the Latin tongue, in plays which were given for the entertainment of a learned king. Earlier successes like the Latin comedies

---

[1] The organization of the masque in Jonson's day was intrusted not to the Revels Office, but was under the direct supervision of the Lord Chamberlain himself—Chambers, i, 100.

[2] See the complete account of the cost of Her Majesty's masque at Christmas, 1610, Daniel's *Tethys' Festival*, Reyher, 509.

THE ROYAL DIVERSION

Pedantius and *Victoria* aside,[1] the famous decade of the
'nineties had produced several English satirical plays,
notable among them *Club Law*, 1599, in which Cambridge
townsmen were ridiculed in their own borrowed habits on
the stage before their own eyes; and secondly, the interesting trilogy, *The Pilgrimage to Parnassus* and the *1
and 2 Return from Parnassus*, 1598 to 1602, cleverly satirical pictures of the life of the Elizabethan student and the
disenchantments attending the scholar's career.   Their
greatest interest now lies in their several allusions—partly
ironical—to contemporary poets, Shakespeare prominent
among them, and the light which these passages throw
on university opinion and information as to current
drama.   Jonson, for example, is "the wittiest fellow of a
bricklayer in England," but likewise "a mere empiric,"
"a slow inventor," and "as confident now in making a
book as he was in times past in laying a brick."   Marston,
mainly as to his satire,

> Cuts, thrusts and foins at whomsoever he meets
> And strews about Ram Alley meditations;

and Marlowe is lamented as one possessed of

> Wit lent from heaven, but vices sent from hell.

"Sweet honey-dropping Daniel" is praised for his "sugared sonneting" (what of Shakespeare's "sugared sonnets
among his private friends"?); and Drayton is distinguished as wanting "one true note of a poet of our time
. . . he cannot swagger it well in a tavern or domineer in
a hothouse."   Shakespeare seems less known for his plays
than for his erotic vein, which is much quoted by Gullio,
an upstart courtier.   For, despite the allusion to the poet's
relation to the "war of the theaters," already quoted, in
which it will be remembered that he is represented as "put-

[1] By Edward Forsett, see Moore Smith in *Times Literary Supplement*,
October, 1918, and Abraham Fraunce, respectively; *Club Law* is by
George Ruggle.   All are Cambridge plays.   See especially Boas, *Uni-
versity Drama*, 822.

243

ting Ben Jonson down," this is the academic summary of
his achievement:

> Who loves not Adon's love or Lucrece rape?
> His sweeter verse contains heart-throbbing life,
> Could but a graver subject him content,
> Without love's foolish languishment.

Oxford plays

This in the year 1601, or possibly even 1602![1]

A more intimate and less conscious picture of the drama
at the universities is to be gleaned from a merry boys'
trifle called *Narcissus*, a burlesque given at St. John's
College, Oxford, Christmas, 1602; or from the theatromania which raged in the same college five years later,
staging eight or more plays, Latin and English, and lasting for months.[2] In 1605 James visited Oxford and was
regaled with three Latin dramas. It was in one of these
that Inigo Jones introduced the device of a *machina versatilis* by which "the stage did vary three times in the
acting of one tragedy"; and Jones did not fail to employ
a like device, somewhat later, in staging the royal masques
at court. Italian comedy had long remained the popular
example for university imitation whether in Latin or
English, pastoral or satirical. Of the college pastorals,
those of Christopher Brooke and Phineas Fletcher, already
mentioned, are favorable examples. A satirical comedy of

Ignoramus at Cambridge

great repute was the Latin *Ignoramus* by George Ruggle,
a fellow of Clare Hall, Cambridge; a favorable English
example, acted during the same royal visit, in 1615, is
Albumazar, by Thomas Tomkis of Trinity College.[3] Both
were derived from Italian comedies by the almost con-

[1] For a summary of the Parnassus plays, see *ibid.*, 332, and also G. C.
Moore Smith, *Modern Language Review*, 1915, x, 162.

[2] *Narcissus* was printed from MS. by Miss M. L. Lee, with a valuable
introduction, 1893. The prologue declares the academic attitude in the
words: "We are no vagabonds, we are no arrant rogues that do run
with plays about the country." As to theatromania at Oxford, see "The
Christmas Prince," *Malone Society Reprints*, 1922.

[3] Tomkis is also the reputed author of the elaborate dramatic allegory
Lingua, which has been thought to have been acted as early as 1602 and
to contain contemporary allusions. G. C. Moore Smith, in *Modern
Language Review*, iii, 146.

temporary Gianbattista Porta. The clever satire and broad obscenities of *Ignoramus* so delighted King James that he journeyed back to Cambridge to see the comedy acted again. And it was the same godless play that drew from Milton, some years later, his scathing attack on matter such as this displayed in action and put into the mouths of young intending divines.[1]

Drama at the universities continued in its former courses throughout the reign of King Charles, who succeeded his father in 1625. But from a school exercise justified in its pedagogical bearings, the giving of a play at the university had now become a sumptuous social event, fit, it was thought, with elaborate professional setting and handsome costuming, for the entertainment of royalty. The academicians took themselves very seriously, and treated with the condescension of the amateur, as we have seen, the efforts of the great professional dramatists who were making their age memorable. The records of professional performances at the universities are unsatisfactory. We know that the authorities generally frowned upon them, and even paid London players at times to take themselves off without acting.[2] But the title page of the first quarto of *Hamlet* declares that tragedy as "diverse times acted in the city of London and also in the two universities," however agnostic doubt has sought recently to dispute it.[3] *Volpone* was so well received by academic audiences that Jonson dedicated his play on publication "to the two most noble and most equal sisters," Oxford and Cambridge. Indeed, in latter times, it was Jonson, the accepted entertainer at court, honored by his king, authentically learned and the recipient of honorary recognition at both universities, who linked court and university with the drama of the people. And many were the young collegians who, visiting him, like Beaumont, in his literary Bohemia, were encouraged

Hamlet and *Volpone* at the universities

[1] *Apology for Smectymnuus*, American ed., 1851, p. 267.
[2] F. S. Boas, "Three Hundred Years of Shakespeare at Oxford and Cambridge," *Shakespeare and the Universities*, 1923, p. 42.
[3] *Ibid.*, "Hamlet at Oxford," 14.

and adopted in time as the "sons of Ben" on approval of their poetic and dramatic talents.

Among the "sons of Ben," especially to be mentioned, is Thomas Randolph, a precocious young scholar in whose making the two universities conspired. True to academic standards, his work includes a fine pastoral play, *Amyntas*, in which he surpasses Daniel in wit, spirit, and even poetry, a comedy, *The Jealous Lovers*, in the Plautine manner, and a dramatic satire, *The Muses' Looking Glass*, in which he proclaims his allegiance to Jonson. Randolph died in 1635 before he had completed his thirtieth year, and with him was eclipsed the one university playwright whose work ranks with the greater professional dramatists of his time. Hausted, Strode, Cowley, destined to become a distinguished poet, and Cartwright are among Randolph's contemporaries who were writing drama at the universities in the 'thirties; and two of these greeted King Charles on his visit to Oxford in 1636 in plays that are memorable if not for dramatic excellence, at least in the history of the stage. *The Floating Island*, by William Strode, reports Anthony à Wood,

was acted on a goodly stage . . . and had on it three or four openings on each side thereof, and partitions between them, much resembling the desks or studies in a library, out of which the actors issued forth. The said partitions they could draw in and out at their pleasure upon a sudden, and thrust out new in their places according to the nature of the screen, whereon were represented churches, dwellings, palaces, etc., which for its variety bred very great admiration. Over all was delicate painting resembling the sky, clouds, etc. At the upper end a great fair shut [shutter] of two leaves that opened and shut without any visible help." [1]

Clearly we have here the *scena ductilis* or scene run in on grooves from the flies and arranged to produce the effect of perspective, all to become familiar in Restoration times. But Wood's further statement that this ("as I have been informed") was the first use of such scenery on the English

[1] *History of Oxford*, ed. 1796, ii, 409.

stage, is as unfounded as his claim that the device was "originally due to the invention of Oxford." In a later passage concerning the same events, Wood praises "the great wit of Inigo Jones" in devising the "variety of scenes" which characterized the presentation of Cartwright's tragicomedy, *The Royal Slave*, acted the next evening, a feature of which was the varying of the scene seven times.[1] But already as far back as 1605, Jones had experimented with change of scene, but this was by means of "revolving triangular screens of Italian design." [2] Miss Campbell considers these stagings of the royal visit to Oxford of 1636, in their use of "shutters" as marking the change from the two-sided "houses" to flat scenes; and she calls attention to the employment, "within the arch," in *Microcosmus*, 1634, of "a continuing perspective of ruins" drawn before other scenes while they are changed.[3] In Davenant's masque, *Salmancida Spolia*, 1640, the "border that inclosed the scene" and "the curtain flying up" have become familiar features, and the original drawings of Jones for the setting of this masque disclose a stage "divided by back shutters run in grooves" providing "four complete changes of scene."

Later stages at Oxford

It remains to trace the masque in the reign of Charles. While none attempt the exposition of a story, Jonson at least endeavored to keep the antimasque, which he had invented, coherent in the contrast which it offered to the masque proper. But his successors, losing sight of this, introduced two, three, or more antimasques, which they often conceived of as antic-masques; and they soon came to be little better than the series of "stunts" of a modern vaudeville. Jonson's own activity continued when masquing, dropped for a season, was revived in 1631, Charles himself heading the masquers in *Love's Triumph*

Jonson's and others' masque of Charles's reign

[1] *Ibid.*, 411, *The Royal Slave* is the earliest play to denote change of scene in print.

[2] Chambers, i, 233, and see Reyher, *Les Masques anglais*, 332.

[3] *Scenes and Machines*, 179-194. The designs of Jones are reproduced on p. 181. *Microcosmus*, by Thomas Nabbes, is described as "a moral masque."

through Callipolis in the person of Heroic Love; and a queen's masque, *Chloridia,* followed in the next year. In both, Jonson worked once more in harmony with his old co-worker, Inigo. But soon their quarrel broke out anew, and Jonson was supplanted for the nonce by Aurelian Townshend (who had learned his art of him) in two creditable efforts;[1] and the now bedridden poet wrote only twice thereafter for the king. Charles seems to have been kind to his father's old laureate, whose splenetic temper towards the end must have been trying at times. But Jonson was constrained to see Inigo Jones, in a new partnership with the young and promising dramatist, James Shirley, outdo at least the splendors of the Jacobean masque. In Shirley's *Triumph of Peace,* 1634, the four Inns of Court combined to honor the king and queen and to protest against the outrageous attack which William Prynne, in his stupendous and fanatical *Histriomastix,* had recently launched against the stage in general and acting and masques at court in particular.[2] Prynne represented the Puritan attitude in its most belligerent and malignant mood, and the accidental circumstance that Queen Henrietta Maria did actually take a part in a harmless pastoral play, *The Shepherds' Paradise,* penned by one of her gentlemen in waiting especially to give Her Majesty and her French ladies some exercise in the difficult English language, gave to certain passages of Prynne's book the character of a personal attack. The unhappy zealot was cruelly punished; and this, together with the heartless and ill-timed gayety of the court in this masque, marks one of those points of breaking, soon to bring the nation to civil war.

Masques of Shirley, Carew, and Davenant This year of Shirley's masque, 1634, was signalized by a return masque to that of the young lawyers, acted at court and the work of the king's cup-bearer, the courtly

[1] *Albion's Triumph* and *Tempe Restored,* both 1632; ed. E. K. Chambers's *Aurelian Townshend's Poems and Masks,* 1912, provided with an informing Introduction.
[2] Printed in 1632.

lyrical poet, Thomas Carew. *Cœlum Britannicum,* for such was the title, was staged by Jones, and William Lawe furnished the music. The work contains no less than eight antimasques, necessitating eight changes of scene. It is of no great merit. Clearly, in a loosely strung series of novelties, such as these of Shirley and Carew, the masque reverts to chaos. To this very year, too, belongs the first performance of Milton's *Masque,* "presented at Ludlow Castle before the Earl of Bridgewater, Lord President of Wales." This famous poem in masque-like form was subsequently called *Comus,* from "the god of cheer" of that name employed by Jonson in his masque, *Pleasure Reconciled with Virtue.* And here again Lawe furnished the music. More genuinely poetical and infinitely more coherent than its congeners, this celebrated production, like its forerunner, *Arcades,* lacks that dramatic life with which Jonson contrived to endow even his lesser efforts. In the year preceding the closing of the theaters, Davenant, who had succeeded Jonson in the laureateship, became the leading writer of masques for the court. Of his several efforts in this kind, *The Temple of Love* is the best. In it there is an endeavor to return to a measure of simplicity and coherence at least. But the war was shortly on England, and there was an end of masqueing.

The measure of the influence of the masque on the popular drama is by no means easy to determine. It is always to be remembered that the masque was only the royal form, so to speak, of innumerable like occasional and quasi-dramatic productions. Aside from the masque-like quality of many plays written for court performances —prominent among them *The Sun's Darling* of Dekker and Ford, and Heywood's *Love's Mistress*—the collected works of the latter, for example, and of Shirley, too, exhibit several short pieces, more or less dramatically cast into dialogue, the occasions for the writing of which have been mostly lost; and men like Jonson and Campion may well have written many private entertainments, never pre-

Minor entertainments and masques in plays

served to be collected in their works.[1] Nor should a mention be omitted here of the Lord Mayors' Pageants, given yearly between 1580 and 1639, more than thirty remaining extant to exhibit the adaptability, if not the better talents, of the dramatists Peele, Dekker, Middleton, Heywood, Webster, and Shirley.[2] To return to influences of the kind on actual drama, it could escape not even a careless reader of Shakespeare that in representing his age, like his fellows, he again and again employs diversions of this kind in his plays. These vary from amateur theatricals like Bottom's and Hamlet's calculated *Mouse-Trap*, professionally acted, to the historical maskings of Henry VIII and the wedding devices, antimasque and symbolic dreams of *The Winter's Tale, The Tempest*, and *Cymbeline*.[3] These latter alone may be safely referred to the contemporary vogue of the veritable masque. Elements of the masque have been found in sixteen of the Beaumont and Fletcher plays; and upwards of eighty plays have been counted as containing masques from Kyd to Shirley.[4]

Effect of court presentation on the public stage The degree to which popular staging was affected by the novel devices at court is less readily determined. We may agree that there was "no general adoption of the stage and shifting scenes of Inigo Jones in the London theaters."[5] This change was not complete until after the Restoration. But Jones extended his art to the staging of several regular dramas, usually those acted before royalty at court or at the universities. Scenic plays at Oxford have been mentioned in a preceding paragraph. For Heywood's *Love's Mistress* in 1633 and a highly successful revival of *The Faithful Shepherdess* in the next

[1] See, for example, Heywood's *Pleasant Dialogues and Dramas*, 1637; Shirley's poetic *Triumph of Beauty*, of the same year, and his *Contention of Ajax*, 1640.
[2] Fairholt's *Lord Mayors' Pageants*, 1843; Greg, *List of Masques*, 1902; and R. Withington, *English Pageantry*, ii, 1-25.
[3] *Winter's Tale*, iv, 3; *Tempest*, iv, 1, a masque; and iii, 3, a species of antimasque; *Cymbeline*, v, 4.
[4] R. S. Forsythe, *The Relations of Shirley's Plays*, 1914, p. 79.
[5] Thorndike, A. H., Influence of Court Masques," *Modern Language Publications*, N. S., viii, 116.

year, Jones likewise devised scenery; both were acted at court like the pastoral *Florimene*, given in French by ladies in waiting of the queen. Thorndike is of opinion that when these scenical novelties were repeated, as some of them were in the London playhouses, little or none of the scenery which had made them attractive at court was employed or imitated.[1] And he bases this opinion on the absence of indications of such scenes or allusions to them in the texts of plays which we know were so reacted and in others, like those of Cartwright, the well-known university playwright. But can the mere absence of such directions possibly be accepted as settling such a point? Authority seems on firmer ground in the words: "That backgrounds were frequently used [in the public theaters] and that occasionally painted flats were substituted seems to me probable."[2] In the absence of the possibility of proof, it may be surmised that the pre-Restoration popular stage exhibited far more eagerness to imitate, as far as possible, the new stage devices at court than we have any means of proving. Considering the bareness of the texts in these matters, it is wiser to have a modicum of faith and believe that the usages of the stage, like other human conventions, developed gradually and more or less logically, rather than to accept the repugnant idea of any long continuance side by side of a picture stage, scenically set at court, and a platform, bare of perspective, in the London playhouses.[3]

[1] *Shakespeare's Theater*, 191-195.
[2] *Ibid.*, 198.
[3] The valuable and scholarly Descriptive Catalogue of *Designs by Inigo Jones for Masques and Plays at Court*, by Percy Simpson and C. F. Bell, Oxford 1924, was received too late for a specific consideration in the text of this chapter. The admirable distinguishing feature of this work is the reproduction of fifty plates of designs, sketches and drawings chiefly by Inigo Jones, illustrating the masques of Jonson and his successors. Other reproductions of the collection will be found in *The Works of Ben Jonson*, edited by C. H. Herford and Percy Simpson, now issuing.

CHAPTER XIII

THE CAVALIER DRAMATISTS

Playwrights of the reign of Charles

OUR concern in this chapter is with the playwrights whose work falls within the reign of Charles I and comes to an abrupt end with the Puritan closing of the theaters. In the quarrel that was ripening during these years, the stage was, almost to a man, with the king; for whatever the value of popular approval, the court was the ideal patron and arbiter of taste, and the Puritan was recognized, now as never so fully before, the implacable enemy of the theater. Our consideration of the masque at court and the plays at the universities has already taken us into the reign of the new king; but there are one or two threads still entangling our narrative with the past which call for a moment's explication. These are the career of Massinger, whose association with Fletcher carries on in his own dependent work; and the collaboration of Middleton with Rowley in several plays, superior in certain respects to anything that it was possible for either to achieve independently. Although each of these topics has its roots chronologically in the former reign and although Middleton died but two years after Fletcher, Massinger and Rowley survived almost to the closing of the theaters, and the activity of the former at least continued nearly as long.

William Rowley

William Rowley was born in 1585, and he was thus fifteen years Middleton's junior.[1] At first an actor in Queen Anne's company, Rowley rose to be financial manager of the Prince's men and at last to a prominent place in the King's company. He was for years in great request

[1] William is not to be confused with Samuel, who is probably the Rowley praised by Meres for comedy in 1598 and whose *When You See Me You Know Me,* a play on Henry VIII, is his best known work.

252

as a collaborator, and we find him associated with Day and Wilkins, with Dekker, Webster, and Heywood, and later with Fletcher, Ford, and especially with Middleton. Rowley's name was even coupled on the title page of one play, *The Birth of Merlin*, with that of Shakespeare. We learn that he was beloved by the great poet as well as by Fletcher and Jonson. On the stage, Rowley's parts were commonly those of good-humored, boisterous clownage. He acted Plum Porridge in a masque of Middleton's and similar humorous personages in his own plays and those of others. On this it has been argued that it was Rowley's personality and his talents in such parts that led him into authorship; and that he was, in much of his collaboration, intrusted with the preparation of scenes in which he was personally to appear.[1] Rowley was active for a score of years and his name has been traced in upward of twenty extant plays. The best of them is *All's Lost by Lust*, 1619, a vigorous tragedy on the story of *El Rey Rodrigo*, last of the old Christian kings of Spain. An elemental simplicity and rightness of feeling characterizes this tragedy, qualities none too common in plays which fall close to the novel allurements of Fletcher. What we can identify certainly as Rowley's displays a ready conversancy with the stage, quickness, and buoyancy, if a lack of the higher and more literary qualities of his art.[2]

The collaboration of Rowley with Middleton began about 1616. It is traceable in several important plays. Notable among them is *The Spanish Gipsy*, a romantic tragicomedy of a power and effectiveness able to abide comparison with the best of Fletcher; while *A Fair Quarrel*, equally effective if in a contrasted type, presents, without squeamishness or false perspective, a question in virile

Collabora-. tion of Rowley and Middleton

[1] See on this E. N. S. Thompson, "Elizabethan Dramatic Collaboration," *Englische Studien*, xl, 41.

[2] Other plays, thought to be Rowley's unaided, are *The Birth of Merlin*, *The Shoemaker a Gentleman*, which is a romantic chronicle of ancient British times, *A New Wonder*, a biographical comedy of London life of considerable merit, and *A Match at Midnight*, which is pure Middletonian comedy of manners. These plays range from 1617 to 1631.

ethics, as veritably a problem in those healthier days as are the eternal trivialities and casuistries of our contemporary novelists as to the psychology of the sexes.[1] Even greater than these, for its repulsive but compelling figure of De Flores, who stands with Webster's Bosola not far below Iago, is *The Changeling* in the terrible truth of its psychology of perdition; for Middleton alone, in the greatest of his tragedies of temptation, *Women Beware Women*, scarcely equaled it. The thread of Rowley unraveled from the tangled skein of Elizabethan collaboration will be found both vivid in color and strong of fiber. Though it is not to be denied that to this collaboration Middleton added ease and grace of style and a general competency to cope successfully with dramatic material.[2]

A Game at Chess

It was in all but the last year of the reign of King James that the most striking event of Middleton's life overtook him. It will be recalled that late in 1623 Prince Charles, in company with the king's favorite, Buckingham, returned from a fruitless journey into Spain, undertaken to further a darling project of his royal father, a match between the prince and the Infanta Maria. This match was exceedingly unpopular in England, and Middleton took occasion to satirize the situation on the stage in *A Game at Chess*, in which the scene was set for a chessboard and royal as well as other personages, both English and Spanish, were represented as white and black chessmen. On complaint of the Spanish ambassador the play was suppressed, the actors reprimanded, the author only escaping imprisonment by being conveniently "not found." The king was not very seriously displeased, however, for the match had been broken, and the company was soon acting as usual. *A Game at Chess* is not a political satire of any unusual merit; but it achieved the success of a nine days' wonder, affording us an interesting example of current stage comment on passing events, a practice which

[1] *Works of Charles and Mary Lamb,* ed. E. V. Lucas, 1904, p. 114.
[2] On this collaboration see Miss P. G. Wiggin, *The Middleton-Rowley Plays,* 1897.

we have reason to believe was more widely characteristic of the drama of Elizabeth and the Stuarts than is usually recognized.[1] Without accepting the notion that no subject of either of these sovereigns ever wrote without casting a shadow, more or less dense, of allegory, anagram, or cryptogramic allusion, we must admit that the age delighted in analogies, to us often trivial, far beyond what has been usually suspected. Long before Middleton's representation of James as the "white king," that sovereign had figured, and that not allegorically, in a lost play touching an exciting episode of his life, the conspiracy of Gowry:[2] we cannot but regret that we are unable to know just how; and in 1619 a fine play on John Van Olden Barnavelt, by Fletcher and Massinger, was prohibited, "some great counsellors" being "much displeased with it," perhaps less because it related comparatively recent political happenings in a foreign country than because it seemed to parallel somewhat the fate of Raleigh, recently executed on a very old charge. In 1631, Sir Henry Herbert, Master of the Revels, refused to license a play of Massinger's because it contained "dangerous matter" concerning the deposing of Sebastian, King of Portugal. Soon after a play entitled *Believe As You List* was staged, its subject the pathetic story of the return of Antiochus, thought to have been slain in battle, with the denial of his kingship and identity at the behest of Rome; and the author, Massinger, apologizes in his prologue with pointed irony for his ignorance of geography and his accidental lighting on the parallel of "a late sad example." [3] *Believe As You List* is almost certainly the play staged by Herbert in an earlier form, and "the late sad example" may well be that of the Pals-

Other plays of alleged political import

---

[1] On the general subject, see T. S. Graves, "Political Use of the Stage During the Reign of James I," *Anglia*, xxxviii, 1914, p. 137. In Bullen's *Middleton*, 1885-86, vii, 1, will be found an account of this play, to which E. C. Morris has added in *Englische Studien*, xxxviii, 1907, p. 39.

[2] Played by the King's men in December, 1604. Winwood's *Memorials* of State, 1725, ii, 41.

[3] See S. R. Gardiner, "The Political Element in Massinger," *Contemporary Review*, 1876, xxviii, p. 495, who finds political allusiveness in some five of the author's plays.

grave, husband of the Princess Elizabeth, who had lost not only his kingdom of Bohemia, but his Electorship in the empire under the imperial ban, and was now little befriended by his royal father-in-law in his time of misfortune. As to Massinger, the historian has found political allusions in others of his plays; and we may believe that the poet was only in this respect somewhat more daring than some of his fellows.

Philip
Massinger

Philip Massinger, the son of a gentleman attached to the service of the Earl of Pembroke, was born at Salisbury in 1584, the year of the birth of Beaumont. He quitted Oxford without a degree in 1606, and we next hear of him about 1613, petitioning Henslowe, with Field and Daborne, for a release from prison (doubtless for debt) on promise of a play.[1] Fletcher and Massinger were personal friends of long standing, and the latter had more hand in the body of plays that go under the names of Beaumont and Fletcher, as we have seen, than had ever Beaumont. But Massinger was likewise an independent dramatist. His earliest work was for the Lady Elizabeth's and the Queen's men; his work with Fletcher and the plays which he wrote independently and subsequent to Fletcher's death were for the King's company with which he remained associated until his death in 1640. Massinger began, like his fellows, in the revision of older work; for example, *The Virgin Martyr*, originally possibly Dekker's; and his hand has been traced by some in *Henry VIII* and *The Two Noble Kinsmen*, which we have found already associated with both Fletcher and Shakespeare.[2] To Massinger should logically have fallen the mantle so regally worn by Fletcher since Beaumont and Shakespeare had ceased to write. But Massinger, with all his talents, was less amenable to the public taste; and he was soon supplanted by the subtler fascinations of Ford and the pleasing and inventive unoriginality of Shirley. A tone suggesting pov-

[1] Greg, *Henslowe*, ii, 110.
[2] A. H. Cruickshank, *Philip Massinger*, 1920, denies Massinger's hand in either, 84-104.

erty and the want of success marks some of Massinger's
later dedications; and it has even been questioned whether
he was contemporaneously very popular on the stage.[1]

While in his unaided tragicomedies especially, Mas- The plays
singer carried forward faithfully the traditions of Fletcher, of Massinger
his was no spirit of servile imitation. Massinger's is a
certainty of touch and an earnestness, intent on subjects
neither frivolous nor pandering to a degenerate taste.
The Maid of Honor, 1622, and *The Renegado*, a couple
of years later, are both of them fine plays, sustained by a
noble sense of ethics, neither strained nor perverted; they
are well constructed and admirably written in a free and
rapid blank verse, abounding in the long phrase carried
over, and different from the firmer-fibered versification of
Beaumont as well as from the darting hendecasyllables of
Fletcher. In *The Renegado* a beneficent Jesuit figures;
the *dénouement* of *The Maid of Honor* sends Camiola, the
dignified and high principled heroine, into a convent; an
earlier theme of Massinger's is the martyrdom of Saint
Dorothea. These things, his friendships, and other indications have been thought to point to an affiliation, on the
poet's part, with the Roman faith; but this Massinger's
most recent appreciators deny.[2] Massinger's method is
eclectic. In an early play, *The Great Duke of Florence*,
he rewrote an old play into an excellent drama in the contemporary fashion.[3] Often he refashions old and hackneyed romantic material, as in *The Bashful Lover*, half
Shakespeare, half Fletcher, into something both animated
and justified in the difference. When he undertakes a
classical subject, such as his tragedy, *The Roman Actor*,
Massinger is true to the ideals of his school; the play
becomes the romance of the imperious empress Domnitia
and her passion for a common player, whose situation
raises him to the heroic. The boldness of this topic and

[1] A. W. Ward in *Encyclopœdia Britannica*, ed. 1914, article Massinger;
denied by M. Chelli, *Le Drame de Massinger*, 1924, p. 50.
[2] *Ibid.*, 62 and 337; and Cruickshank, as above, p. 3.
[3] The source is *A Knack to Know a Knave* of Henslowe's repertory.

257

the excellence of the handling of it justify the poet's own estimate of this as the best of his plays. *The Fatal Dowery* and *The Unnatural Combat*, too, this last on the terrible story of the Cenci, but putting the emphasis on murder, not incest, are tragedies full of eloquence and action vividly realized on the stage.

Massinger's dramatic art Massinger has been criticized for a tendency to exalt virtue into Quixotic absurdity and blacken villainy into incomprehensibility. This is, of course, merely the Fletcherian art of exaggerated contrast. A more serious defect, likewise the later Fletcher's, is the conception of good and evil as less innate than a matter of extraneous circumstances. The idea that all human virtue as potentially soluble in the acid of temptation, provided only the acid be strong enough, is scarcely a conception peculiar to Massinger, or even to his age. Perhaps it is a certain inability on Massinger's part to rise in situations of passion on the wings of poetry, and his habitual substitution of rhetoric, effective enough in itself, but not always where it belongs, that causes the critics who accept Fletcher often to do less than justice to Massinger. Among plays not already mentioned, *The Guardian*, 1633, is an excellent example of what this adaptive and yet independent talent of Massinger's could do with Spanish material such as that employed by Fletcher in *The Pilgrim* or *The Chances;* and in its admirable manipulation of old romantic stuff, its liveliness, humor, and extravagance, it stands a good second to these more famous plays. It has been truly remarked that Massinger is an author to be read in large draughts, if we are to get into his spirit; and, thus read, he is likely to claim the reader for his own. Two critics of diverse nationality and outlook have recently illustrated this: Canon Cruickshank, who finds in the poet consummate stagecraft, a dexterous style distinguishable for dignity and lucidity and a melodious versification; and the late young French scholar, Maurice Chelli, who, affirming especially Massinger's essential independence of Fletcher, recognizes in the subject of his study a genius ruled by the spirit of order and coherency, "an intelligence attentive and calm, and, if a stranger to sudden moments of illumination, as void of chaotic hesitancy." [1]

Let us return to comedy, especially the comedy of manners, latterly refined, in the superficialities of the intercourse of gentlemen at least, in the hands of Fletcher, whose later plays of the type seek foreign rather than English scene, however Jonson and Middleton still reveled frankly in the vulgarities of London city life. With Middleton's death, in 1627, the older realistic comedy of London citizen life disappears except for occasional examples. Both Massinger's efforts in this species were on the stage before that event, and both are creditable in their effort to preserve an older mode by the infusion into it of a new spirit. *A New Way to Pay Old Debts* is one of the few plays, outside of Shakespeare, which, written in the seventeenth century (1625), still holds the professional stage. And the earlier *City Madam* is almost as good, however it repeats with new variations the picture of the rich city merchant, his foolish wife and daughters, a theme already well executed in *Eastward Ho*. Among writers of comedy still contemporary with Middleton and these plays of Massinger was Thomas May, better known for his tragedies on classical subjects, and Robert Davenport, whose able effort to revive the old chronicle history in *King John and Matilda*, in 1624, is his best claim to remembrance. Heywood's comedies continue, too, throughout this time and far into the reign of Charles. His pleasing and modern adaptation of Plautus, *The Captives*, falling in this very year, and the interesting domestic drama, *The English Traveller*, which in a way repeats the situation of *A Woman Killed with Kindness*, in 1630. [2]

Almost coincident with the accession of Charles, Jonson returned to the stage with *The Staple of News* in which

Comedies of manners of Massinger and others

Jonson's last comedies

---

[1] *Le Drame de Massinger,* 342.
[2] *The Captives* has recently been reprinted by A. C. Judson, 1921.

the poet's satire hardens into allegory in his hands. *The New Inn*, an effort at lighter comedy, was ill received, four years later, and *The Tale of a Tub*, which soon followed, fared little better. In 1633 Jonson closed the cycle of his plays with *The Magnetic Lady or Humors Reconciled*, holding to his theories, his personal enmities, and satirizing Inigo Jones in particular to the end. This is not the Jonson of *Volpone*, for age, ill health, and poverty was doing each its work. But there is now and then in these later dramas a flash of the old spirit, that telling power in words, that searching satire and sturdy moral stamina. Jonson died universally lamented in 1637 and left not his peer behind him. To comedy he bequeathed the method of humors illuminated with a saturnine play of satirical and ironic comment and the conception of a close-knit and rational constructiveness in plot which affected the practices of the stage for generations.

Of "the sons of Ben," from Beaumont to Randolph and Cartwright, we have heard somewhat, and of the joys of their literary Bohemia,

> those lyric feasts
> Made at the Sun,
> The Dog, the triple Tun,
> Where we such clusters had
> As made us nobly wild, not mad.

Less on the plane of convivial equality were Jonson's generosities to lesser men, his self-assumed preceptorship of Field, a fatherless boy, and of Brome,[1] who was his body servant, in the art of play-making; and his tender little epitaph on Salathiel Pavey, a child-actor who died "when scarce thirteen":

[1] A. Thaler, *Modern Language Notes*, February 20, 1920, finds Brome an actor in 1628 and believes that Jonson called Brome his "man" metaphorically. Does Brome call himself "a serving creature" in the commendatory verses prefixed to the Beaumont and Fletcher folio, 1647, "metaphorically" also?

THE CAVALIER DRAMATISTS

Yet three filled zodiacs had he been
The stage's jewel;
And did, what now we moan,
Old men so duly,
As, sooth, the Parcæ thought him one,
He played so truly.

The influence of Jonson on his fellows was altogether the most profound and immediate of his age; an affirmation the more fully to be realized in that Fletcher's art of an emphasized contrast and of personage distinguished by salient trait, as we have seen, is really an outgrowth of the Jonsonian theory of humors, and an application of that theory to a wider field.

Foremost among faithful disciples of Jonson was Richard Brome with his "low, homespun" stuff, as he himself called his dramatic endeavors. If we are seeking adjectives descriptive, the humble, the deprecatory, the apologetic Brome will best describe him; for he is always harping on his lowliness, his unworthiness to intrude into the company of greater men. Trickery, disguise, "humors," often degenerated into mere eccentricity of conduct, abundant bustle, and much grossness are the elements which go to make up the comedies of Brome; we miss not only distinction of style and diction, but likewise that hold upon reality which contrived to keep Jonson, with all his "humors," prevailingly sane even in his lesser work.[1] One comedy of Brome rises above the general level, and this is *The Northern Lass*, the story of the honest infatuation of a simple country girl for a fine gentleman who has laughingly suggested himself as a fit husband for her, with her actual winning of him by her constancy and honest devotion. This comedy enjoyed a long term of life on the stage, and deserved it. Among other "sons of Ben" may be named Shakerley Marmion, who catches at times the spirit of Jonsonian railing; Jasper Mayne, who imitates

Richard Brome and younger "sons of Ben"

[1] H. F. Allen, *The Comedies of Brome*, Michigan Thesis, 1912; E. C. Andrews has treated more fully *The Life and Works of Brome*. Yale Thesis, 1913.

261

his hilarity and intricacy of plot; Henry Glapthorne and William Cartwright, each of whom repeats his situations, with less verve and success, however, than Brome. Thomas Nabbes was a stronger playwright than these and a respectable poet outside the drama; and Sir Aston Cockayne, friend of Beaumont, like the Duke of Newcastle and his duchess, a veritable bluestocking, were literary people of rank, measurably removed from the realities and pleased to play with play-making for a diversion. The story goes that Jonson and Shirley were personal literary advisers of the ducal pair, and that some of their comedies owe more than was acknowledged to these experts. The results in any case are not remarkable. Of this entire group we could spare all but a play or two of Brome and *The Bride* of Nabbes, a cleaner, more natural, and less labored comedy than the type had seen for many a day.

James Shirley

Our knowledge of Shirley, like that of Shakespeare, depends on whether we assume the pose of agnostic small scholarship and question every "fact," not actually documented or corroborated by at least two witnesses under seal or under oath. In this case we "know" half a dozen trifles. On the other hand, if we accept ordinary human probabilities on the basis of information derived from those, like excellent old Anthony à Wood, who had no reason in the world to play dishonest tricks upon posterity, we know enough to "place" Shirley, learn what he was about, and go about our other business.[1] On these latter premises, James Shirley was born in 1596, in London, educated at the Merchant Taylors' School, Cambridge, and likewise Oxford, became a schoolmaster at St. Albans, and went over to the Roman Church, finally coming up to London and settling into dramatic authorship about the time that King Charles came to his throne. His first work was for the Queen's men playing at the Phœnix, but before long he

[1] J. Schipper, "Shirley, sein Leben und seine Werke," *Wiener Beiträge,* xxxvi, 1911; A. H. Nason, *James Shirley,* and R. S. Forsythe, *The Relation of Shirley's Plays,* both 1914; and A. C. Baugh, "Some New Facts about Shirley," *Modern Language Review,* xvii, 1922.

was writing for the leading King's men, and rose by his abilities, his steady industry and adaptability to the tastes of his audiences, to the leadership in play-making left vacant by the death of Fletcher. Shirley, while in all likelihood of no important family, lived on terms of intimacy with the court and was personally esteemed by King Charles, who suggested to him the subject of one of his most popular plays, *The Gamester.* The dramatist was at the height of his career in 1634, when the writing of the splendid masque, *The Triumph of Peace,* was intrusted to him by the four Inns of Court. Two years later he visited Ireland under the patronage of the Earl of Kildare and wrote for the new theater which Ogilby had recently founded in the Irish capital. But 1640 saw Shirley back again in London, and when the war broke out he served his king under the immediate command of another patron, the literary Duke of Newcastle, sharing in the royal defeat at Marston Moor. The theater closed to his activities, Shirley returned to his first profession, that of schoolmaster, publishing his poems and individual plays, collecting those of Beaumont and Fletcher, and laboring at school books and hack writing. Shirley lived on until the great fire of 1666, dying with his wife of exposure in consequence of their enforced flight into the fields on the destruction of their home. Neither quarrels nor enmities are recorded against Shirley. He was a partisan in the cause of his patrons and as unfair to the virtues of Puritanism as many have been since his time without his reasons.

Shirley wrote about as many plays as Shakespeare, and, save for what must have been rather refashioning than collaboration in the case of two plays originally Chapman's, this work was done alone.[1] The dramatic work of Shirley ranges widely and includes comedies of manners, by far the largest class, a pastoral, extravaganza, and Spanish comedy of intrigue, many tragicomedies more or

The dramatic activity of Shirley

[1] These plays are *Chabot Admiral of France* and *The Ball*, a comedy. The former was revised about 1635, the latter written in 1632, and probably in no part Chapman's.

less pseudo-historical, and finally, four tragedies. Shirley was a diligent student of the great dramatists who had preceded him. From them he learned his art; and his stagecraft, his conception of personage, his diction and his poetry proclaim him of the mighty brotherhood. This involves the confession that Shirley is to a greater degree than most of his predecessors a man of books; but it should not deny him a marked originality in giving a new turn to his material, nor genuine power, in his comedies of manners at least, of drawing on the life about him. Shirley is at his best in representing a certain phase of the social life of that new class, neither wholly noble and courtly nor yet entirely bourgeois, out of which has evolved what is now known in English-speaking countries as "society." Shirley's first comedy, *Love Tricks*, is a composite of several kinds of drama; in *The Wedding*, Jonson rules; in *The Brother*, Fletcher. These, too, were early. But after this the poet asserts his individuality, and in *The Witty Fair One*, a clever comedy of surprise, displays an originality and constructive excellence second to none. In general it may be said that Shirley simplified plot, clarified diction, and escaped singularity. The difficulties of language, allusion, and construction so usual in the earlier dramatists have all but disappeared from his dialogue. He has none of the mannerism of Fletcher, little of the rhetoric of Massinger, and he produces his effects without stirring our horror and loathing as do Marston and Webster at times. Ease, moderation, taste, and poetry of spirit at need, no poetry by way of garniture—these are some of the qualities of Shirley.

Plays and dramatic art of Shirley

The best of several excellent tragicomedies is *The Politician*, in which some have found a situation suggested by Hamlet. Among lighter romantic dramas few are more effective in a certain unexpectedness—which is better than surprise—than *The Opportunity*, the plot of a Spanish source. Of Shirley's tragedies *The Traitor*, a story of daring intrigue, and *The Cardinal*, in which those whose pursuit is ever of the eternal likeness of things have found similarities to *The Duchess of Malfi,* are by far the best. There is nothing more certain about Shirley than that he is not a disciple of Fletcher. He recurs to an earlier, a sounder view of even the romantic relations of life and keeps measurably closer to the actualities. Once more, Shirley is no decadent either in the larger ethics underlying his conception of the world of men or in pandering to the lower tastes of his auditors. Indeed, despite the notorious example which Charles Kingsley made of Shirley, taking, somewhat unfairly, mainly one of his plays, *The Gamester,* as his illustration, Shirley is distinctly cleaner in this respect than Fletcher.[1] Of course no dramatist could transfer to his scenes the actual fast life of his day, the races, as in *Hyde Park,* the mania for gambling, the life of pleasure, in several examples, and not speak with an openness which we now consider vulgar, or did at least before the war. But Shirley's was no degenerate's outlook on life, and his favorite situation, that of the *roué* reclaimed by the steadfastness of a good woman, is not the favorite with such. Shirley's comedies of manners, *Hyde Park, The Lady of Pleasure* (from which Sheridan disdained not to borrow his Lady Teazle), *The Ball, The Example,* are delightful reading to-day to one whose palate has not been vitiated by the insinuating improprieties of some of the drama which we praise in this our purer age.

Acceptance on the stage in the time of King Charles was not so easy a matter. There were not only contemporaries to rival. The great dramas of the past, Shakespeare, Jonson and Fletcher at least, still held the boards, strong in an acting tradition handed down for a generation; and their performance was demanded, as the annals abundantly prove, from time to time, by the London play-goers as well as the court. Shirley's solution of the problem was to ring new changes on old and tried material and in the

The problem of the Carolan dramatists

---

[1] C. Kingsley, *Plays and Puritans,* 1873, ed. 1889, pp. 57-61; also S. R. Gardiner, *History of England,* vii, 331.

process avoid, as he does almost uniformly, the charge of plagiarism. Massinger followed Fletcher, but with a seriousness and in a manner his own; lesser men were either frankly imitative of the past or *nil*. There was another, a bolder, a more daring solution, and that was Ford's. To employ an obvious figure, the Jacobean theater-goer had long become accustomed to a highly seasoned diet, dashed with stimulants. Neither the simple fare of old times wholly satisfied him nor the coarser provender of terror and brutal crime. The age loved to be thrilled rather than physically horrified, and it demanded novelty, especially the novelty of surprise, a solution unforeseen, a disaster unpresaged. Now this was exactly what Ford gave to his time; and more, a problem left to the auditor to puzzle over; the solution has become unimportant. To accomplish this Ford set before his patrons a meat, to return to our figure, high in flavor and dangerously close to being tainted, delicately dressed with sentiment and exquisite poetry to make it seductively palatable. The art of Ford is almost as conscious as that of Jonson, as deliberate, as calculated. But Ford begins by accepting Fletcher and the implications of Fletcher. With much show in his utterances of a scholarly contempt for the common crowd (a trick of Jonson's), Ford plays on the feelings and addresses his subtle casuistry to the understanding of his auditors, predicating his success as designedly as a George More.[1]

John Ford As to John Ford, the man, once more we are constrained to repeat the futile formula confessing our all but total want of information. A Devonshire man, of good family and born in 1586, somewhat connected with the law, possibly of Exeter College, Oxford, certainly of the Middle Temple in 1602, a dramatic writer between 1626 and 1639, then lost for any work or any mention. This is all we "know" of Ford. Tradition relates that he was of a mel-

[1] See the excellent monograph of Professor S. P. Sherman, "Ford's Contribution to the Decadence of the Drama," *Materialien*, xxiii, 1908.

ancholy cast of mind, obviously fitting in a tragic poet; and, his own prologues and prefaces declare, as already suggested, an attitude of independence and contempt for the general opinion which may well have been a pose. Ford's name has been associated with *The Sun's Darling*, a poetical "moral masque" of Dekker's in which the younger poet's part was doubtless chiefly that of revision. His hand, too, is avowed on the title page with the same collaborator and William Rowley in the fine domestic tragedy, *The Witch of Edmonton*, here also probably in a *The Witch of Edmonton* later revision. This tragedy mingles the motif of a forced marriage with the supernatural, giving us, as a result, a drama of much tenderness and truth. The skill with which the two are interwoven and the sympathy of feeling for the old hag, Mother Sawyer, the reported witch, are both much in contrast with the grosser picture of the popular delusion of witchcraft which Heywood and Brome presented in *The Late Lancashire Witches*, when that subject was holding public attention about 1633. It may well be that Ford's part in the former play was referable to a revival of it in view of its contemporary timeliness. About all these Stuart contributions to witch-lore, it is to be remarked that, following the royal opinion of King James, not one of them called into question the reality of the delusion. Reference has been made above to Robert Davenport's attempt to revive the old-fashioned chronicle play in his able *King John and Matilda*. This was in 1624. Nearly ten years later, Ford likewise turned back to this attractive, if now antiquated, form to give to the stage, in *Perkin Warbeck*, an historical drama of much dignity and *Perkin Warbeck* dramatic power. It will be recalled that Perkin was an impostor, who aspired to the throne of Henry VII on the pretense that he was in reality one of the two youthful sons of Edward IV, who tradition affirms were murdered in the Tower by the procurement of their wicked uncle, Richard Crookback. The bones of the little victims had not been found in the time of Ford, buried as they were beneath the stairs in the Tower; and the cue of the playwright and the novelty of his play was the presentation of the story by way of a problem, raising the question was Perkin Warback really an impostor, or possibly a veritable prince? [1]

Ford's contribution to the drama

But neither these works nor his contributions to comedy, which are often despicable in their coarseness and pruriency, constitute the real Ford.[2] Passing *The Lovers' Melancholy*, a story of melancholia and its remedy derived from the popular book of the moment, Robert Burton's *Anatomy of Melancholy*, and the really fine tragicomedy, *The Lady's Trial*, Ford's latest work, we have in *Love's Sacrifice* and *'Tis Pity She's a Whore*, the distinctive and original additions of Ford to the topics of the stage. It is the point in each that our sympathies are sentimentally enlisted to palliate, if not to excuse, what we should ordinarily revolt at as indefensible and morally to be reprobated. In *Love's Sacrifice* two lovers struggle against an illicit infatuation which leads them all but to extremity, and the struggle is presented as a triumph of "heroism." In *'Tis Pity* we have a tale of the incestuous passion of a brother and sister, suffused with a false and sentimental pathos and obscured in casuistry and a beauty of diction which must have carried many an auditor with it. If decadency in art have anything to do with a loss, so to speak, of the sense of that moral direction which guides mankind, like the compass, in his perilous passage through life, and preserves for him an elemental conception at least of the right and honorable direction and the wrong, then Ford's is emphatically decadent art. On the other hand, this notorious tragedy—and it is something that it does remain a tragedy—is beautifully written, full of poetry and possessed of a strange power of pathos despite the repellent coarseness inseparable from such a topic. *The*

The Broken Heart

Broken Heart, this last aside, is Ford's most famous play;

---

[1] Compare the similar question raised in Massinger's *Believe As You List*, on the stage about the same time.

[2] See especially as to this *Fancies Chaste and Noble*, a repulsive example.

and except for the grotesque figure of a preposterously jealous husband, which the age may have accepted as comic, but which we emphatically can not, we have a master tragedy of extraordinary force and beauty. The surprising and original climax in the last act, which, described in cold blood, strikes the hearer as wholly artificial and unnatural, read with the careful preparation of the preceding scenes, carries artistic conviction. Ultra-romantic, supremely original, and cast in a no-man's land of a most unclassical Epire, with oracles consulted and the manners of a court of the renaissance, *The Broken Heart* creates in the reader, none the less, a truer sense of reality than most of the romantic dramas of Fletcher or Shirley and is reminiscent in its gnomic wisdom and passages of poetry of the hand of Webster or Shakespeare.[1]

The lesser dramas of King Charles's reign, where they were not Jonson vulgarized, as we have seen, were all but wholly Fletcher. Especially true was this of Brome, whose industry and inventiveness, backed with honest sentiment, produced, in several plays, a fair imitation of Fletcherian tragicomedy; however, no ray of poetry illuminate any of it. Cartwright, Glapthorne, Wilson, and many more turned out acceptable journey work of this kind, although we weary of material grown stale and a decadence in verse and diction which the licenses in these particulars of Shakespeare, Fletcher, and Massinger had fostered. Among the horde of gentlemen and courtiers who wrote, the cavaliers' dramatists—for they wrote only for such—Sir William Davenant holds an important place as the successor of Jonson in the laureateship and the link between two ages, both for his plays and for the position which he took at the Restoration as one of the two royal patentees, charged with the revival of the stage. Davenant, who was born

Sir William Davenant and lesser cavalier dramatists

---

[1] To the category of Ford we may now add *The Queen, or the Excellency of her Sex,* printed anonymously in 1653; as three authorities unite in this opinion, the editor in *Materialien,* 1906, W. Bang; S. P. Stuart, in *Modern Language Notes,* xiii, and now H. D. Sykes, *Notes and Queries,* December, 1920.

in 1606, was the son of an Oxford inn-keeper and godson of Shakespeare. Service with Fulke Greville, Lord Brooke, the friend of Sidney and a writer of literary tragedies, may possibly have turned young Davenant from intended trade to play-writing. At any rate, he began just when the death of Fletcher seemed to leave no one to follow in his steps. Davenant's earliest efforts were tragic, suggesting reading in the old drama of revenge, a vein of his own much tempered with Fletcher. After an illness which interrupted his career, Davenant returned to the stage, in 1630, with a novel emphasis on one of the features of previous drama that was destined later to develop, in the hands of Dryden, into one of the most distinctive varieties of the drama of the Restoration, the heroic play.[1]

Davenant and the beginnings of the heroic play

In a former chapter we found certain plays of Fletcher discovering a new and artificial code of conduct derived from popular French romances which were the contemporary reading of cultivated people and referable in part at least to Spanish ideals. It was out of this that the followers of Fletcher, first in this respect among them Davenant, developed the heroic play, which seems mainly distinguishable from other romantic drama in that it has displaced the hero of deeds superhuman and the hero passionate with the hero supersensitive, "the paragon of virtue and the pattern of noble conduct." *Love and Honor*, Davenant's earliest play of the type, dates 1634, and involves the generosity, disinterestedness, the loyalty and exaggerated courtesy which are the salient features of its kind. And *The Fair Favorite*, 1638, maintains the type, including in its theme as well an attendant feature of the new cult of honor, that of Platonic love. Historically a recrudescence, in precious and literary form, of mediæval asceticism and chivalrous love, the Platonic cult finds its immediate inspiration in the heroic novel, *L'Astrée*, by Honoré D'Urfé, in which is expounded this whole phil-

[1] Dryden expressly declares Davenant "for heroic plays, . . . the first light we had of them." "Of Heroic Plays," *Essays of Dryden*, ed. W. P. Ker, i, 149.

osophy of love. The cult made its way into England with the coming of the French queen of Charles I; and its vogue extended to fashionable literary circles such as that of the Duchess of Newcastle, to re-echo satirically in Jonson's *New Inn*, 1629, and in the anonymous *Lady Alimony*, not very long after. In 1634 Davenant glorified the new cult in his masque at court, *The Temple of Love*, apotheo- sizing Her Majesty as the founder of "a new religion of love"; but a year later his *Platonic Lovers*, a drama given over to "love debates," scarcely maintained the ideal which he had labored to create. The two or three other plays of Davenant which preceded the Restoration are not notably of the heroic type. It is perhaps enough for us here to repeat that in the inflated "romance" of Fletcher, with its method of heightened contrast, the heroic idea has its beginnings in English drama; that Shirley, who quite mis- understood heroic passion in his *Parliament of Love*, lent the practice of a simplified plot, the trend of the age suggested the employment of the heroic couplet, and the example of the French romances added the definite con- ception of the hero supersensitive, the ideal of conduct. We have here a development perfectly logical and refer- able back with confidence at least as far as Fletcher.[1]

The Platonic cult of love

No better example of the cavalier dramatist of mediocre ability could be suggested than that of Lodowick Carlell, a member of the king's household, at last Keeper of the Great Forest at Richmond. It was Carlell's life as a courtier that made him a playwright, and he rather depre- cates the idea that his play, *The Deserving Favorite*, 1629, should "travel so far as the common stage." Car- lell's tragicomedies are all of the heroic adventurous type, ranging in scene from legendary Britain to "Burgony"; and he clothes them in a degenerate and hybrid medium of expression, "too fiberless for good verse and too rhyth- mical for successful prose."[2] In Carlell dramatic degen-

Degenerate "romances" of Carlell and others

[1] See B. J. Pendlebury, *Dryden's Heroic Plays*, as cited above, p. 275, for a critique of this view here reaffirmed.
[2] On Carlell, see C. H. Gray's reprint of *The Deserving Favorite*, 1905.

eracy is at least that of form. Even more wildly, grotesquely adventurous, and more irrationally "romantic" are the several tragicomedies of John Gough, Sir William Lower, and the Killigrew brothers who wrote, three of them, and separately. Of these Thomas was reared as a page in the court and retained the personal friendship of Charles II on the Restoration. To this he owed his royal patent for the re-establishment of a theatrical company at that time, Davenant being granted the only other. Thomas Killigrew is also accountable for one of the most ribald comedies that disgraced the English stage, and it is only fair, to the credit of much-abused Restoration times, to remember that Killigrew's play and the vulgarities of Brome were first witnessed and approved by subjects of Charles I. Nor is the list of cavalier dramatists easily exhausted. Sir William Lower, some time governor of Virginia, William Habington, poet in an elder style, Francis Quarles, serious religious poet and author of the popular book, *Emblems*, and the two famous lyrists, Richard Lovelace and Sir John Suckling, all were writers of dramas in their day,[1] the last named, alone distinguished. It is characteristic of what the stage had become that Suckling, who was as rich as he was dissolute and extravagant, should have put his tragedy, *Aglaura*, on the stage more gorgeously costumed than any play before its time. In the same spirit he furnished out a hundred horse for the disastrous Scottish campaign at an expense of £12,000. Suckling was a poet of genuine talent and his *Goblins* is as lively and agreeable a comedy as his *Brennoralt* is an ably-planned and well-written tragedy, albeit both are amateurish. In another age and with a more serious motive, Suckling might have been a great dramatist.

The Killigrews

Sir John Suckling

Thus it was that the old drama, save for the productive ingenuity of Shirley and the sensational genius of Ford,

[1] The plays of Lovelace have perished. Of the several dramatic romances of the Killigrews *Cicilia,* 163, drawn from *Le Grand Cyrus,* is typical.

dwindled away into amateurish rococo romance and unabashed vulgarity. And now militant Puritanism rose in its might against the stage and its veritable abuses. The very first year of the reign of Charles I witnessed the prohibition by Parliament of plays on Sunday, and Nathaniel Giles, who had recruited the stage for thirty years with boys under an abuse of the privilege of the crown "to take up singing children" for the service of the royal chapel, was forbidden the continuance of this notorious practice. The trial and condemnation of Prynne, who voiced Puritan anathema against the stage in his stupendous *Histriomastix*, was only a temporary victory for the cavalier party, and in the upshot embittered the quarrel. *The Lady's Trial*, the latest play of Ford, was licensed in 1638; and Shirley's *Cardinal*, 1641, was the last great tragedy to be tried out on the stage, his comedy, *The Sisters*, April, 1642, practically ending the long list of plays licensed by the Master of the Revels. In 1636 and 1637 the plague had shut up all places of assembly for a time; and, in 1642, the theaters were finally closed by order of a triumphant Puritan Parliament; and soon after, all players were declared rogues within the meaning of existing statutes.

Puritanism closes the theaters

273

CHAPTER XIV

The Drama in Summary

The drama
as a social
institution CONSIDERED as a social institution, many were the changes in English drama from the days of its use as an illustrative feature of the Church's service to the time when triumphant Puritanism declared it an ungodly and frivolous thing and decreed that it should be no more. In the Middle Ages the drama became a spectacle, the most conspicuous feature of a religious festival and an authentic utterance of lay civic life. The Reformation turned it into a powerful controversial weapon; the humanists into an educational instrument offering an example of conduct and an aid in the study of language, enunciation, and ease of carriage. And during all this time, however latent, it was the picture of life which the drama presented, its power to divert and amuse that carried all these ulterior purposes to success. From the moralists' point of view the drama lost when the teaching function ceased; from an artistic point of view, it gained everything. For however trammeled with the need of pleasing the court or satisfying the rules of the classicist, drama had now become an art with the world to mirror, and that inexhaustible subject, the passions and conduct of men, for its theme. Elizabethan drama could never have been what it became had it remained in the leading strings of the classicists or existed merely to entertain a pleasure-loving court. The literature of a class is often choice and beautiful, but it seldom carries beyond its own age. Elizabethan drama at its height was truly a great national utterance, because its constituency, those whom it represented in its art, ranged through every rank and grade, because its appeal

was thousand-tongued and grounded in the hearts of uni- A great
versal humanity. Stir with tales of love and wonder, national
utterance
rouse with the trumpets of national fame, or linger lov-
ingly or humorously on the every-day life that was his at
his elbow, Shakespeare and his fellow dramatists had their
auditors heart and soul with them, auditors possessed of
a hearty capacity for joy, an insatiable appetite for story,
and a genuine sense of beauty, all of which have never
existed simultaneously to a like degree in those who have
followed them. Marked disintegrating influences that set
in with King James were the new cynical view of life and
the eager effort to outdo the past, not in inventiveness—
that was impossible—but in exaggerated and subtilized
emotion and situation, the thing that led in one direction
to Ford, in another to the heroic play. Another such
influence was, contradictorily, conventionality, which demanded the repetition of personage and plot especially in
the comedy of manners. So the drama narrowed in range
and appeal, first in Fletcher, then in Shirley, until with
Puritanism, standing askant and hostile, the last poet's
constituency scarcely reached beyond the court(and such
as would like to be thought as of the court.

As to source and inspiration, Elizabethan drama finds Sources
its ultimate roots, as we have seen, in the semi-religious inspiration
festivals of the folk and in efforts of the Church to enhance
the interest of its service and instruct in Bible story and
Christian doctrine. Out of this grew the realism, the
humor of comedy and appeal to the ideal by way of sentiment and tragic emotion. With the moral play came the
necessity for greater inventiveness, and the storehouses of
legend and story were ransacked for material and suggestion. The renaissance brought a minuter and a more
popular study of the ancients; and the examples of Roman
tragedy and comedy transformed the shapeless succession
of scenes, which constituted the method of the sacred
drama, into a structure, guided by rules of procedure, at
times restricted by them. The influence of the classics on

English drama is not to be underrated. Where Seneca and Plautus did not offer a pattern to follow, they set up an example to recoil from. The very excesses of romanticism are often begotten in protest against rule. And yet, when all is said, the Elizabethan, as a whole, is a romantic drama, exuberant, imaginative, turbulent, and uncontrolled by precedent, except for Jonson, his followers, and the collegians. And the inspiration, with most of the sources, for all this, comes from renaissance Italy, not the Italy that was or ever had been, but what the enchanted imaginations of Englishmen made her, the beautiful, seductive siren of the ages. But we shall misinterpret Elizabethan drama if we deny its reality, its unapproachable verity and faithfulness to actual contemporary life. It is because of the frankness and obviousness with which all this learning of Rome and this adventure of Italy is assimilated to English conditions, English manners, and English ways of thinking that this old drama remains so vital. It is often amusing to notice how, with every intention to create an exotic atmosphere, the older dramatists fail, and with all their Rialtos and Veronas give us English men and women living under English conditions. Shakespeare is the most contemporaneous of authors. He translates everything into his own present. Studies which seek his discernment in creating Romans, Italians, French, and the like are wasted. Except for the effect of his sources and obvious, outward superficialities, Shakespeare's personages are English men and women. And this is measurably true of his great contemporaries, even Jonson with all his panoply of learning. It was when the drama forgot this honest reality that we substitute, not an accurate Florence or a realization of ancient Greece, but a no-man's land of Fletcherian romance—Austracia, Iberia, Candia, and Bohemia with its circumjacent sea—as mapless territories as the kingdom of Ruritania. Later times opened few sources not already broached. Among them the chief were the passing influences of the contemporary French

prose romances, in the days of King Charles, and the more
lasting draughts on Spanish fiction and drama.

Looking for parallels of latitude and longitude on the
map of our subject, we may note that Lyly was, between
1580 and 1588, the accepted leader in the drama which
he raised to an artistic place at court; that the weight of
example then shifted, under the leadership of Marlowe
especially, to the popular stage until Marlowe's death, in
1593, made way for Shakespeare. Shakespeare's pre-
eminence in romantic comedy and chronicle history was
established between this date and that of the death of
Elizabeth in 1603; and within this period Dekker, Heywood, and Middleton, of the popular eclectic method in
writing drama, and Jonson, Marston, and Chapman, of
the contrasted learned satirical school, rose to success.
From 1603 to 1612 Shakespeare maintained his primacy
especially for his greater tragedies; and Jonson's, too, are
these years for the vogue of his humors and his leadership
in the entertainment of the court. With Shakespeare's
retirement follows the vogue of Fletcher, for his tragicomedies in particular, but for his comedies as well. And
upon Fletcher's death, in 1625, despite the repute of
Massinger and Ford's brief day, comes Shirley, Fletcher's
undisputed successor, to the closing of the theaters in 1642
and the death of the old drama.

Chrono-logical succession of authors

The personnel of the old drama included nearly everybody who might be impressed into the service; for it was,
up almost to the time of Shakespeare, all but wholly
amateur. Except for the minstrel, whose help was at
best occasional, neither priest, craftsman, nor other citizen
was a professional player. Later civic entertainments of
princes on progress, theatricals at the universities or at
the several Inns of Court, especially, were, all of them,
purely amateur; and at their beginnings the boy companies, whether at school or of the royal chapels or other
choirs, were no more. It may be assumed that the professional player is, after all, the lineal descendant of the

Amateur and pro-fessional actor

minstrel, whether, loosely banded, he wandered about, bearing his fardel a pickaback, or became attached by patronage to some noble. Before the end of Elizabeth's reign, the actor had often become a personage of wealth and recognized place. Edward Alleyn, who created the title rôles of the great plays of Marlowe, through a combination of the return for his universally applauded acting and the inheritance of Philip Henslowe's money, died a rich man, able to found his College of God's Gift at Dulwich with £10,000, and supplement that gift with others. Richard Burbage, even greater in his day for his acting for the first time Romeo, Hamlet, Lear, and Macbeth, died also a man of wealth, gained in part through his inheritance from his father, James, of half an interest in the Globe and Blackfriars. There were other actors whose repute was only measurably less. Nathan Field, a boy of the Chapel children, acted important parts in plays of Jonson and, with the King's men, as an adult, boasted successes in rôles of Fletcher and as Bussy D'Ambois; William Kempe, an older man, succeeded to the popularity of Tarleton as a clown and, with Richard Cowley, was one of the "humorous men" of Shakespeare's company. John Lowin was noted as Falstaff and also for Henry VIII; and Joseph Taylor succeeded Burbage, combining fame in parts as diverse as Hamlet, Iago, Ferdinand of *The Duchess of Malfi* and Face in *The Alchemist*. As to those who took women's parts, we know less. Field is alleged to have been such; but I find no proof of it. We do not know the name of the "squeaking Cleopatra" whose business it was "to boy" Egypt's greatness on the stage, nor the Rosalind who says: "*If I were a woman,* I would kiss as many of you as had beards that please me." Amateur playing continued throughout the period of the regular drama. The posing in sumptuous costume of noble gentlemen and ladies and their premeditated grouping and dancing in the masques, at court, in Stuart times, was decorative rather than histrionic. The acting parts in the masques were habitually given to professionals. But the presentation of plays, at schools, the universities, and the Inns of Court continued, and in all of this the setting was amateur endeavor. There is evidence of amateur undertakings of serious plays in lower walks of life. A play called *The Hog hath Lost his Pearl* was "divers times publicly acted [in 1615] by certain London apprentices at Whitefriars." The audience in this latter case is described by a contemporary as "made up rather of the apprentices's mistresses than their masters," and by reason of certain offense the performance was broken up by the sheriffs who carried off some of the actors "to perform the last act in Bridewell [in jail]."

The personnel of the authors of these old plays has been set forth at large in the previous pages. From complete anonymity there was progress gradually to a recognition of the dignity, if not the property rights, of authorship. This last in its fullness is yet to come. No literary habit was more confirmed than that of collaboration, sometimes by several writers; and the texts of plays in the possession of the companies were open, on revival, to incessant change, interpolation, and rewriting in which apparently almost anybody conveniently at hand might participate. The idea of preserving plays in print was a gradual growth, fostered more by the eagerness of printers to turn a penny on a momentarily popular stage success than by any desire on the part of dramatists "to be in this wise voluminously read." Indeed, among the playwrights, literary consciousness was conspicuous in its absence, until Jonson set up a new ideal in editing works of his own and seeing them through the press; and Jonson in this was ahead of his age and little followed. Chambers lists the extraordinary number of one hundred and seventy-odd "playwrights," and this only up to the death of Shakespeare. But this comprises writers of shows and pageants and translators, and includes my lord Bacon, deviser and condescending patron of "masques and triumphs" in their proper functions as

Playwrights amateur and professional

"toys" for the entertainment of royalty, as well as gentlemen, like Percy and Barry, drawn by its glamour to
experiment with the public stage in veritable plays.
Analogous to the actor, the professional playwright was
late to emerge. Students of law or in the universities
wrote, as they acted, for the fun of the thing. Masters
of schools and of chapels stretched the limits of their obli-
gations to their posts in writing plays for their children.
Lyly wrote dramas, as he wrote fiction, as a means to
preferment. It is only when the professional actor tries
his hand at authorship that we reach the verge of professional play-writing. And it was because the actor had
his hand, directly or indirectly, so constantly in Elizabethan drama, that these plays are so alive and still act, on
trial, so well. Greene relates a pleasing anecdote of a
successful actor, "able at his proper cost to maintain a
windmill"—admirable title for the octagonal playhouses
of the day or any theater, for that matter; and how he
found the poet in distress and engaged his "university
wit" to make plays for the common stages. But even
Greene, like Lodge, Nash, and Kyd, was a pamphleteer
or general prose-writer turned playwright. Marlowe and
Shakespeare are our first genuinely professional dramatists, and they were soon followed by Dekker, Heywood,
and Middleton, although none of these gave up wholly
the vocation of pamphleteer. Jonson was much more than
a playwright, and might have maintained the distinction
of his carpers between his works and his plays. Fletcher
and Shirley all but wholly wrote alone for the stage and
were neither actors nor otherwise concerned in the business
of running the theater. In later Stuart times the writing
of plays fell again more and more into amateur hands.
Randolph, Cartwright, Suckling, and their like were
gentlemen trifling with the drama, not men seriously following a vocation. Davenant had a serious side and went
into evasion of Puritan laws against the performance of
plays during the Commonwealth quite professionally, to

be rewarded by Charles II with one of the two patents which he granted by way of monopoly to players' companies. But the other patentee was Thomas Killigrew, gentleman trifler with the best, or rather the worst, of those who had been Charles's fellow exiles.

As to the plays themselves the history of the drama at large represents a series of experiments in novelty, evolving species after species, each to have its vogue and be succeeded by something else. Types arise only to be modified and combined in a new conjunction. Definite enough are Marlowe's conqueror play and Kyd's tragedy of revenge, both of them belonging to times before the defeat of the Armada in 1588, the latter continuing in many modifications practically to the end. The 'nineties evolved chronicle history in the hands of the Shakespearean "predecessors," which the master carried forward, with others following, to the close of Elizabeth's reign and little further. In the same decade Shakespeare found his bent in romantic comedy and tragedy, drawing practically the whole drama after him in the next decade with Fletcher's added weight. And towards the end of the same fruitful 'nineties came Jonson with his comedy of humors, a defined and delimited species of the comedy of manners, which, mingled with Middleton's looser conception of the same kind of play and applied to picture London low life, dominated English comedy for nearly three centuries. The first decade of King James witnessed the rise of tragicomedy, its guiding spirits Beaumont and Fletcher, and this compromise between the rigors of tragedy and the amenities of high comedy, narrowed in range and heightened in flavor by means of subtilized sentiment and strained situation, led on to the heroic drama of Dryden with its spectacle, its unreality, its inflated rhetoric and rhyming couplets. Without naming here any of the minor varieties evolved out of these major classes, it is clear that with its roots deep in moral, interlude, and story, this drama grew into a remarkable complexity in kind in its heyday,

Successions of kinds of drama

281

the score of years of Shakespeare's activity; and that, in the hands of Fletcher and his followers, it was resolved into practically two major varieties, romantic serious drama, which tended more and more to the unrealities of the heroic, and realistic comedy of manners, conventional, repetitious and successful only as, from time to time, it made new drafts, as did Shirley, on the actual life of the moment.

Development in staging

The staging of the old drama, it is sufficient to epitomize here, underwent a gradual modification. Mediæval conditions, it will be recalled, admitted several places scattered about the church edifice on platforms, moving in vans or arranged simultaneously on one great stage. The action took place, according to circumstance, either on one or other of these places of scenic structure ("houses," they were called) or in the neutral space or spaces between them. And this general arrangement continued to be the usual one in England up to and including the plays of Lyly. Under the influence, however, of classical lore, edited and experimented on both theoretically and practically in Italy, a new conception of staging plays came into vogue, involving the continuity of one setting for one play, a dignified architectural assemblage of temples, arches, and vistas for tragedy, the like, only more familiar, for comedy, a sylvan landscape for pastoral, a recognized form in Italy. This Italian setting involved structures of at least two sides and perspective, and led on obviously to the change and shifting of scenes either by means of the *scena versatilis* or the *scena ductilis;* and all of these features came in time, mainly through the study and practice of Inigo Jones at court and at the universities, profoundly to modify the popular stage. In Shakespeare's time plays were presented on the public stage in various degrees of disregard or conflict between the old idea of simultaneous properties, unity of scene and change of scene, this last effected by the bringing on and taking off of objects, furniture, and even painted cloths to suggest the character

of the place. And it is not to be denied, as Mr. Gran-
ville-Barker, a practical and successful producer as well
as author of plays, has recently pointed out, that in the
popular drama, as staged vigorously in the early inn-
yards especially, there was a healthy disregard, if not a
complete innocence of all these matters, the acting of a
story with the passion involved so absorbing interest,
that where it was set or how it was set was matter of little
moment. The old notion of a neutral place between the
houses persisted in scenes the locality of which is undetermined or unimportant; but the tendency was towards
elasticity in change and as constant a use of the whole
stage as possible. It is not to be successfully denied that
the Elizabethans used painted cloths stretched on frames,
brought in and set to produce scenic effects, and this even
in public theaters. And it cannot be maintained that such
settings were confined to the inner stage, to be cloaked by
a curtain when not pertinent, or that the free dramaturgy
of the age was at any time seriously restricted by considerations of scenic exigency. In the presence and conduct
of a great play, stage setting is always amazingly unimportant. However, there were a plenty of plays, then as
now, that needed all that the carpenters and wig-makers
could do for them.

Lastly, from a literary point of view, it is not to be **Essential
qualities**
denied that this old drama is exceedingly unequal. There
is slovenly writing, incompetent handling, and careless
plotting in it. There is—what is worse—brutality, sen-
sationalism, pandering to low tastes, and pruiency in these
old plays. And these defects are not confined to inferior
authors, but blot at times work which we cannot but wish
were without them. The age was coarse. Elizabethan
manners were not our manners. But it is easy to lay
too much up to this charge; though it is perhaps worth
recalling that this drama was written and acted by men
before audiences composed, in earlier times, on the popular
stage at least, almost wholly of men. And yet, when all

this has been allowed, as we look at the drama at large, our wonder is that it is prevailingly ethically so sound. These taints are, for the most part, superficial and do not strike in vitally; and none deny the straight seeing, the grasp of right, the lofty ideality, and the sustaining poetry of the best of these plays. The present writer finds it difficult to be patient with theories that deplore the imperfect psychological perception, the limited political and social vision, the lack of scientific insight among Elizabethans. There is one sovereign remedy for this state of mind: read the old drama, instead of theorizing about it; and we find that Shakespeare and his fellows are to be trusted in that which they touched—if not in what we think that they ought to have busied themselves about—in that which they knew, the nature, conduct, and passions of men, acting and reacted upon in a world marvelously the same, in the great essentials, as our own.

Means of expression The style and medium of expression of the old drama is as varied almost as its contents. Rhyming verse, often elaborate in stanza, was habitually employed in the Middle Ages in drama of every sort; and the tumbling rhyming long line,

> As long liveth the merry man, they say,
> As doth the sorry man, and longer by a day,

the verse of *Gammer Gurton* and *Roister Doister*, still crops up in passages of *The Comedy of Errors*. Prose in drama was first used for a whole play by Gascoigne; and Lyly employed and perfected this medium of comedy, somewhat euphemistically at first, using it habitually except in one play. Despite some earlier passages by Peele, it was Marlowe who first demonstrated how pliable and efficient a medium for drama blank verse might become; and his example was followed habitually in tragic and romantic drama, while prose came to be the commonly accepted medium for comedy. The dramatic prose of men like Shakespeare and Jonson, while closely representative of

the daily speech of the time, is highly organized and as
artistic a mode of expression in its field as blank verse.
It is familiar in all the school books how Shakespeare's
blank verse developed from a certain rigidity and consciousness of the line to a freedom of phrasing, a litheness
and variety unequaled. In this regard Shakespeare is
representative of the development of dramatic versification
in his age at large, from his "predecessors," whose general
manner was much that of Shakespeare's youth, to the
freedom of his manhood, shared by his equals in years,
and to the license and decay which that freedom presaged.
Fletcher especially invented a new and distinctive blank
verse in which a more frequent license as to the number
of syllables (especially at the end of the line) combined
with a more or less strict observance of the line itself. For
example, the famous passage of Wolsey in *Henry VIII*
beginning:

> Farewell! a long farewell, to all my greatness!
> This is the state of man: to-day he puts forth
> The tender leaves of hopes; to-morrow blossoms
> And bears his blushing honors thick upon him, etc.,

is distinctly in the Fletcherian manner in the added final
syllable and other features, whether Fletcher wrote these
lines or Shakespeare imitated them. Different is the manner of undoubted Beaumont:

> I have a boy,
> Sent by the gods, I hope, to this intent,
> Not yet seen in the court. Hunting the buck,
> I found him sitting by a fountain's side,
> Of which he borrowed some to quench his thirst
> And paid the nymph as much again in tears;

in which we notice a strict observance of the number of
syllables, but freedom as to the phrase and the running
of it over the line into the next. It was the combination

285

of these two licenses with a gradual breakdown of the fiber of verse into merely measured prose that marks the history of decadent blank verse in the Stuart era. Massinger wrote a loose but fluent verse of his own. Ford recovered, for the nonce, much of the vigor and music of earlier dramatic verse; and poets, like Shirley and Suckling, stood out against the tendency to confuse verse and prose which came to characterize the work of minor dramatists, their contemporaries. But the Carlells, Killigrews, and Lowers lost any sense of the line distinguishing the two mediums of expression, and the reaction to the regular tread of the decasyllabic couplet with its return to rhyme came none too soon in Davenant and Dryden.

The grand style

The language of serious Elizabethan drama, in its heyday, has been denominated the grand style. A romantic drama in its essentials, romantic raiment was appropriate; and argument as to the abstract superiority of plain language is little to the point. Moreover, the life at court and the life of noble and substantial citizen was conducted with ceremony, dignity, attention to grace and a certain inflation, shall we call it, above the ordinary; and not to reflect this faithfully in the drama, which was the mirror of that life, would have been injustice to the truth. Accepting these conventions and those which inhere otherwise in the time, there is no literature which still retains so much of the quality of universality to carry it over the ages as does this great drama, there is no body of writing so uniformly successful in its picture of the doings, the passions, and ambitions of men, and so sustained by the glow of eloquence and the radiance of poetry.

BIBLIOGRAPHY

A LIST OF BOOKS

(more especially of those published since 1908)

INTRODUCING THE READER TO ENGLISH DRAMA UP TO THE
CLOSING OF THE THEATERS, 1642

This list makes no pretensions to completeness; and,
for the most part, takes no account of the many valuable
contributions in periodical publications such as *The Modern Language Review* in England, *Anglia, Englische
Studien* and the *Shakespeare Jahrbuch* in Germany, and
Modern Philology, Studies in Philology, and the *Publications of the Modern Language Association* in America.
References of this kind, where necessary, will be found in
footnotes in their appropriate places. For earlier and
fuller bibliographies, see the present writer's *Elizabethan
Drama,* 2 vols., 1908; *The Cambridge History of English
Literature,* Vols. V and VI, 1910; and the incidental bibli-
ographies contained in E. K. Chambers's two works, *The
Mediæval Stage,* 2 vols., 1903, and *The Elizabethan Stage,*
4 vols., 1923.

SOCIAL ENGLAND, LONDON AND THE PLAYHOUSES

Adams, J. Q., Shakespearean Playhouses, 1917.
Albright, V. E., The Shakespearean Stage, 1909.
Campbell, L. B., Scenes and Machines on the English
Stage, 1923.
Chambers, E. K., The Elizabethan Stage, 4 vols., 1923.
Chambers, E. K., The Mediæval Stage, 2 vols., 1903.
Gildersleeve, V. C., Government Regulations of Eliza-
bethan Drama, 1908.

Graves, T. S., The Court and the London Theatres During the Reign of Elizabeth, 1913.

Lawrence, J. W., The Elizabethan Playhouse, 2 vols., 1912, 1913.

Murray, J. T., English Dramatic Companies, 2 vols., 1910.

Onions, C. T., Shakespeare's England, 2 vols., 1916.

Reynolds, G. F., Some Principles of Elizabethan Staging, 1905 (*Modern Philology*, v).

Reynolds, G. F., What We Know of the Elizabethan Stage, 1911 (*Modern Philology*, ix).

Sheavyn, P., The Literary Profession in the Elizabethan Age, 1909 (*Manchester University Publications*).

Stephenson, H. T., Shakespeare's London, 1905.

Stopes, C. C., Burbage and Shakespeare's Stage, 1913.

Thompson, E. N. S., The Controversy Between the Puritans and the Stage, 1903.

Thorndike, A. H., Shakespeare's Theater, 1916.

Wallace, C. W., Shakespeare, the Globe and Blackfriars (privately printed, 1909; *Nebraska Studies in English*, x, 1910).

Wallace, C. W., The Children of the Chapel at Blackfriars, 1908.

HISTORIES OF OLDER ENGLISH DRAMA, OF PARTS OF IT AND DOCUMENTARY AND SOURCE MATERIAL

Adams, J. Q., The Dramatic Records of Sir Henry Herbert, 1917 (*Cornell Studies in English*).

Arber, E., Transcript of the Stationers' Company, 1894.

Boas, F. S., University Drama in the Age of the Tudors, 1914.

Boswell-Stone, W. G., Shakspere's Holinshed, 1896.

Brooke, Tucker, Shakespeare's Plutarch, 1909.

Brooke, Tucker, The Tudor Drama, 1912.

Cambridge History of English Literature, The, edited by A. W. Ward and A. R. Waller, 14 vols., 1907-1916.

of Stuart times. Other collections are explained in their titles.

Adams, J. Q., Chief Pre-Shakespearean Dramas, 1924.

Belles Lettres Series, The English Drama, edited by Baker, G. P., individual volumes by various editors, 1902-1908.

Bond, R. W., Early Plays from the Italian, 1911, contains *Supposes, Bugbears* and *Misogonus.*

Brandl, A., Quellen des weltlichen Dramas in England vor Shakespeare, 1898, reprints chiefly moral plays and earlier comedy.

Brooke, Tucker, Shakespeare Apocrypha, 1908, contains *The London Prodigal, Cromwell, Oldcastle, The Puritan Widow, The Yorkshire Tragedy, Locrine.*

Bullen, A. H., A Collection of Old English Plays, 4 vols., 1882-1885; new series, 3 vols., 1887-1889.

Chester Plays, edited by H. Deimling, *Early English Text Society,* 1893.

Cunliffe, J. W., Early English Classical Tragedies, 1912, contains *Gorboduc, Jocasta, Gismond of Salerne.*

Digby Plays, edited by F. J. Furnivall, *Early English Text Society,* 1882.

Dodsley, R., A Select Collection of Old Plays, 12 vols., 1744; fourth edition by W. C. Hazlitt, 15 vols., 1874-1876.

Evans, H. A., English Masques, 1897, masques of Jonson, Daniel, Campion and others.

Fairholt, F. W., Lord Mayor's Pageants, 2 vols., 1843-1844 (*Percy Society,* xxxviii, xliii).

Farmer, J. S., The Tudor Facsimile Texts, 184 vols., 1907-1914.

Farmer, J. S., Recently Recovered Plays, 1906.

Gayley, C. M., Representative English Comedies, 3 vols., 1903-1914.

Interlude, see *Moral Play* in the present group, below, and also John Heywood, below.

Ludus Coventriæ, edited by K. S. Block, *Early English Text Society*, 1922.

Manly, J. M., Specimens of Pre-Shakespearean Drama, 2 vols., 1897.

Malone Society, Collections, vol. i, 1907-1911; vol. ii, pt. 1, 1913 (in progress).

Malone Society, Reprints, 46 vols., 1907-1924 (in progress).

Materialien zur Kunde des älteren englischen Dramas, edited by W. Bang, Louvain, 43 vols., 1902-1914.

Mermaid Series, The Best Plays of the Old Dramatists, 22 vols., 1887-1895.

Miracle Plays can be fully studied in the editions of the four cycles as indicated under the headings of the present group, *Chester Plays, Ludus Coventriæ, Towneley Miracle Plays, York Mystery Plays*. For a less complete survey, see Pollard, English Miracle Plays.

Moral Plays are, many of them, reprinted in Dodsley, the earlier volumes, Brandl, Pollard, Manly and Adams, as above. See also *Digby Plays* in this group and John Bale, below.

Neilson, W. A., The Chief Elizabethan Dramatists Excluding Shakespeare, 1911.

Pollard, A. W., English Miracle Plays, Moralities and Interludes, 7th ed., 1923.

Schelling, F. E., Typical Elizabethan Plays (in press).

Towneley Miracle Plays, edited by A. W. Pollard, Early English Text Society, 1897.

York Mystery Plays, edited by L. T. Smith, 1885.

WORKS OF THE CHIEF INDIVIDUAL PLAYWRIGHTS

BIOGRAPHIES AND MONOGRAPHS

BEAUMONT, FRANCIS (c. 1584–1616), and FLETCHER: Works, ed. A. Glover and A. R. Waller, 10 volumes,

1905-1912. Selected plays, *Mermaid Series*, ed. J. S. L. Strachey, 2 vols., 1887; *Belles Lettres Series*, ed. A. H. Thorndike, 1907, R. M. Alden, 1912; *Masterpiece Series*, ed. F. E. Schelling, 1912; single plays in *Temple Dramatists* and elsewhere. *Philaster* and *The Maid's Tragedy* are reprinted practically in all of these. Collectively they also include *King and No King, Valentinian, Bonduca, The Faithful Shepherdess, The Knight of the Burning Pestle, Barnavelt, The Spanish Curate, The Wild-goose Chase*, and other plays. On these authors and their relations, see A. H. Thorndike, The Influence of Beaumont and Fletcher on Shakespeare, 1901; O. L. Hatcher, John Fletcher, 1905; G. C. Macauley, in *Cambridge History of English Literature*, volume vi, 1910; C. M. Gayley, Beaumont, the Dramatist, 1914; L. Wann, in *Wisconsin Shakespeare Studies*, 1916.

CHAPMAN, GEORGE (c. 1560-1634): Plays, ed. T. M. Parrott, 2 vols., 1910-1914. *Mermaid*, 1895, ed. W. L. Phelps, contains *All Fools*, the two plays on Bussy D'Ambois and the two on Byron; *Belles Lettres*, ed. F. E. Schelling, 1903, F. S. Boas, 1905, and T. M. Parrott, 1907, add to these *Eastward Ho* and *The Gentleman Usher*.

DANIEL, SAMUEL (c. 1563-1619): Complete Works, 5 vols., ed. A. B. Grosart (vol. iii contains *Cleopatra, Philotas, The Queen's Arcadia* and the masques); the first of these is reprinted in *Materialien*, xxi, ed. M. Lederer, 1911; *The Vision of the Twelve Goddesses*, Evans, English Masques.

DEKKER, THOMAS (c.1572-c.1632): Dramatic Works, 4 vols. (*Pearson Reprints*), 1873. *The Shoemaker's Holiday* and *Old Fortunatus* are reprinted in several collections, the former, for example, in Gayley, vol.

ii, 1914, the latter, ed. O. Smeaton, in *Temple Drama-tists*, 1904. Both of these, with *The Honest Whore* and *The Witch of Edmonton*, appear in the *Mermaid, Dekker*, ed. E. Rhys, 1887; *The Sun's Darling*, in the same, volume *Ford*, 1888, *The Virgin Martyr*, in the same, volume *Massinger*, 1889. *Satiromastix* is reprinted in *Belles Lettres*, ed. J. H. Penniman, 1913. M. L. Hunt, Thomas Dekker, a Study (*Columbia Studies*), 1911; the collaboration of Dekker is vari-ously treated in *Yale Studies*, 1919; *Anglia*, 1912, *Modern Language Review*, 1920. *The Gull's Horn-book*, ed. R. B. McKerrow, 1904.

FLETCHER, JOHN (1579-1625): See BEAUMONT.

FORD, JOHN (1586-1639): Complete Works, ed. A. Dyce, 3 vols., 1869; *Mermaid*, ed. H. Ellis, 1888, contains *Love's Sacrifice, 'Tis Pity, Perkin Warbeck* and *The Broken Heart;* this last is also reprinted in *Temple Dramatists*, ed. O. Smeaton, 1905, and with *'Tis Pity,* in *Belles Lettres*, by S. P. Sherman. See also by the same, Ford's Contribution to the Decadence of the Drama (*Materialien* xxiii), 1908, which also reprints most of the plays.

GREENE, ROBERT (1558-1592): Plays and Poems, ed. J. C. Collins, 2 vols., 1905; *Mermaid*, ed. T. H. Dick-inson, 1909, contains *Alphonsus of Arragon, A Look-ing-glass for London and England, Orlando Furioso, Friar Bacon and Friar Bungay, James IV*, and *George a Green*, which last appears also in Adams. *Friar Bacon* is reprinted in most collections and in *Temple Dramatists*, 1904; and *Selimus*, attributed to Greene, by A. Grosart, 1898. J. C. Jordan, *Robert Greene*, 1915 (*Columbia Thesis*).

HEYWOOD, THOMAS (c. 1570-1641): Dramatic Works, 6 vols. (*Pearson Reprints*), 1874; *Mermaid*, ed. A. W. Verity, 1888, contains *A Woman Killed With Kind-*

ness, The Fair Maid of the West, The English Trav-
eler, The Wise Woman of Hogsden and *The Rape of*
Lucrece; the first of these is frequently reprinted,
Temple Dramatists, ed. A. W. Ward, 1897; *Belles*
Lettres, ed. K. L. Bates, 1919, with *Fortunes by*
Land and Sea, and contains new material in the
introduction.

JONSON, BEN (1572-1637): Works, ed. W. Gifford, re-
vised by P. Cunningham, 9 vols., 1875; *Mermaid,* ed.
B. Nicholson and C. H. Herford, 3 vols., 1894, contains *Every Man In His Humor, Every Man Out of*
His Humor, Poetaster, Bartholomew Fair, Cynthia's
Revels, Sejanus, His Fall, Volpone, Epicoene, The
Alchemist. Of these the first and the last three are
also reprinted in *Masterpiece Series,* ed. E. Rhys,
1912; while others appear variously collected in ed.
H. C. Hart, 2 vols. completed, 1906; *Everyman's*
Library and elsewhere. In *Materialien,* in the *Ma-*
lone Society and in the *Yale Studies in English* (between 1905-1920) some eight or ten of Jonson's plays
are variously and critically edited. Other popular
editions are those of *The Alchemist* and *Eastward Ho,*
ed. F. E. Schelling, *Sejanus,* ed. W. D. Briggs, and
Poetaster, ed. J. H. Penniman in *Belles Lettres,* 1903,
1911, 1913. Ten of Jonson's masques are reprinted
by H. A. Evans, English Masques, 1897. See also,
Baskerville, C. R., English Elements in Jonson's
Early Comedy, 1911; Castelain, M., Ben Jonson,
l'Homme et l'Œuvre, 1907; Penniman, as above, for
the "War of the Theaters"; and Simpson, P., The
Portraiture of Humors, his edition of *Every Man In*
His Humor, 1919.

KYD, THOMAS (1558-1594): Works, ed. F. S. Boas, 1901;
The Spanish Tragedy is reprinted in several collections; *Temple Dramatists,* ed. J. Schick, 1898.

LYLY, JOHN (1554-1606): Complete Works, ed. R. W. Bond, 3 vols., 1902. *Endimion* and *Compaspe* are the most frequently reprinted in collections, the former especially by G. P. Baker, 1894; the latter in *Temple Dramatists* and by Adams. Feuillerat, A., John Lyly, 1910.

MARLOWE, CHRISTOPHER (1564-1593): Works, ed. Tucker Brooke, 1910. *Tamburlaine, Doctor Faustus, The Jew of Malta* and *Edward II* appear in *Mermaid*, ed. H. Ellis, 1887; and likewise in *Masterpiece Series*, ed. W. L. Phelps, 1912. *Faustus* and *Edward II* are contained in several collections, and are separately edited in the *Temple Dramatists* and elsewhere. J. H. Ingram, Marlowe and his Associates, 1904; the earlier bibliography of *Faustus* will be found in A. W. Ward's edition of that play, 4th ed., 1901.

MARSTON, JOHN (c. 1575-1634): Works, A. H. Bullen, 3 vols., 1887. *Antonio and Mellida*, both parts, *Malone Society*, ed. W. W. Greg, 1921; *The Malcontent* in Works of Webster; E. E. Stoll, Shakespeare, Marston and the Malcontent Type, *Modern Philology*, 1906.

MASSINGER, PHILIP (1583-1640): Works, ed. F. Cunningham, 3 vols., 1871; *Masterpiece*, ed. L. A. Sherman, 1912, contains *The Roman Actor, The Maid of Honor, A New Way to Pay Old Debts* and *Believe as You List; Mermaid*, ed. A. Symonds, 2 vols., 1887-1889, contains several other plays, among them *The Unnatural Combat, The Fatal Dowery* and *The City Madam; A New Way to Pay* is in most collections and separately in *The Temple Dramatists*, 1904. Recent criticism of Massinger is that of A. H. Cruickshank, Philip Massinger, 1920; and M. Chelli, Le Drame de Massinger, 1924.

MIDDLETON, THOMAS (c. 1570-1627): Works, ed. A. H. Bullen, 8 vols., 1885-1886; *Masterpiece*, ed. M. W. Sampson, 1915, contains *Michaelmas Term, A Trick to Catch the Old One, A Fair Quarrel, The Changeling; Mermaid*, ed. H. Ellis, 2 vols., 1887-1890, contains, besides, several other plays, among them *The Roaring Girl* and *A Chaste Maid in Cheapside*. P. G. Wiggin, An Inquiry into the Authorship of the Middleton-Rowley Plays, 1897.

PEELE, GEORGE (c. 1557-1596): Works, A. H. Bullen, 2 vols., 1888; *The Arraignment of Paris, David and Bethsabe* and *The Old Wives' Tale* appear in Plays of Peele, ed. H. Morley, 1887; the first and third are often reprinted in the collections, the former appearing likewise separately in *Temple Dramatists*, 1905.

ROWLEY, WILLIAM (? -c. 1625): No separate ed. Rowley's chief collaborator was Middleton, under which see *All's Lost by Lust, Belles Lettres*, ed. E. P. Morris, 1907; and *Publications of the University of Pennsylvania*, ed. E. W. Stork, 1910, each with another play.

SHAKESPEARE, WILLIAM (1564-1616): Complete Plays (in one volume), ed. W. A. Neilson, 1906; University Press Shakespeare, ed. S. Lee and other editors, 20 vols., 1906-1908; Shakespeare's Principal Plays, ed. Brooke, Cunliffe and MacCracken, 1922, contains *Midsummer Night's Dream, Romeo and Juliet, The Merchant of Venice, Richard II, 1* and *2 Henry IV, Henry V, Much Ado About Nothing, As You Like It, Twelfth Night, Julius Cæsar, Hamlet, Othello, King Lear, Macbeth, Antony and Cleopatra, Coriolanus, Cymbeline, Winter's Tale, Tempest*. Editions of the single plays by various authors, among them the *Temple*, ed. I. Gollancz, 1895; *Arden*, ed. J. Craig, 1899, *Yale*, ed. W. L. Cross and Tucker Brooke.

1908. Among innumerable books on Shakespeare the following may be named: A. H. Thorndike, The Relations of Hamlet to Contemporary Revenge Plays, 1902; A. C. Bradley, Shakespearean Tragedy, 1904; and the more recent: A. W. Pollard, Shakespeare Folios and Quartos, 1909; W. A. Neilson and A. H. Thorndike, The Facts About Shakespeare, 1913; A. W. Pollard, Shakespeare's Fight with the Pirates, 1917; J. D. Wilson, The Copy for Hamlet, 1918; S. Lee, Life of Shakespeare, revised ed. 1919; H. D. Sykes, Sidelights on Shakespeare, 1919; L. Winstanley, Hamlet and the Scottish Succession, 1921; R. M. Alden, Shakespeare, 1922; J. Q. Adams, Life of Shakespeare, 1923; F. S. Boas, Shakespeare and the Universities, 1923; W. W. Greg, and others, Shakespeare's Hand in the Play of *Sir Thomas More*, 1923.

SHIRLEY, JAMES (1596-1666): Complete Works, ed. A. Dyce, 6 vols., 1833; *Mermaid*, ed. E. Gosse, 1888, includes *The Witty Fair One, The Traitor, Hyde Park, The Lady of Pleasure, The Cardinal, The Triumph of Peace.* Shipper, J., Shirley, sein Leben und seine Werke (*Wiener Beiträge* xxxvi), 1911; Forsythe, R. S., The Relations of Shirley's Plays, 1914; Nason, A. H., James Shirley, 1914.

TOURNEUR, CYRIL (? -1624): Plays and Poems, ed. J. C. Collins, 2 vols., 1873; *Mermaid Series*, ed. J. A. Symonds, 1888, *Webster and Tourneur*, contains *The Revenger's Tragedy* and *The Atheist's Tragedy*, as does *Masterpiece Series*, ed. A. H. Thorndike, 1912.

WEBSTER, JOHN (? -1634: Dramatie Works, ed. W. C. Hazlett, 4 vols., 1857; *Mermaid Series* and *Masterpiece Series*, both as above, reprint *The White Devil* and *The Duchess of Malfi;* which latter play appears also in *Temple Dramatists*, ed. C. E. Vaughan, 1896, and in several collections. Stoll, E.

E., John Webster and the Periods of His Work, 1905; Brooke, R., John Webster and the Elizabethan Drama, 1916.

WORKS OF A FEW MINOR PLAYWRIGHTS AND MORE IMPORTANT SINGLE PLAYS

ANONYMOUS: *Arden of Feversham, Temple Dramatists*, ed. R. Bayne, 1897; *Calisto and Melibea* (J. Rastell), *Malone Society*, ed. F. Sidgwick, 1908; *Everyman, Materialien* iv, ed. W. W. Greg, 1904; *Gammer Gurton's Needle* (W. Stevenson), in Gayley; *Pilgrimage from Parnassus*, ed. W. D. Macray, 1886, and *Temple Dramatists*, ed. O. Smeaton, 1905; *Sir Thomas More*, ed. T. Brooke, 1908; most of these are to be found likewise in collections.

BALE, JOHN (1495-1563): *King Johan*, with other works, ed. J. S. Farmer, 1907.

BROME, RICHARD (? -1652?): Dramatic Works (*Pearson Reprints*), 3 vols., 1873, contains *The Northern Lass* and other plays.

CHETTLE, HENRY (c. 1560-1607): *Hoffman*, ed. R. Ackerman, 1894.

DAVENANT, SIR WILLIAM, ed. Maidmont and Logan, 5 vols., 1872-1874, *Love and Honor* and *The Siege of Rhodes*, ed. J. W. Tupper, *Belles Lettres Series*, 1909.

DAY, JOHN (c. 1574-c. 1640): ed. A. H. Bullen, 2 vols., 1881, *Mermaid Series*, ed. A. Symonds, *Nero and Other Plays*, 1888, reprints *The Parliament of Bees* and *Humor Out of Breath*.

FIELD, NATHAN (1587- ?): ed. A. W. Verity in the same volume, reprints *Woman Is a Weather-cock* and *Amends for Ladies*.

GASCOIGNE, GEORGE (1535-1577): Complete Works, ed. J. W. Cunliffe, 1907, who also reprints *Jacasta* and *Supposes* in *Belles Lettres* Series, 1906.

GREVILLE, FULKE, LORD BROOKE (c. 1554-1628):

Works, ed. A. B. Grosart, 4 vols., 1870, contains both *Mustapha* and *Alaham*.

HEYWOOD, JOHN (1497-1578): Dramatic Writings, ed. J. S. Farmer, 1905, includes *The Four PP, The Pardner and the Frere* and other interludes.

HAUGHTON, WILLIAM: *Englishmen for My Money* (*Publications of the University of Pennsylvania*), ed. A. C. Baugh, 1917.

LODGE, THOMAS (c. 1557-1625): *The Wounds of Civil War*, is reprinted by the *Malone Society*, ed. W. W. Greg, 1910. This is Lodge's only acknowledged unaided play.

LYNDSAY, SIR DAVID: *Satire of the Three Estates*, ed. D. Laing, 1879.

NABBES, THOMAS (fl. 1628): is reprinted as to his plays entire in Bullen's *Old Plays*, new ed., 2 vols., 1887.

NASH, THOMAS (1567-1601): *Summer's Last Will and Testament* (the only unaided play of Nash) is reprinted in Dodsley, viii.

PORTER, HENRY, *The Two Angry Women of Abingdon*, in Gayley, as above.

PRESTON, THOMAS (c. 1569-c. 1589): *Cambyses* in Dodsley, iv; and Adams.

RANDOLPH, THOMAS (1605-1635): ed. W. C. Hazlitt, 2 vols., 1873, includes *Amyntas*.

SACKVILLE, THOMAS (1536-1608): *Gorboduc* is reprinted in Manly, ii.

SUCKLING, SIR JOHN (1609-1642): ed. W. C. Hazlitt, 2 vols., 1874, contains *Aglaura* and *The Goblins*.

UDAL, NICHOLAS (1505-1556): *Ralph Roister Doister* in Gayley, and *Temple Dramatists*, ed. Williams, 1901, and in Adams.

(Many of these plays will be found elsewhere also, in other collections, noted above.)

A Chronological List of Important Dates

Dates which precede the titles of plays denote the probable year of performance. They are necessarily merely approximate. Dates in parentheses following titles are those of earliest publication.

1110 Miracle play of St. Catherine.

1125 Latin saints' plays of Hilarius.

1170–82 Fitzstephen's mention of sacred plays in London.

1200 Passion play at Sienna.

1250 *The Harrowing of Hell.*

1264 Feast of Corpus Christi instituted; confirmed 1311.

1340–50 *York Mysteries* (MS. 1430–40).

1350 *Towneley Mysteries* (MS. about 1450).

1378 Lost play of the paternoster.

1390–1420 *Chester Plays* (MSS. 1500–1607).

1416 *Ludus Coventriae* (MS. 1468).

1427 Lost plays of Plautus recovered.

1450 *The Castle of Perseverance* and other early moral plays.

1461–83 Edward IV.

1476 Caxton, first English printer.

1485–1509 Henry VII: *Hickscorner, Youth, the World and the Child,* etc.

1486–1500 Medwall's Interlude of *Nature* and romantic comedy *Fulgens and Lucres* (1923).

1495 *Everyman* (1509–30).

1499 Erasmus at Oxford.

1500 Wager's *Mary Magdalene* (1566).

1509–47 Henry VIII.

1515 Skelton's *Magnificence* (1529–33); Trissino active in Senecan tragedy in Italy; More's *Utopia.*

1516 Cornish Master of the Chapel.

1517 Rastell's *The Nature of the Four Elements* (1519).

1520–47 Activity of John Heywood in comedy interlude.

1530 *Calisto and Melibea.*

1534 Udall writing plays.

1535 Death of More.

1538–48 Activity of Bale in controversial plays, *King Johan.*

1540 Lindsay's *Satire of the Three Estates* (1602); Palsgrave's *Acolastus;* Buchanan's Latin tragedies at Bordeaux.

1540–47 Grimald's Latin plays.

1545 Sir Thomas Cawarden, Master of the Revels.

1545 Henry VIII's proclamation against "vagabonds, ruffians, idle persons and players."

1547 Wever's *Lusty Juventus* (1550).

1547–53 Edward VI.

1553 *Gammer Gurton's Needle* (1575) acted at Oxford. Jodelle and Garnier active in Senecan tragedy in France.

1553 *Respublica* (1866); *Ralph Roister Doister* (1567).

1553–58 Queen Mary.

1554 Lyly, Greville born; Bandello's *Novelle.*

1557 Stationers' Company incorporated, registering printed books; Peele born.

1558 Kyd, Greene and Lodge born.

1558–1603 Queen Elizabeth.

1559 Chapman born.

1560 *Misogonus* (1898); *The Bugbears,* (1896–97).

1561 Edwards Master of the Chapel.

1562 *Gorboduc* (1565·).

1563 Drayton and Daniel born.

1564 Birth of Marlowe (Feb.) and Shakespeare (Apr.); Elizabeth visits Cambridge, Udall, Preston and Legge contribute to her entertainment.

1565 Cinthio's *Hecatommithi.*

1566 Elizabeth visits Oxford, Edwards, Master of the

Chapel, contributes to her entertainment; Hunnis succeeds Edwards; Gascoigne's *Supposes* (1573) acted at Gray's Inn; Painter's *Palace of Pleasure*; Edward Alleyn born.

1567 Richard Burbage and Nash born; Fenton's *Tragical Discourses*.

1568 Mary Stuart takes refuge in England.

1569 Preston's *Cambyses* (1569-84).

1570 Thomas Heywood and Middleton born. Hostility of the City against plays.

1572 Actors without patrons declared rogues and vagabonds; James Burbage a member of Leicester's company of players; Jonson and Dekker born.

1574 Royal patent issued to Leicester's players.

1575 Royal festivities at Kenilworth, Gascoigne and Hunnis contributors; Marston and Tourneur born.

1576 James Burbage builds the Theater in Shoreditch, first public playhouse in England; Farrant converts rooms in the priory of Blackfriars into a private theater for the Children of the Royal Chapel.

1577 The Curtain playhouse built in Holywell Lane; Northbrooke's *Treatise against Plays*; Gascoigne dies.

1578 Whetstone's *Promos and Cassandra*; Sidney's mask *The Lady of May*; Holinshed's *Chronicles*.

1579 Sir Edmund Tilney Master of the Revels; Spenser's *Shepherds' Calendar*, Lyly's *Euphues*, North's *Plutarch*; Gosson's *School of Abuse* and Lodge's answer.

1580–88 THE PERIOD OF LYLY

1580 A playhouse at Newington Butts; Fraunce's *Victoria*, Wingfield's *Pedantius* and other plays at Oxford; Webster born. Belleforest's *Histoires Tragiques*; Montaigne's *Essais*.

1581 The Master of the Revels commissioned to license all plays; Hunnis and Newman succeed Farrant at

Blackfriars; Translation of Seneca's *Ten Tragedies;*
Lyly's *Campaspe* acted before Elizabeth.

1582 Plague in London; Lyly's *Sapho and Phao* (1584)
at court and at Blackfriars; Gager's Latin *Meleager*
and other plays at Oxford.

1583 Sidney's conservative criticism of the stage and
praise of *Gorboduc;* the Earl of Oxford acquires
the lease of Blackfriars and gives it to Lyly, Hunnis
and Evans running the company. The Queen's
players organized to control the profession; the fall
of a scaffold kills several at a play at Paris Garden,
Bankside.

1584 Peele's *Arraignment of Paris* acted by the Chapel
Children before the queen. First Blackfriars re-
converted into tenements; Massinger born.

1585 Thomas Giles, Master of Paul's, given a special
royal commission "to take up singing boys" for the
Chapel.

1586 Mary Stuart tried and executed; Sidney dies. Lyly's
Endimion (1591) acted by Paul's boys before the
queen; Kyd's *Spanish Tragedy* (1592) and *Arden
of Feversham* (1592) on the stage. William Rowley and Ford born.

1587 Shakespeare comes up to London; the Rose playhouse built by Henslowe in Southwark. Marlowe's
Tamburlaine (1590); *The Famous Victories of
Henry V* (1598); Lodge's *Wounds of Civil War*
(1594).

1588-93 THE PERIOD OF MARLOWE

1588 Defeat of the Armada; the Marprelate Controversy
to 1590. Marlowe's *Doctor Faustus* (1604); Peele's
David and Bethsabe, (1599); Greene's *Orlando*
(1594) and *George a Greene* (1599); *The Troublesome Reign of John* (1591). Death of Leicester
and Tarlton.

LIST OF IMPORTANT DATES

1589 Strange's players at the Cross Keys Inn; *The Faery Queen* I–III; Marlowe's *Jew of Malta* (1594); Lyly's *Midas* (1592); Greene's *Friar Bacon* (1594); *Locrine* (1595).

1590 Paul's boys suppressed. Lyly's *Mother Bombie* (1594); the Countess of Pembroke's *Antonie* (1592); Greene's *James IV* (1598); Peele's *Edward I* (1593) and *Old Wives' Tale* (1595); *1 Contention of York and Lancaster* (1594); *Edward III* (1596); *Mucedorus* (1598); *Laelia* at Cambridge. Lodge's *Rosalynde*.

1591 Elizabeth goes on progress into Sussex and perhaps witnesses *Love's Labor's Lost* (1598) at Titchfield in September. *The Comedy of Errors, The Two Gentlemen of Verona* and *1 Henry VI* (all 1623) on the stage; Gager's *Ulysses* (1592) at Oxford. Tasso's *Aminta* and Guarini's *Il Pastor Fido* printed in London.

1592 Elizabeth visits Oxford; the miscellaneous theatrical data of Henslowe to 1603 and later; Kyd's *Cornelia* (1594); Marlowe's *Edward II* (1600); Peele's *Battle of Alcazar* (1594); Nash's *Summer's Last Will* (1600); *Cromwell* (1602); *King John* (1623); Greene dies.

1592–93 The plague closes the playhouses.

1593–1610 THE PERIOD OF SHAKESPEARE AND JONSON

1593 Marlowe's *Massacre at Paris* (1596–1600), Marlowe and Nash's *Dido* (1694). Marlowe dies. Greene's *Groatsworth of Wit*; Southampton receives the dedication of *Venus and Adonis*; Dekker begins playwright. *Richard III.*

1594 *Titus Andronicus* (1594) acted at the Rose by Sussex men as a new play; *King Leir* registered 1605; The Swan playhouse licensed for erection; Shakespeare joins the Chamberlain's men who act ten days in June at Newington Butts with the Admiral's

men; *Richard II* and *Romeo and Juliet* (both 1597)
probably on the stage; *Gesta Grayorum*, entertainment of Elizabeth, Bacon and Campion among the
devisers; performance of *The Comedy of Errors*
(1623); Lodge's *Wounds of Civil War* printed;
Heywood's *Four Prentices of London* (1615); Munday's *John a Kent* (MS. 1595); *Look About You*
(1600); *The Taming of a Shrew* (1594).

1595 The group of pre-Shakespearean chronicle plays,
Henry VI, etc., in print by this year; *A Midsummer
Night's Dream* and *The Merchant of Venice* (both
1600); Lyly's last play, *The Woman in the Moon*
(1597).

1596 Shakespeare resides in St. Helen's Bishopsgate, later
in the liberty of the Clink, Southwark; Johannes de
Witt visits the Swan and from his description van
Buchell transcribes the extant picture of that play-
house; Richard Burbage builds the second theater in
Blackfriars. Dekker's *Old Fortunatus* (1600);
Porter's *Two Angry Women* (1599); Middleton's
Mayor of Queenborough (1661). Peele dies; Shirley
born.

1597 The Chamberlain's men at the Theater, Pembroke's
at the Swan; Nash and Jonson's *Isle of Dogs* there
acted sends the authors to jail; *1 Henry IV* (1598);
The Birth of Merlin (1662). Richard Burbage
dies.

1598 Meres, in his *Wit's Treasury*, mentions a dozen plays
of Shakespeare and his unpublished sonnets; *2
Henry IV* (1600); *The Merry Wives of Windsor*
(1602); *Much Ado About Nothing* (1600) and per-
haps *Hamlet* (1603) on the stage. Munday's *1 2
Huntington* (1601); Jonson's *Every Man in His
Humor* (1601), Shakespeare acting a part; Chap-
man's *Bussy D'Ambois* (1607); *Oldcastle* (1600);
The Merry Devil of Edmonton (1608); Haughton's
Englishmen for My Money (1616); *A Warning for*

Fair Women (1599), all on the public stage; *The Pilgrimage to Parnassus* (1886) at Oxford. The Burbages remove the materials of the Theater to the Bankside and project the Globe playhouse.

1599 The Globe opened with the Chamberlain's men, a sharing company, Shakespeare and Burbage members; *Henry V* (1600) and *As You Like It* (1623) on the stage. Marston's *Histriomastix* (1610), and *Antonio and Mellida* (1602); Jonson's *Every Man Out of his Humor* (1600); Dekker's *The Shoemaker's Holiday* (1600), his *Old Fortunatus* acted before the queen. *Club Law* (1907) acted at Cambridge; Rainold's *Overthrow of Stage Plays.*

1599–1602 "Poetomachia" or War of the Theaters, Marston, Jonson and Dekker chiefly engaged.

1600 Alleyn builds the Fortune playhouse in St. Giles Cripplegate for the Admiral's men; Paul's boys are revived, Marston, Dekker, Chapman, Webster writing for them; and Evans takes over the Children of the Chapel at Burbage's Blackfriars. *Julius Caesar* (1623); Dekker's *Patient Grissel* (1603); Jonson's *Cynthia's Revels,* (1601); Daniel's *Philotas* (1604); Greville's *Alaham* (1633).

1600–01 Young Clifton kidnapped by Giles and Evans to act at Blackfriars; an inquiry by Star Chamber closes the theaters in 1602.

1601 *Richard II* privately acted before the Essex conspirators; Jonson's *Poetaster* (1602); Dekker's *Satiromastix* (1602); Marston's *Malcontent* (1604); *1 Return from Parnassus* (1886) at Oxford. Execution of Essex.

1601–07 Shakespeare resides with Mountjoy in Silver Street.

1602 Worcester's players at the Rose, Kempe, Lowin, Beeston among the actors, Heywood, Day and Webster their poets. The Duke of Stettin praises the music at Blackfriars. *Troilus and Cressida* (1609);

Chettle's *Hoffman* (1631); *2 Return from Parnassus* (1606) at Cambridge; *Narcissus* (1893) at Oxford. The playhouses closed.

1603–1625 James I.

1603 The Chamberlain's men receive a new patent as the King's company; the Admirals become Prince Henry's; Worcester's the Queen's. Shakespeare acts in Jonson's *Sejanus* (1605); *Measure for Measure* (1623); Heywood's *A Woman Killed With Kindness* (1607); Dekker's *The Honest Whore* (1604); Marston's *The Malcontent* (1604); *Lingua* (1607). Stow's *Survey of London*.

1604 A grant for liveries to the King's players for James's entry into London, Shakespeare among them; the King's players attendant as grooms of the chamber at Somerset House. The Children of the Chapel become the Queen's Revels, Daniel appointed to license their plays and Marston a playwright for them. Daniel writes the first Jacobean masque, *The Vision of the Twelve Godesses* (1610), and his *Philotas* excites suspicion at court. *Othello* (1622); Samuel Rowley's *When You See Me You Know Me* (1605); Chapman's *Revenge of Bussy D'Ambois* (1613); Marston's *The Dutch Courtesan* (1605); Dekker's *Whore of Babylon* (1607); and *Westward Ho* (1607); Heywood's *If You Know Not Me* (1605, 1606); Fletcher's *The Tamer Tamed* (1647), Middleton's *The Family of Love* (1608).

1605 The Red Bull playhouse erected in St. James Clerkenwell and occupied by the Queen's men under Thomas Greene, Heywood chief playwright. Difficulties because of satire on the Scotch in *Eastward Ho* (1605) acted at Blackfriars by the Queen's Revels, Jonson and Chapman jailed for it; Marston sells out. James visits Oxford, where Inigo Jones uses triangular scenes in Daniel's *The Queen's Arcadia* (1606) for his entertainment; Jonson's

Masque of Blackness (1608) at court. *King Lear* (1608); Chapman's *Monsieur D'Olive* (1606); Wilkins' *Miseries of Enforced Marriage* (1607); *A Yorkshire Tragedy* (1608); the Gunpowder Plot. Randolph born.

1606 The Children of the Revels under Keysar at Blackfriars. Day's *Isle of Gulls* (1606) gives offense at court. *Macbeth* (1623), Jonson's *Volpone* (1607) and *Hymenaei* (1606); Dekker and Webster's *Northward Ho* (1607); Tourneur's *The Revenger's Tragedy* (1607); Greville's *Mustapha* (1609); Middleton's *A Trick to Catch the Old One* (1607); Beaumont's *The Woman Hater* (1607). Lyly dies, Davenant born.

1607 *Antony and Cleopatra, Timon of Athens* (both 1623); Heywood's *Fortune by Land and Sea* (1655); Tourneur's *The Atheist's Tragedy* (1611); Beaumont's *Knight of the Burning Pestle* (1613); Stirling's *Four Monarchic Tragedies*. Theatromania at Oxford. Campion's *Masque at Lord Hayes Marriage* notable for its music.

1608 Lease of Blackfriars surrendered to Burbage, the King's men act there thereafter in winter; the French ambassador complains of the representation of the French court on the stage in Chapman's two plays on Byron (1608), and both boys' companies are forbidden to act. *Pericles* (1609); Fletcher's *Faithful Shepherdess* (1610); Jonson's *Masque of Beauty* (1608). A playhouse in Whitefriars occupied by the Children of the King's Revels organized by Drayton, other poets and sharers Barry, Mason. Day's *Humor Out of Breath*; Mason's *The Turk* (1610), Barry's *Ram Alley* (1611).

1609 Drayton's Whitefriars fails, Keysar and Rossiter secure the lease and reassemble the Blackfriars troupe there. Jonson's *The Silent Woman* (1612);

and *Masque of Queens* (1609); *Coriolanus* (1623); Beaumont and Fletcher's *Philaster* (1620).

1610–1625 THE PERIOD OF FLETCHER

1610 Rossiter reorganizes the troupe at Whitefriars with Daborne as the Children of the Queen's Revels, Field the chief actor; the King's men agree with Rossiter to keep St. Paul's playhouse silent at a dead rent. Daniel's *Tethys' Festival* (1610) at court; Sir George Buck Master of the Revels. *Cymbeline* (1623); Beaumont and Fletcher's *The Maid's Tragedy* (1619); Jonson's *The Alchemist* (1612); Webster's *The White Devil* (1612).

1611 *The Winter's Tale, The Tempest* (both 1623); Jonson's *Catiline* (1611); Beaumont and Fletcher's *King and No King* (1619); Field's *Amends for Ladies* (1618); *The Second Maiden's Tragedy* (1824); Jonson's *Masque of Oberon* (1616).

1612 Shakespeare signs a deposition in the case of Bellot vs. Mountjoy; Beaumont ceases to write for the stage; probable collaboration of Shakespeare with Fletcher. *Henry VIII* (1623); Fletcher and Shakespeare's (?) *The Two Noble Kinsmen* (1634); Jonson's *Love Restored* (1616). Heywood's *Apology for Actors;* Prince Henry dies.

1613 The Globe playhouse destroyed by fire during a performance of *Henry VIII*, rebuilt in 1614. The marriage of the Princess Elizabeth signalized by grand masques by Beaumont, Chapman and Campion. Webster's *The Duchess of Malfi* (1623); Middleton's *No Wit, No Help Like a Woman's* (1657).

1614 The Hope playhouse opened by Henslowe and Rossiter, Jonson's *Bartholomew Fair* (1631) acted by the Lady Elizabeth's men, and later at court. Jonson's *The Sad Shepherd* (1641); Fletcher's *Bonduca* and *Valentinian* (both 1647).

1615 James visits Cambridge; Phineas Fletcher's *Sice-lides* (1631). John Fletcher's *The Chances.*

1616 Deaths of Beaumont and Shakespeare. First Folio of Ben Jonson. Middleton and Rowley's *A Fair Quarrel* (1617).

1617 The Phoenix or new Cockpit opened in Drury Lane by the Queen's men under Beeston. Fletcher and Massinger's *Thierry and Theodoret* (1624); Heywood's *The Fair Maid of the West* (1631).

1618 Alleyn leases the Fortune at £200 per annum to the Palsgrave's men. Fletcher's *The Loyal Subject* and *Bonduca* (1647). The Execution of Raleigh.

1619 Abortive effort to collect the plays of Shakespeare; Burbage dies. W. Rowley's *All's Lost by Lust* (1633); Jonson's *Pleasure Reconciled* (1640); Massinger and Field's *The Fatal Dowery* (1632); Fletcher's *The Little French Lawyer* (1647); his *Barnavelt* (1883) prohibited.

1620 Alleyn founds Dulwich College. Massinger and Dekker's *The Virgin Martyr* (1622); Fletcher and Massinger's *The False One* (1647); Webster's *The Devil's Law Case* (1623).

1621 Actors entertain the Spanish ambassador at the Fortune, later destroyed by fire; re-erected in 1622. The Red Bull enlarged. Fletcher's *The Wildgoose Chase* and *The Pilgrim* (1647), Dekker and Ford's *The Witch of Edmonton* (1658).

1622 Massinger's *The Maid of Honor* (1632); Fletcher and Massinger's *The Spanish Curate* (1647).

1623 Sir Henry Herbert Master of the Revels. Prince Charles and Buckingham in Spain. The First Folio of Shakespeare. Fletcher's *The Lover's Progress* (1647); Massinger's *The Renegado;* Middleton and W. Rowley's *The Changeling* (1653) and *The Spanish Gipsy* (1653); Middleton's *The Witch* (1778).

1624 Tourneur dies. Middleton's *A Game at Chess* (1625), Fletcher's *Rule a Wife and Have a Wife*

(1640); Ford's *The Sun's Darling* (1656); Davenport's *King John and Matilda* (1655).

1625–42 THE PERIOD OF SHIRLEY

1625 Charles I; Plague in London. Massinger's *A New Way to Pay Old Debts* (1633). Lodge, Fletcher, William Rowley die.

1626 Massinger's *The Roman Actor* (1636); May's Roman tragedies. Alleyn dies.

1627 Ford's *'Tis Pity She's a Whore* (1633); Massinger's *Great Duke of Florence* (1636); Heywood's *The English Traveller* (1633). Middleton dies.

1628 Ford's *The Lovers' Melancholy* (1629).

1629 Salisbury Court private theater built in St. Bridges, Farringdon Without, Marmion and perhaps Shirley the authors. Ford's *The Broken Heart* (1633); Carlell's *The Deserving Favorite* (1629).

1631 Massinger's *Believe As You List* (1832) refused a license.

1632 The Second Folio of Shakespeare; Lyly's *Six Court Comedies*. Randolph and Marmion active playwrights; Shirley's *The Ball* (1639), and *Hyde Park* (1637); Masques of Townshend at Court; Charles visits Cambridge, Prynne's *Histriomastix*. Dekker dies.

1633 Ford's *Perkin Warbeck* (1634); Heywood's *Late Lancashire Witches* (1634); Shirley's *The Gamester* (1637); Jonson's *The Magnetic Lady*, his last play (1641); Massinger's *The Guardian* (1655); Marston's *Tragedies and Comedies*.

1634 Nabbes' *Microcosmus* employs a "continuing perspective of ruins within the arch." Shirley's *Triumph of Peace* a masque by the four Inns of Court. Milton's *Comus*, Carew's *Coelum Britannicum* for both of which Lawe wrote the music. Jonson's *Pleasure Reconciled* (1641); Shirley's *The Opportunity* (1640); Randolph's *Amyntas* (1638); Davenant's *Love and Honor* (1649) and his masque *The Temple of Love* (1635). Webster dies.

1635 Shirley visits Dublin and writes for the Irish stage; his *Coronation* (1640), and *The Lady of Pleasure* (1637), Davenant's *The Platonic Lovers* (1636); Plague in London; general shifting among theatrical companies; law-suits among the heirs of Richard Burbage.

1636 Charles visits Oxford and is entertained among others by Cartwright in his *The Royal Slave* (1639) in which "the scene varied seven times."

1637 Suckling's *Aglaura* (1638). Jonson dies.

1638 Plays at the Red Bull in disrepute for "base plots and noise." Cowley's *Naufragium Joculare* (1638); Suckling's *The Goblins* (1646).

1639 Ford dies.

1640 Massinger dies. The Long Parliament. Davenant's *Salmacida Spolia* (1640).

1641 Thomas Heywood dies. Brome's *The Jovial Crew* (1652); Shirley's *The Cardinal* (1652). Outbreak of the Civil War.

1642 The Puritan Parliament orders the playhouses closed.

INDEX

INDEX

This Index is selective and confined to the text. It includes major topics, the names of authors, actors and others connected with the drama, and the titles of plays, these last italicized.

INDEX

Bacon, Francis, prepares dumb shows, 39; 40; supports the masque, 242

Bagehot, Walter, 117

Balcony, the, 201, 202

Bale, John, 23, 24, 40, 108

Ball, The, 265

Bandello, 95, 135, 170

Bankside, the, 64, 77, 195, 214

Barker, Granville, 283

Barnes, Barnabe, 86

"Barriers," 45, 235, 237

Barry, David, Lord, 188, 196, 197, 280

Bartholomew Fair, 190, 195

Bashful Lover, The, 257

Battle of Alcazar, The, 85, 93

Bear-baiting, 64, 73, 78

Bear Garden, the, 77

Beaumont, Francis, 94, 212-219, and Fletcher, 216; features of, 220, 221; his masque, 225, 241, 242; 256, 257, 260, 263, 281, 285

Beaumont, Sir John, 214

Beeston, Christopher, 116, 195

Believe as you List, 255

Bell Inn playhouse, 65

Bell Savage Inn playhouse, 65

Bestrafte Brudermord, Der, 100

Birth of Merlin, The, 114, 253

Blackfriars theater (Farrant's), 51, 53, 66, 74, 76

Blackfriars theater (Burbage's), 75, 76, 79, 139, 193, 196-198, 226, 278

Blackness, The Masque of, 136

Blank verse, 59, 83, 182, 217, 218, 284-286

Blind Beggar of Alexandria, The, 144, 181

Blind Beggar of Bethnal Green, The, 144, 184

Blurt Master Constable, 186

Boar's Head Inn playhouse, 65

Boas, F. S., 108

Boccaccio, 95, 158, 223

Boleyn, Anne, 33, 124

Bonduca, 204, 228

Boy Bishop, 4

Brandon, Samuel, 161

Brennoralt, 272

Bride, The, 262

Bridges, John, *see Gammer Gurton*

Broken Heart, The, 268

Brome, Richard, 193; and Jonson, 260, 262, 269, 272

Brooke, Christopher, 244

Brooke, Rupert, 172

Brooke, Samuel, 240

Brother, The, 264

Browne, William, 242

Bruno, Giordano, 30, 190

Buchanan, George, his tragedies, 30

Buck, Sir George, Master of the Revels, 169

Bugbears, The, 49

Bull Inn playhouse, 65

Burbage, Cuthbert, 74, 79, 139

Burbage, James, 51, 66, 68, 70, 74, 76, 139, 278. And *see* Theater

Burbage, Richard, 72, 74, 79; represented on the stage, 179; 192, 197, 198; acting of, 207; and Shakespeare, 227. And *see* Blackfriars.

Burleigh, Lord, 61, 62

Burton, Robert, 268

Bussy D'Ambois, 103

Byron, Conspiracy and Tragedy of Charles, Duke of, 103, 196

Caesar's Fall, 169

Caesar and Pompey, 163

Calisto and Melibea, 40, 41, 45, 93

320

INDEX

INDEX

Merry Wives of Windsor, The,
47, 128, 135, 141, 143, 144,
183
Messalina, 198
Michaelmas Term, 186
Microcosmus, 247
Midas, 54
Middle Temple and Lincoln's
Inn, Masque of the, *see*
Chapman's masque
Midsummer Night's Dream,
56, 60, 61, 87, 118
Middleton, Thomas, 148; in
tragedy, 172, 173; his come-
dies of low life, 184-187;
281; and Mayors' pageants,
250; and Rowley, 252-254;
his parody of political event,
254, 255
Milton, John, and the drama,
245; his masque, 249
Minstrel and mime, 1, 2, 4, 5,
46
Miracle play, 10-12, 13-18, 19;
the cycle of the, 14-16
Mirror for Magistrates, The,
107
Miseries of Enforced Marriage,
89, 146, 223
Misfortunes of Arthur, The,
37, 39
Misoganus, 30
Monsieur D'Olive, 182, 183
Monsieur Thomas, 206, 231
Montaigne, 170
Montemayor, 46, 134
Moral play, 19, 21-26, 108
More, George, 266
More, Sir Thomas, 26, 41, 112;
the literary circle of, 25, 26
More, Sir Thomas (the play),
112, 120
Morton, John, Cardinal, 25
Moryson, Fynes, 80
Mother Bombie, 54, 55
Mountjoy, Christopher, 226
Mucedorus, 129, 140

Much Ado About Nothing, 46,
135, 136
Mulleasses the Turk, 161, 197
Mumming, 5, 13, 28, 44
Munday, Anthony, a t t a c k s
plays, 67; his play writing,
114, 123, 130
Murder play, the, 88, 89
Muses Looking Glass, The,
246
Music, 233, 240, 241
Mussato, his *Ecerinis,* 29
Mustapha, 160, 161
Mystère du Viel Testament, 15
"Mystery play," 13

Nabbes, Thomas, 262
Narcissus, 244
Nash, Thomas, his touch with
the drama, 60, 93, 180; and
Marlowe, 84; allusion to
Kyd's *Hamlet,* 88; allusion
to *1 Henry VI,* 110, 119
Nature, Medwall's, 26
*Nero, Tragedy of Claudius
Tiberius, The,* 165
Newcastle, Duke of, 262, 263
Newcastle, Duchess of, 271
New Custom, 24
New Inn, 260, 271
*New Way to Pay Old Debts,
A,* 259
Newington Butts, the theater
at, 64, 72, 78
Northbroke, John, 67
Northern Lass, The, 261
Northward Ho, 185
Norton, Thomas, *see Gorboduc*
Nottingham's men, the, Earl
of, 73
*No Wit, No Help Like a
Woman's,* 187

Ogilby, John, 263
Old Fortunatus, 60, 125, 132
Old Wives' Tale, The, 59, 94,
129
Opportunity, The, 264

INDEX

Poetomachia, see "War of the Theaters."

Political allusion, see Allusiveness.

Politician, The, 264

Pollard, A. W., 141

Poor Man's Comfort, The, 240

Pope, Thomas, 139

Porta, Giambattista, 245

Porter, Henry, 145, 183

Porter's Hall (playhouse), 197

Praesepe, the, 7, 8

Preston, Thomas, 42, 43, 58

Pride of Life, The, 22

Privy Council and the drama, 67, 68

Problem play, the, 253, 254, 266-268

Progress, the royal, 42, 43, 60, 61

Promos and Cassandra, 49

Properties, 57, 199, 202; shift of, 203; symbolic and portable, 203-205; 285. And see Scene.

Prophetae, 8, 10

Prophetess, The, 228

Prose in drama, 48, 49, 55, 184, 191, 284, 285

"Prospective," see Scene, Scenery.

Protestant plays, 23, 24

Proteus, The Masque of, 234

Prudentius, his *Psychomachia,* 21

Publication, Elizabethan, 140-142

Puritanism and the Stage, 66-68, 76, 78, 190, 197, 248, 263, 273, 275

Quarles, Francis, 272

Quartos, "good" and "bad," 140, 141

Queen Anne's players, see Anne of Denmark.

Queens, The Masque of, 236, 238

Queen's Arcadia, The, 239

Queen's players, the (Elizabeth), 72, 131, 133; and see Anne of Denmark.

Queen's Revels, The, 99, 160, 195

Queen's Revels, Rossiter's second, 195, 197

Queen's Revels, third, 197

Quem quaeritis, or Easter trope, 7

Radcliff, Ralph, 21

Rainolds, John, attacks plays, 67

Raleigh, Sir Walter, 126

Ralph Roister Doister, 33, 34, 39

Ram Alley, 188, 197

Randolph, Thomas, 246, 260, 280

Rankins, William, 130

Rape of Lucrece, The, 165

Rastell, John, *The Four Elements,* 25, 26, 41; his "playhouse," 26

Red Bull playhouse, the, 74, 194

Renegado, The, 257

Respublica, 24

1, 2 Return from Parnassus, The, 179, 243

Revels' Accounts, The, 50-52, 56, 57

Revels, Office of the, 5, 45, 50, 52

Revenge of Bussy D'Ambois, The, 102, 103

Revenge plays, see Tragedy.

Revengers Tragedy, The, 104, 169

Richard II, 96, 117, 120; and the Essex conspiracy, 124; 162

Richard III (Shakespeare), 96, 110, 120, 123, 162

Richard III, The True Tragedy of, 109

INDEX

Supposes, 48, 49
Sussex, Lord, his players, 69, 89
Swan playhouse, the, 64, 77, 198

Tacitus, 165, 190
Tale of a Tub, The, 260
Tamburlaine, 82-87, 132, 156, 161
Tancred and Gismund, 37, 39
Tamer Tamed, The, 145, 214
Taming of a Shrew, The, 48, 135
Taming of the Shrew, The, 39, 48, 145, 208, 215
Tarlton, Richard, 65, 70, 80, 278
Tasso, 135, 140
Taylor, Joseph, 278
Tempest, The, 223, 226, 250
Temple of Love, The, 249, 271
Terence, Christianized, 29; 30, 36, 46, 48
Textor, Ravisius, 30
Theater, the (earliest playhouse), 63, 66, 70, 76-78
Thetys' Festival, 241
Thierry and Theodoret, 228
Thomas Aquinas, 12
Thorndike, A. H., 8, 251
Thracian Wonder, The, 143
Tilting, 44, 45
Timon of Athens, 166, 222
'Tis Pity She's A Whore, 268
Titus Andronicus, 71, 86, 88, 92, 95, 118
Tompkis, Thomas, 244
Tourneur, Cyril, 169, 222
Townshend, Aurelian, 248
Towneley Plays, 14, 15, 16, 25, 26
Tragedies and Comedies of Marston, 142
Tragedy, 82; of Marlowe, 83-90; of revenge, 86, 96-105, 169; romantic, 93-96; 150;

Shakespeare in, 151-155, 157-159, 166-169; of classical topic, 155-166; Webster in, 170-173; Fletcher in, 228-230; of Middleton and Rowley, 253, 254; Shirley in, 264; of Ford, 268, 269. And see Senecan influence, Murder play.
Tragicomedy, 182, 212; of Beaumont and Fletcher, 219-221; 228, 230; of Massinger, 257; 272
Traitor, The, 264
Travel plays, 184
Travels of Three English Brothers, The, 218
Trick to Catch the Old One, A, 186
Trissino, 35
Triumph of Peace, The, 248, 263
Troilus and Cressida, 141, 150, 155, 157-159, 179
Trope, the, 2-8, 12
Turkish Mahomet, 161
Twelfth Night, 135
Two Angry Women of Abingdon, 144, 183
Two Gentlemen of Verona, The, 46, 119, 134, 222
Two Merry Women of Abingdon, 145
Two Noble Kinsmen, The, 225, 256
Tumbling measure, 83, 284
Turkish "histories," 161
Tylney, Sir Edmund, 50, 70, 73
Types in the drama, 47, 220, 221, 231, 281, 282

Udall, Nicholas, 31, 43
Ulysses and the Sirens, 242
Unities, the, 48
Universities, drama at the, 31, 34, 43, 108, 156, 165, 242, 244-246

INDEX